Red Moons and Silent Truths

Lydia Goldman

Copyright © Lydia Goldman, 2025

All rights reserved. No part of this publication may be reproduced, stored or transmitted in any form by any means, electronic, mechanical, photocopying or otherwise, without the prior written permission of the publisher or author.

First published in Great Britain in 2025 by Sleepy Lion Publishing.

(Trading name of Sleepy Lion Limited)

Text Copyright © Lydia Goldman, 2025

Cover © Mecob Designs, 2025

Editing © Sleepy Lion Publishing, 2025

The right to be identified as author of this work has been asserted in accordance with the Copyright, Designs and Patents Act, 1988.

ISBN: 978-1-917563-04-8

www.sleepylionpublishing.com

DEDICATION

*For Myanmar—a country that captured my heart.
And David Evans—who never got to finish his own memoir.*

Contents

The Coup 1
Chapter 1. The Summer Before 3
Chapter 2. "Hands, Space, Face" 11
Chapter 3. The Sun Shines 15
Chapter 4. Farewell London 23
Chapter 5. Flight 727 28
Chapter 6. Four Walls 37
Chapter 7. Making Home in a Foreign Land 52
Chapter 8. Henry's Village 60
Chapter 9. Do Not Believe the Rumours 64
Chapter 10. Typhoid, a Massage, and Power Cuts 72
Chapter 11. Winter in the Sun 80
Chapter 12. It's All Falling into Place 91
Chapter 13. 16th Street 93
Chapter 14. Emerging from Lockdown 100
PART TWO 107
Chapter 15. First of February, 2021 108
Chapter 16. Rumblings of Rebellion 113
Chapter 17. Bitter Truths 124
Chapter 18. The Weight of Uncertainty 131
Chapter 19. Ruminations 139
Chapter 20. Fifty Things to Do in an Internet Blackout 141
Chapter 21. Privilege and Protest 147
Chapter 22. Broken Promises and Deceptive Hopes 152
Chapter 23. "Miss, it's so loud." 160
Chapter 24. Finding Courage in the Chaos 166
Chapter 25. Red Moons 175
Chapter 26. One Cockroach Too Many 180
Chapter 27. Hiding in Plain Sight 186

Chapter 28.	A City Under Siege	192
Chapter 29.	The Great Traffic Jam Protest	198
Chapter 30.	Voices of the Rohingya	206
Chapter 31.	Don't Be Long	211
Chapter 32.	Electric Days, Sleepless Nights	218
Chapter 33.	Blood-Stained Pavements	220
Chapter 34.	A Risky Mission	224
Chapter 35.	Murder in the Night	232
Chapter 36.	The Revolution Has Begun	236
Chapter 37.	His Sealed Fate	247
Chapter 38.	Terror at Twilight	251
Chapter 39.	The Shadows of Paranoia	253
Chapter 40.	A Decision Made	257
Chapter 41.	In the Eye of the Storm	262
Chapter 42.	The Deadliest Day	269
Chapter 43.	A Dangerous Game	276
Chapter 44.	Safe House	281
Chapter 45.	The Final Day	291
Chapter 46.	"Please, tell our story."	296
Chapter 47.	Thirty-Three Hours	299
Chapter 48.	Home	303
Chapter 49.	Healing and Hope	308
Chapter 50.	Trauma	312
Epilogue.	Myanmar Present Day	317
Personal Stories		320
Nilar		320
Kyi		323

ACKNOWLEDGMENTS

Writing *Red Moons and Silent Truths* has been an incredible and long journey, and I am deeply grateful to everyone who supported me along the way.

First and foremost, I want to thank Hope Haven* for welcoming me into the charity and teaching me the importance of resilience and compassion. Your work has been a beacon of hope and has profoundly influenced my perspective.

Nilar and Kyi*, thank you for allowing me to share your stories and for being brilliant friends while living in Yangon. Our late-night conversations and shared laughter amidst the chaos were invaluable. I still cherish our bubble tea dates and my first ride with you on public transport. Your courage and friendship have been truly inspiring.

To the Sanchaung Crew—Ella, Maeve, Ivy, and Amie*—who became sisters to me, thank you for your unwavering support and camaraderie. The countless evenings we spent by the poolside, at our weekend retreats, and at our movie nights kept me grounded and hopeful.

I want to thank my family and friends for their unwavering support and encouragement. To my parents, thank you for your love and patience. Ben, thanks for the late-night calls while you were in Tokyo, and Zach, thank you for reading and re-reading my endless manuscript drafts.

I would also like to acknowledge Summer and Freya (I promised your names would be in my book), who kept my creativity alive while playing make-believe during nannying sessions and brought joy to my writing process.

A special thank you to Sleepy Lion Publishing and my editors, Michael Amos and Dr. Bob Rich. Thank you for believing in my story and for making this dream a reality.

To my colleagues at Virgo Health and Golin, whose support and encouragement helped me complete this book, thank you for cheering me on.

Finally, to my readers, thank you for taking the time to read my story. Your support and interest mean the world to me, and I hope this book resonates with you as much as it has with me.

*Names have been altered.

To explain the book title, *Red Moons and Silent Truths*, it captures the essence of life in Yangon during the coup. The colour red represents the Myanmar Democratic party, the moons signify the nocturnal protests (at night on our balconies, drumming with pots and pans, singing in unity), and the silent truths refer to the hidden realities of the country that were uncovered; the corruptness and lies of the military.

The Coup

Shortly after departing Myanmar, six weeks after the onset of the devastating military coup, I found myself compelled to start writing this book. Determined to capture every detail, I aimed to preserve the memories and stories that unfolded during those early days.

Back in England, as I sat down to write, I felt myself oscillating between determination and anxiety. This book is the culmination of that determination, albeit tempered by the anxiety.

My decision to move halfway across the world had surprised many. Friends and family raised their eyebrows, questioning the wisdom of my choice. "Why Myanmar?" they asked. I'd often retort, "Who wouldn't leap at the chance to explore a Southeast Asian paradise with flights paid?"

But paradise had its own secrets. As I stepped off the plane onto the sweltering tarmac, the roar of jet engines and masked attendants hurrying us along drowned out any excitement. Fresh masks were handed out inside, and multilingual signs reminded us of the familiar COVID messages that had become part of our global lexicon in 2020.

Months blurred together—a haze of quarantine, isolation, and IV drips. My mental well-being eroded, and the idyllic vision of my time abroad shattered against harsh truths. Yet, amidst the trials, glimmers of hope and beauty found their way into my heart.

Myanmar captivated me with its scorching heat, stifling humidity, exotic flavours, and breathtaking landscapes. Despite the hardships, Myanmar captured my soul in ways I never imagined possible.

Then came a different darkness—the Myanmar military coup. The initial media frenzy faded, leaving untold suffering and fear in its wake. I vowed to share their stories—the harrowing experiences of those I'd grown to adore.

The coup d'état became a pivotal moment, awakening my consciousness. Ignorance transformed into certainty as I realised that coups were woven into Myanmar's history, a thread of oppression stretching back to 1962.

Writing became my lifeline—a way to process, to give a voice to the silenced. But this book can only scratch the surface. Since the coup, themes and voices have echoed across a vast spectrum of activism. I implore readers to delve deeper, research, and keep the story of Myanmar close to their hearts.

Names have been altered, and I have occasionally modified identifying details throughout this book for privacy and protection. My intention is to safeguard individuals while ensuring their stories are still shared, and their voices are still heard.

Chapter 1. The Summer Before

I should have been packing my suitcase instead of sitting on my mother's lap and sobbing. My flight was just two days away, yet I hadn't made any progress for a week.

Yangon, that vibrant city I'd visited in August the previous year, now haunted me. Back then, I'd never imagined I'd be in such disarray. I knew what I needed to pack—the essentials, the memories—but the act of doing so felt impossible. My mind had become a tangled web of indecision, and I couldn't even decide which underwear to take.

It was July 2020, nearing the end of the first COVID-19 lockdown. No travel vaccinations, no open clothing shops. I couldn't even purchase a pair of sandals for the beach, and that realisation alone brought me to tears. This wasn't how it was meant to be.

Finally, I peeled myself away from my mother's lap and retreated to my small room. Casting my gaze upon the familiar surroundings that had been mine since infancy, I felt suffocated. The delicate fairy statues, gifts from my nana, still sat on the windowsill. Pink cushions and bed sheets remained, and a sweet smell lingered—a constant reminder of my need to escape.

Yes, I lived in a large home with a large garden, surrounded by loving friends and family. But it felt like I was on a conveyor belt, moving predictably through life. The privilege weighed heavily, like an anchor.

Restlessness gnawed at me. My brothers and I would playfully jest with our parents, blaming our wanderlust on our expatriate upbringing. I first earned the term "expatriate" at seven years old, just before our move to The Netherlands. Before that, life in London was sheltered and serene—a happy routine of schooldays, weekends filled with bike rides and swimming, and annual holidays in the South of France. But everything changed weeks before my seventh birthday when Eindhoven became our new home. The world suddenly expanded, and so did my longing for adventure.

I remember our grand, creaky house in Eindhoven and its spacious garden, which was shared among neighbouring homes. However, I can't recall ever seeing anyone else use the communal swing set except us. I attended my first international school there, which was divided into two systems: one for Dutch nationals and the other for expatriates like me. It felt peculiar not to wear a school uniform anymore; we traded conformity for individuality. Wednesdays were half-days, and Fridays were pizza days.

Yet, just as I settled into the rhythm of life, we uprooted once more eighteen months later. The Hague beckoned—a British school with a stricter curriculum. Our new school was larger, and our new house had an English shop nearby, selling the Cadbury chocolate bars we drooled over and chewy English toffee.

The next five years were wonderful and adventurous. Summers were filled with beach outings in Scheveningen, the sun warming our backs as we built sandcastles and chased waves. We decorated pavements with colourful chalk drawings and roller-skated with the neighbourhood children. Winters brought frozen lakes, ice skating and cosy cafes where hot chocolate danced with marshmallows. There were annual street parties where competitions, such as the sunflower growing contest, were held (we never won). The Hague quickly became my home. By then, half of my life had been spent in the UK—a place that had begun to fade from memory—and the other half abroad. I had become a fully-fledged third-culture kid.

Leaving The Hague at thirteen was heart-wrenching. With only a few weeks' notice, we found ourselves back in Bromley. The freedoms I'd known in The Netherlands clashed with England's rigidity. The international friendships I'd forged, transient yet profound, whispered their goodbyes. My friends from "home" seemed to have moved on.

Still, I clung to hope. Each of my father's "announcements" fuelled my anticipation for further moves. And then, at sixteen, Indonesia materialised. Despite the uncertainty, I eagerly embraced the change. I knew very little about my new home, Jakarta, but I was desperate for a change of pace and lifestyle.

The following two years in Indonesia were tumultuous yet transformative, leaving an indelible mark. Returning to England for university, in comparison, felt like stepping into a sepia photograph—a life less vivid, less wild.

Now, back in my childhood bedroom, the walls pulsing with anticipation, I prepared for a new adventure: Myanmar. Why Myanmar? It wasn't the typical tourist haunt, not a postcard-perfect paradise. Yet fate led me there—a last-minute detour from my planned graduation trip during the summer of 2019. Initially bound for Bali, China, and Japan, Myanmar wasn't on my radar until friends working in Yangon as teaching assistants beckoned me over.

"I am going to Myanmar!" I exclaimed to my parents over FaceTime, their pixelated faces staring back at me.

"Isn't that Burma?" my mother queried, uncertain.

'Yes…' I faltered, realising I needed to brush up on my geography.

My short visit to Yangon at the tail end of August 2019 was eye-opening. The moment I stepped off the plane, the humid air enveloped me like a warm embrace. The airport, with its echoes of Indonesia, felt strangely familiar. But the lack of tourists struck me; the city's secrets guarded by silence, its atmosphere serene and untouched by the frenzy of mass tourism.

Despite my late arrival, my friends Sophie and Megan awaited me, teaching since dawn.

I sighed in relief. "Thank you so much for picking me up."

"Don't be silly," they said. "You would probably never make it to our block if we hadn't."

As we piled into a Grab car (Myanmar's version of Uber), my suitcase thudded in the boot. Our driver, engrossed in a conversation on his phone, which was not hands-free, occasionally spat a weirdly smelling liquid out of the window. His phone use and the peculiar smell emanating from his drink unnerved me as we swerved through the streets, but Sophie and Megan seemed unfazed. They'd adapted swiftly to the country's idiosyncrasies during their few weeks there.

We wound through sparse traffic and reached "Teacher Towers," an apartment complex exclusively reserved for new teachers at the school. Guards greeted us warmly, and a friendly dog wagged its tail. Inside, the building was under construction, and its interior was dimly lit. But hints of a small pool promised relief from the sweltering heat.

Ascending two floors, we entered Megan's flat. Though spacious, the interior was shrouded in shadow, the absence of windows casting a shadowy veil over the apartment's somewhat gloomy and uncomfortable atmosphere. However, Megan had injected bursts of vibrancy into the space with colourful paintings from a nearby market—pieces that would carry a hefty price tag in England.

"It is not the best," Sophie admitted. "But it's decent, and we have our own space."

During my stay, I explored Yangon—a city of golden pagodas piercing the sky and hidden alleys. Each morning, melodic chants echoed through the streets as children sang unfamiliar words. Loudspeakers blared instructions, and car horns joined a distant drilling—a symphony of urban cacophony.

Intrigued by the girls' new lifestyle, I visited their school. Two security gates stood between me and the entrance, but lush greenery softened the edges. Towering palm trees whispered secrets, and the school became an oasis—a place where language barriers dissolved in smiles and gestures.

The school sprawled out, and the bustling corridors echoed with the cheerful chatter of students from diverse backgrounds—largely Burmese children but also those from Europe and the US. A small cafe nestled in the heart of the campus provided solace amidst the whirlwind of activity.

I settled into a cosy corner, cradling a hot beverage to warm me up in the cold-air-conditioned room. Children of all ages hurried past, their footsteps echoing. Some dashed to final lessons, while others headed for end-of-day registration. The little ones were energetically playing in the spacious early years centre.

Teachers strolled by, exchanging warm smiles with colleagues. I observed Sophie and Megan in their element, their laughter seamlessly blending with the joyous sound of children at play. They seemed happy and seeing them in that state also brought me happiness.

As my stay in Yangon drew to a close, an unexpected opportunity presented itself—a chance to work with Sophie and Megan as teaching assistants at the school. It was a serendipitous combination of circumstances: a shortage of teaching assistants, a parent's eagerness, and my willingness to say yes.

Tempted by the prospect of living abroad and embarking on a new adventure, I grappled with the decision, weighing the allure of independence and exploration against the certainties ahead.

However, there was a slight predicament regarding the job's starting date, a detail I had glossed over in my excitement when sharing the news with my mother.

"I got the job!" I exclaimed eagerly, but I was met with a pregnant pause on the other end of the line.

"I got the job!" I'd repeated, hoping for any response.

"Really?" my mother finally replied, her tone lacking the expected enthusiasm. "We didn't think you were serious. But, uh, that's great!"

Though her lukewarm reaction had been slightly disheartening, the overwhelming support from my friends buoyed my spirits. Meanwhile, distant relatives expressed surprise upon hearing my plans to move to Myanmar. My aunt, in particular, voiced concerns about civil unrest.

"Have you researched the country?" she'd asked.

"Of course," I lied, concealing my ignorance. "I have already done some research and will look into it further."

Unaware of the significance of her warnings, I remained oblivious to her hints. During a lengthy layover between connecting flights, I watched a BBC documentary titled 'Burma with Simon Reeves.' The screen flickered to life, and Simon's raw emotions—shock and sorrow—etched themselves into my memory. The harrowing Rohingya conflict unfolded before me, vivid and unrelenting.

Rakhine State—the epicentre of suffering. Denied access to the Rohingya areas of Burma, Simon's crew persisted. They navigated jungles, evaded army patrols and witnessed the world's largest refugee camp—Kutupalong-Balu Khali. Here, hundreds of thousands of Rohingya Muslims sought refuge, their lives upended by violence or persecution.

As Simon's footsteps traced the path of despair, I thought of Yangon's apparent calm juxtaposed against Rakhine's turmoil. I reassured myself—I wouldn't venture far, wouldn't take unnecessary risks. Yangon was safe, far from the troubled regions.

But shadows have a way of stretching. And as I watched Simon's journey, I wondered if safety was an illusion—one that crumbled with each passing frame.

Chapter 2. "Hands, Space, Face"

Upon my return from my first visit to Myanmar, the months from October to Christmas merged into a disorientating blur of post-holiday malaise. England's dreary weather intensified my longing for Yangon's vibrant streets—the colours, the chaos, the life.

I took up a temporary nanny job with a nearby family to earn money. Initially enjoyable, the role soon became bitter as the parents revealed their unkindness. And, as the skies turned grey and frost clung to the air, my enthusiasm waned. Waking up at 5 a.m. to trudge through frosty air for a forty-five-minute walk, followed by two hours of childcare before school drop-off, became a daily struggle I begrudged.

In January, an offer arrived—the teaching position in Yangon. But fate had other plans. The NHS waiting list held me captive, an impending operation forcing me to decline for the time being. By February, I decided to quit my nanny job. The intimacy of the role—the threads woven into a family's fabric—had frayed. Hurt and resentment simmered as I gave my month's notice, culminating in a tearful departure marked by sharp words and accusations.

A weight lifted from my chest as I stepped out of their home for the last time. Despite the emotional turmoil, I felt optimistic, hoping for stability in my declining mental health. I also prayed for the opportunity to travel to Yangon during the Easter holidays, hoping for a potential job start date.

However, a month later, COVID-19 struck. I brushed off the panic until Boris Johnson's announcement on March 23, 2020, echoed through our living room, ushering in a nationwide lockdown. His words—simple yet seismic—started a new reality.

"Only six deaths," I complained. "What is this country-wide panic?"

My mother's insistence cut through. We gathered around the TV, hushed. Boris Johnson's historic, weighty announcement pierced the air.

"From this evening," he declared, "I must give the British people a very simple instruction: You must stay home."

"Stay at home?" I gasped. "What does that mean?"

And so began our collective isolation—a chapter unlike any other. The echoes of World War II broadcasts reverberated, and we clung to the safety of our homes, waiting for the storm to pass.

While researching the novel virus, I stumbled upon chilling articles and simulations that painted a grim picture of the pandemic's potential impact on humanity. Little did we know then that it would soon spread like wildfire, leaving hundreds of thousands of people dead in its wake.

One article, "*Global pandemic could wipe out 900 million*

people," published in 2018, captured my attention. Johns Hopkins University had conducted a virus simulation—a parainfluenza strain transmitted by coughing. The parallels between this simulation and the unfolding COVID-19 crisis were distressing. The simulations revealed that a novel pathogen had the potential to claim the lives of up to nine hundred million people within a few years. Unfortunately, the world was ill-prepared for such a catastrophic event. This fictional virus was intentionally designed to be no more dangerous than existing illnesses like SARS.

Moreover, in October 2019, months before the first COVID-19 outbreak in China, "Event 201" was organised in collaboration with the Bill and Melinda Gates Foundation. This simulation aimed to test coordinated policy responses to a theoretical pandemic scenario. Business leaders, government officials, and public health experts were invited to devise strategies and contingency plans. Despite these preparations, our government appeared woefully unprepared for the actual crisis. After all, that simulation was based on a coronavirus.

As I absorbed these findings, a sense of unease washed over me. The Johns Hopkins Centre's simulation had ignited a storm of speculation, weaving threads of conspiracy theories and murmurs of uncanny coincidences. While some conjectured that the institution had somehow foreseen the outbreak, I clung to the belief that it merely showcased forward-thinking and highlighted our lack of preparedness.

The notion of overpopulation loomed large; a concept that makes people uncomfortable. It was the proverbial elephant in the room, an unspoken truth—our planet strained under the weight of burgeoning humanity. Could its finite resources and limited space truly sustain an ever-expanding population? Lost in contemplation, I toyed with a harsh lesson: perhaps we needed a wake-up call. Greed and self-centeredness had eroded nature's delicate balance, as Gandhi's words echoed: "The world has enough for everyone's needs, but not enough for everyone's greed."

The annals of catastrophe etched their mark: Haiti's 2010 earthquake, Japan's 2011 Tohoku disaster, and the wrath of Hurricane Harvey and Maria in 2017. Were these mere coincidences or nature's inexorable response? The Ebola outbreak and the ongoing coronavirus pandemic seemed urgent messages urging us to reckon with our planetary transgressions. After all, humanity had already obliterated over sixty percent of animal populations in the past five decades.

In geography class in 2014, I fixated on a grim forecast: By 2050, oil and gas reserves would dwindle to near depletion. Our teacher also warned us that by 2030, without swift action, we'd need two Earths to sustain our voracious appetites. "What will happen when these resources run out, Miss?" I asked.

She paused for a moment, then replied with a touch of resignation, "Who knows? Hopefully, somebody will sort it out."

But who, I thought, my mind wandering into the dystopian realms of resource wars and chasms between haves and have-nots. A real-life Silo.

Chapter 3. The Sun Shines

"Before the coronavirus, I loved being alone."

The first lockdown in the UK eased in early June. My initial dismissal of the virus, fuelled by its distant origin of over seven thousand kilometres, revealed my naivety about our modern world's interconnectedness.

Engrossed in evolving lockdown measures, boredom clashed with the historical gravity of the moment. April and May stretched endlessly, as did the lockdown. "We still don't have the infection rates down as far as we need to," Boris said gravely.

I vividly recall the first week of lockdown, a blur of desperate attempts to lend a helping hand. Armed with gloves and masks, my younger brother Zach and I took to the streets with flyers that said, "Call us if you are shielding and need help! We will collect groceries, walk dogs, and collect medication." Yet, our altruistic gestures were met with suspicion and even hostility. "Stay away," the sharp rebuke pierced the air.

We abandoned our mission and headed to the supermarket for the first time since the lockdown began. Our mother had become overly cautious about us leaving the home, monitoring our every move. Zach and I expected to receive a phone call if we were out of the house longer than the permitted sixty minutes of exercise. We endured scrutiny and interrogations about our precise whereabouts. Eventually, our mother realised that the month-long wait for an Ocado delivery and the minimal fresh food in the house would not sustain us. Therefore, we were granted permission to go food shopping.

The queue to the local shop snaked around the building, a testament to the collective anxiety gripping the nation. As we waited, I observed the psychological ballet of fellow shoppers, each movement a delicate dance of fear or defiance against an invisible foe. I watched as people stifled coughs into scarves and jackets, attempting to conceal any signs of illness. Others awkwardly manoeuvred to maintain distance from other shoppers. At the same time, some seemed unconcerned and even scoffed at the perceived ludicrousness of the situation.

"It is a virus,' someone moaned. "The flu is a virus. This is bloody ridiculous."

At that point, so much about the virus was unknown. No one wore masks, and I wondered if I should have been in the queue at all.

After sixty minutes, we eventually reached the storefront. Entering the supermarket felt like crossing the threshold into a dystopian nightmare. Once abundant shelves now lay barren, stripped bare by the panic-driven hoarding of essentials. Eggs, milk, flour, and sugar had all disappeared as if every household was now practising for *Bake-Off*. The stockpiling of toilet paper seemed particularly irrational, as the virus did not appear to cause diarrhoea or vomiting. But the whole country had entered a fight or flight mode.

We managed to secure the few remaining fruits and vegetables and a single pack of pasta. Fortunately, my mother had clearly foreseen some sort of lockdown, and I was grateful for her foresight in stocking our freezer with a dozen pre-prepared meals. Although the dates on those meals remained a mystery, they offered a modicum of relief.

With each passing day, the illusion of normalcy faded, replaced by the harsh glare of unemployment and uncertainty. Envy gnawed at me as I watched my brother languish in the safety of furlough while I grappled with the spectre of job insecurity. Without a signed contract, the opportunity could be snatched away at any moment.

"If only I had stayed at my dreaded nanny job," I lamented. "I would be on furlough like everybody else."

My mental health began to decline, along with my lack of control exacerbated by the government's constantly shifting directives that left me feeling powerless. Days melted into weeks, marked by a monotonous cycle of solitary walks and constant unease over the changing rules. After disregarding the imposed one-hour limit, I sought refuge in long, two-hour strolls, buoyed by the bright and sunny weather. I walked to the park nearby, where families sat, distanced, in the ample open space. I observed as queues formed at the post office and irate customers were turned away promptly at five in the evening. All non-essential shops had been ordered to shut at the end of March, leaving only supermarkets, pharmacies, and post offices open, their operating hours gradually diminishing each passing week. Getting a doctor's appointment soon became impossible, and in July, masks became mandatory for everyone. The whole country had become a ghost town, and despite the physical presence of family, the walls of our home became suffocating. My world had narrowed, and I had to retrain myself to breathe and find solace in the limited scope of my daily life.

I read a quote by Professor Paul Crawford in his book, *Cabin Fever*, "Whilst we have faced the greatest period of isolation in our lifetimes, we must remember that cabin fever is not new. It happens at sea, on land, in the air and in space. But perhaps most importantly, it occurs in our minds."[1]

It wasn't until I reached out to friends during a group WhatsApp call that I realised I was not alone. The following day, I established a routine with Zach, starting our mornings with yoga, sometimes followed by a run. We also began volunteering. The simple act of helping an elderly couple with their shopping brought a sense of purpose and connection. I never saw their faces; I would drop their shopping outside their home, ring their doorbell, and then they would wait until I was a safe distance away before they stepped out to retrieve the bags.

The sight of abandoned cafes and vendors peddling hand sanitiser and face masks initially felt surreal. Boris Johnson's

---

[1] Crawford & Crawford, *Cabin Fever: Surviving lockdown in the coronavirus pandemic.* (Emerald, 2021)

attempts to alleviate fears by shaking hands with COVID-19 patients, only to later contract the virus himself, added to the unsettling atmosphere.

Car parks stood deserted, and playgrounds were marked with 'DO NOT ENTER' signs. Virtual communication platforms surged to 300 million daily meetings, ushering in an era of Zoom parties, client calls, and virtual weddings. My purse, once filled with notes and coins, now lay empty as cash became obsolete. This brought a moment of reflection, tinged with sadness, as I thought about the kind-hearted lady who relied on spare change while sitting outside our local coffee shop each day.

We embraced the virtual realm, transforming our homes into offices, classrooms, restaurants, and workout spaces. The delineation between physical and virtual worlds blurred, and I joined a fitness boot camp, where I was guided through a workout from the comfort of my living room. Our homes became more than just shelters; they became hubs of productivity, creativity, and connection.

The relentless grip of the virus tightened, and my adaptation to this new reality unfolded gradually. Yet, a persistent worry gnawed at the corners of my mind. As schools across England swiftly transitioned to virtual platforms—and virtual schools became the norm overseas—I questioned the feasibility of being flown to Myanmar by a company with no physical school to offer.

Sophie and Megan's evacuation from Myanmar, whisked away to their home countries, worried me. Well-meaning friends and family bombarded me with inquiries, their questioning gazes echoing my own doubts. When I responded, "I was told I would be given the details soon," I could almost hear their disappointment.

"I WILL GO TO MYANMAR!" Zachary yelled. "Repeat."

"I WILL GO TO MYANMAR," I'd cry.

"I will be successful."

"I will be successful," I whispered, struggling to believe those words fully.

"Why are you whispering?" he challenged. "You need to believe it."

"But…what if I really don't go to Myanmar? What will I do?"

"Everything happens for a reason," he affirmed. "Whatever happens will happen."

"Thanks, bro," I smiled as we embarked on another meditative walk. Together, we decided to embrace silliness. We danced, connected with our spiritual sides, and welcomed crystals into our home. Sage rituals cleansed our energies, lifting our moods.

"Unreal," I gasped. "Why do I take antidepressants when I could be mindful every day?"

"Maybe you feel great because you are on antidepressants," Zach teased.

And then, a message from the headmistress arrived—an invitation for a catch-up and a discussion about the role in Yangon. Holding my breath, I believed it sounded like the job was mine. But I dared not celebrate prematurely. Thrilled by the email, I kept the news to myself until after the anticipated Zoom call.

"Lydia," the headmistress appeared on my screen. "Are you excited about moving to Yangon?"

Relief flooded me. "I am beyond excited."

Days later, a contract arrived in my inbox. After diligently completing the paperwork, I waited for confirmation from my references. Finally, I could relax and look forward to my enormous adventure ahead.

"The tricky part," she explained, "is that we don't know exactly when you'll be able to enter the country. But rest assured, the school will start virtually until everyone is back in Myanmar."

Weeks later, my inbox overflowed with a flurry of emails from the school. Each message proposed an alternate potential flight date, yet the actual date remained elusive. In early July, one email hinted at a flight scheduled for the following week. The situation was perplexing, exacerbated by Myanmar's stringent COVID-19 regulations.

Unsurprisingly, England topped their list of countries deemed a "definitely no" for entry due to our soaring case numbers. Flying out soon seemed unlikely.

"You'll have to put up with me for another couple of months," I joked with my parents.

"How can you not know when you'll be flying?" My dad asked, his tone edged with conceit.

"The school isn't sure if we'll get visas," I explained. "Only essential personnel can enter Myanmar."

"Well, surely British teachers are non-essential," he remarked. "You could all work online. Are the schools open in Yangon?"

"No," I mumbled.

"Well, you could be here until after Christmas, then," he sighed.

"I know."

Later that same day, an email confirmed my father's prediction, setting only a slightly earlier timeframe than Christmas:

> Dear all,
>
> The feedback from Myanmar Embassies worldwide is that any visa issue is suspended until 31st July. So, we need to wait and see what the authorities agree. We are working with a local travel agent to explore options for August flights back in as a group booking.

And so, I continued to wait, caught in the limbo of uncertainty, my adventure postponed but not abandoned.

Chapter 4. Farewell London

July 2020

"Mum," I shouted, "I've just received a very, very stressful email."

She hurried into the room, her eyes widened with concern. "What does it say? Let me see." I thrust my phone into her hands, heart pounding.

As she read, her eyes widened. "The Myanmar Embassy? A relief flight on July 26th. That's just seven days away."

"I know," I choked out. "That's why I'm freaking out."

"What's happening?" my dad asked, joining us in the living room.

"I might be going to Myanmar next week," I said, tears welling up. "Or maybe not. I don't know."

My father, always the optimist, cheerfully remarked, "That's fantastic. You've been waiting for this news!"

"No," I sobbed, "I'm not ready. It's too soon!"

Perplexed, my father challenged my distress, "What do you

mean too soon? Come on, pull yourself together."

"Andy," my mother intervened gently. "I think it is more that the email is so indecisive. It only says there is a 'possibility', and they don't even know how many seats are available."

"It's simple," he said firmly. "Pack your bags. If you go, you go; if you don't, you don't."

His straightforward advice should have comforted me, but my overanxious nature turned even the most straightforward solutions into complex riddles. I read and reread the email, searching for clarity.

Meanwhile, my new boyfriend, Daniel, was visiting for the first time. With the world gripped by a global pandemic, it was hardly an ideal environment for romance. Yet Matt Hancock made it work, so perhaps there was hope for the rest of us. On that day—our second-ever date—I had assured Daniel we'd have at least a month together before I moved to Myanmar. Now, those plans seemed uncertain.

"I'm not going," I repeated, my words echoing like a broken record.

"But it says possibility," my mum and Daniel chimed in, their voices a feeble attempt to assuage my mounting stress. "It might not happen at all."

Despite their well-intentioned reassurances, stress clung to me. Messages from fellow teachers flooded my inbox. News headlines whispered tales of dwindling air passenger arrivals in the UK, and the stories of desperate travellers turned away at customer service due to inadequate paperwork haunted my thoughts. Overwhelmed by these daunting possibilities, my mind momentarily strayed to the seemingly more straightforward choice of remaining in the comforting familiarity of Bromley.

Summoning the last vestiges of my resolve, I responded to the email, seeking clarity. I asked when visas would be processed and explained that I could not isolate for seven days. The lockdown had ended in London, and I needed to be able to say goodbye to my friends and family. The reply only added to my confusion, assuming my attendance without addressing my concerns.

My fate now teetered in the hands of the British and Myanmar embassies. I silently prayed, hoping that if the flight did materialise, my COVID-19 tests would yield a positive result. The thought of faltering and displaying a lack of commitment in my new job, should the flight come to pass, was unthinkable. The process of arranging tickets alone would take several days, leaving a mere four days to tackle everything else: COVID-19 tests and two embassy visits. This entailed the delicate dance of submitting and retrieving passports, all while navigating the stringent isolation requirements. It all felt impossible.

Of course, I was proven wrong. Doubts were swiftly dispelled. The seemingly impossible transformed into a frenzy of paperwork and meticulous organisation. In record time, we secured a fast-track immigration visit, paving the way for our departure. A commanding email arrived five days before the departure date, telling us we were not invited but rather "expected" to be on that flight. Later that day, a second email followed, even more direct, leaving no room for leniency. It felt like I was already on thin ice before beginning the job.

The email also mentioned the quarantine requirement upon

arrival in Yangon. A full fourteen days of isolation awaited us, divided between a hotel and our new apartments. The apartments at "teacher towers," where I had visited Sophie and Megan, were unfinished. The construction delays caused a ripple in our plans, scattering us across the city instead of uniting us under one roof. I couldn't recall when I had been entirely solitary for so long without the presence of others or even a pet. The prospect of being trapped within four walls, alone with my thoughts, made me shudder. And to my dismay, Sophie and Megan would not be joining me. Megan's journey home to Australia during the early days of the pandemic had been met with immigration restrictions that quashed any hopes of her leaving again. Sophie, living in Wales, chose not to fly. I prayed they would end up on a flight soon after and realised I had to pull up my *big-girl pants* and travel the long journey alone. Once I crossed the immigration barrier at the airport, the responsibility would rest solely on my shoulders.

Despite my reservations, I knew I had to board the flight on 26th July, with friends or without. I had to confront my fears and anxieties, embracing growth and the opportunities that lay beyond my comfort zone. Comfort zones, I realised, were like the fable of the boiling frog—drop a frog in boiling water, and it will immediately leap out to save itself, but place it in cold water that gradually heats up, it remains unaware until it's too late. I had grown complacent, oblivious to the need for change. Life felt stagnant; I had to take that leap, jump out of the water, and find something new.

In the days leading up to the flight, I teetered on the edge of abandoning the job multiple times. The nagging worries and fears tempted me to email the school and declare that the job "wasn't for me." However, I pushed forward, determined to defy that inner voice.

"I am going," I announced to my mother on the Tuesday, five days before the flight.

"Then you better start packing," she responded matter-of-factly.

"Can you help?" I whimpered, on the edge of tears yet again.

"Of course."

The next day, I entered self-imposed isolation. However, it seemed futile since I needed to take the train to the Myanmar Embassy in central London the following morning. I ordered a COVID-19 test, ensuring it was conducted 72 hours before I flew. I dropped the test into the priority post box, fearing the possibility of testing positive for the virus, which I now did not want. My mind was made up, and I needed to be on the flight.

Those next few days became a whirlwind of emotions until, finally, on Thursday morning, three days before the flight, we received official confirmation that the flight was indeed going ahead.

Chapter 5. Flight 727

27th July 2020

"Did you know that the royalty, rich, and famous have their own suite at Heathrow airport?" I exclaimed excitedly to my parents as we cruised along the M25. "It costs at least three thousand pounds, and they get a Michelin-star chef, concierge, and personal shopper!"

"Yes, I've been there," My father replied, his tone playful as he spun exaggerated tales of hand lifters and foot rubbers.

"Ha," I retorted, rolling my eyes, then returned my gaze to the passing scenery outside the window.

"Do you think we will all be allowed in together?" I asked, worried.

"What does the website say?" my mother inquired. "Maybe it depends on how busy it is."

I pulled up the website on my phone and read aloud, 'These are exceptional times, and we must ask that you respect the new government guidance on social distancing and only drop off/collect people who live in the same household as you. Further to this, we would also ask that you only enter the terminal if absolutely necessary, wearing a face covering, and not just to say goodbye to or greet a traveller."

"It is essential," I declared. "You might never see me again!"

"Don't say that!" my mother gasped, glaring through the rearview mirror.

"Do you think we'll make it in time?" I continued.

"Lydia, calm down," my mother sighed. "We have over three hours until check-in closes, and we're only five minutes away from Heathrow."

"My COVID-19 test hasn't even come back yet," I wailed. "Do you think they'll let me fly?"

"It will come through, don't worry."

As I glanced out the window, the rising sun bathed the M25 in a gentle warmth, casting a golden glow that danced among the trees as we drove. I drank in the scene, momentarily lost in the tranquillity of the countryside—the hills' slopes, the crisp country air and the graffiti marks on the bridges and sidewalks. I thought of my new home. Unlike the neatly paved sidewalks I was used to, there would be rugged, uneven paths of dirt and stone. Animals would roam freely through the streets, and a vibrant, chaotic city awaited me.

The atmosphere in the car was heavy, and there was an unspoken sense of loneliness and nervous anticipation. Only the occasional interruptions from the radio—the breakfast show chatter and weather updates—broke the stillness. At least I had hope for some sunny weather in my new home.

"We made it!" I sighed with relief as we reached the terminal car park. "Remember, let's stick together and follow my lead."

I carefully manoeuvred my two suitcases and hand luggage out of the car and onto a trolley.

"Let's watch," I whispered to my parents. Airport security interacted with other travellers' friends and family, turning them away from entering Terminal 2. It became clear that their focus was primarily on verifying suitcases rather than thoroughly checking tickets due to the rush of passengers.

"Pretend you're flying too," I instructed my parents, handing them one of my bags each. "Even if they want to check tickets, I don't have one, so let's just say we're all flying to Yangon."

To our relief, we were granted entry without any scrutiny. My eyes immediately sought out Ella in the check-in queue. She had also made it inside the airport with her parents. Our paths had crossed just days earlier at the Myanmar Embassy in London, where I'd learned she was a fellow teaching assistant.

"You made it," I exclaimed.

Ella appeared just as nervous as I did, offering a comforting reminder that I wasn't alone in this. Suddenly, our moment of solidarity was shattered by a commotion at a nearby check-in desk. An irate man's voice echoed through the terminal as he vehemently argued over excess baggage fees. My heart sank; I, too, had an extra suitcase, foolishly assuming the fees would be reasonable. However, without our flight tickets in hand, I hadn't been able to pre-book the extra suitcase online and, to my shock, I was informed that the extra luggage amounted to a staggering eight hundred pounds.

Panic set in. I needed time to reassess and repack my

belongings, but time was a luxury I couldn't afford due to a much larger problem. My COVID-19 test results, which were supposed to be in my inbox, were nowhere to be found. Throughout my sleepless night the evening before, I anxiously refreshed my email, hoping for a glimmer of relief, but to no avail.

I frantically contacted the school administration for help. They advised me to explain my situation to the airport staff and beg for leniency. But as I surveyed the chaos, with masked travellers and overwhelmed airport personnel, the daunting reality set in—pleading my case would be difficult.

"Fuck fuck fuck," I whispered to my mother. "I swear I saw a man turned away for not having a test certificate."

"Just smile, "she replied. "Act confused."

She pushed me forward, and I stumbled to the smiling, slightly hassled check-in lady.

"Good morning," she said. "Off to Yangon?"

"Yes," I replied.

"Great," she beamed. "Could I please see your passport, visa and test certificate?"

"Here is my passport and visa," I stammered. "My test result hasn't come through yet. They assured me it would arrive today."

"You can't fly without it," she replied, her smile fading.

"Can I go through security? I should have the test result before boarding the flight," I begged. "It's still early."

"You can't enter security without the certificate," she responded. "It's for the safety of our staff."

Desperation filled my voice as I continued, "I don't have the virus, I swear. I need to be on this plane."

To my left, I saw my mother's anger simmering beneath the surface. "This is ridiculous," she spat. "You paid over one hundred pounds for that test."

"Excuse me," the check-in lady interrupted. "I need to check in the other customers. Please step aside."

Feeling defeated, I gathered my suitcases and walked past my colleagues, my head hanging low.

"Dad, they won't let me fly," I muttered.

"This is absurd," he remarked, his voice tinged with disbelief. "Wait here and call the testing clinic."

As my father stormed off, searching for someone he deemed "superior," a wave of dread and humiliation swept over me. Deep down, I knew no saviour was waiting to bend the rules. Rules were rules, and no amount of shouting or stubborn determination could change that. I did as I was told, though, and frantically dialled the number of the testing clinic, each unanswered call intensifying my disappointment. Time was running out, and with it, my chance to leave England. The days of preparation, the endless stress, the goodbyes—they would all mean nothing if I couldn't board that plane.

Would the school be disappointed? Would it be my fault? My room in Bromley had already been emptied, and I had no job waiting for me upon my return. I had said goodbye to all my friends, and the thought of returning to my street with my tail between my legs was unbearable.

Then, amid the panic, an idea took root—a desperate, audacious plan that seemed as reckless as it was brilliant. It was the only option. I thought back to my university days, when a housemate had changed her father's name on her mobile to 'NHS' and requested him to send a text feigning an appointment, a clever ruse to take a sick day or miss a morning of work. Only days prior, I received a negative COVID-19 test text from the NHS, which the airline would not accept. Perhaps if I changed it to that day's date, they wouldn't notice. I urgently told my father the plan: forward him the text, alter his name to 'NHS Operations,' and have him resend it with the flight day.

He jumped at the idea, and although the check-in lady had already emphasised the necessity of a printed certificate, I hoped my tearful plea would stir compassion.

"I will make an exception," she said, her voice softening. "I can see how much you want to be on this flight."

"Thank you, thank you, thank you," I breathed.

"Email me the text," she instructed. "I'll print it out and give it the government stamp of approval."

Only when I held the stamped paper could I relax. My parents' concern melted into relief, and my racing heart slowed. The momentary happiness in my parents' eyes raised a slight suspicion, but I quickly dismissed it. After all, my father had very generously covered the excess baggage fee, not without demanding I get a refund, of course.

In hindsight, the signs were there all along. Delayed test results and unexpected excess fees—subtle warnings from the universe, perhaps urging me to reconsider boarding the flight. But frazzled and desperate, I brushed them aside, wiped away my tears, and drew a deep breath of relief.

When I checked my emails, I found many messages from

the new headmaster asking if I'd managed to check in. I could now respond with the good news.

After triple-checking my belongings, I made my way to the airport security. By the time I said goodbye to my parents, my tears had dried up. I embraced my father and mother in turn.

"Have fun, Liddi," my father smiled warmly.

Then my mum, a longer grip which was hard to tear away from. Reluctantly, I pulled myself away and moved through the security checkpoint. Solitude washed over me—I was truly alone on this journey now.

My delay in checking in meant boarding was imminent. I'd expected social distancing on the plane, excited at the prospect of not being squished like herded animals. But the flight attendants shattered that illusion—the aircraft would operate at full capacity. The COVID-19 tests now seemed pointless. Observing the other passengers already settling into their seats, we were packed together like sardines. Every inch of space was occupied, making the seats smaller, the aisles narrower, and the cabin more confined than ever. The world had shrunk, compressing us into this uncomfortable metal tube hurtling through the sky.

Wearing my PPE, two face masks and a suit, I felt the warmth and suffocation of the fabric against my skin. Protective gear, intended for security, now added to my discomfort. Mentally preparing for the long, uncomfortable eight-hour flight to Doha, I acknowledged that physical comfort would be a luxury I'd have to forego.

Once airborne, the captain's voice crackled through the speakers, outlining enhanced cleaning protocols and safety measures.

The cabin remained subdued, and I shifted in my seat, trying to find comfort within the limited space. The rhythmic clatter of the meal cart broke the monotony. Twice, it made its way down the corridor, offering a reduced service. However, without a flight ticket, I missed out on ordering my usual vegetarian meal, leaving me hungry and weary. Instead of eating, I tried to sleep, seeking respite from the confines of the cramped seat and the turbulence of my racing thoughts. Beside me, a male colleague mirrored my discomfort, his restless movements echoing my own.

When sleep finally claimed me, it was a fitful journey. Nonsensical nightmares disrupted my slumber, causing me to jolt awake at sporadic intervals. The hours stretched endlessly; the dimly lit cabin filled with the steady hum of the plane's engines.

As we descended toward Doha, arriving well past midnight, exhaustion weighed upon me like an anchor. The recycled air and passing hours left my mouth dry and parched. My eyes drooped, and my skin crawled. All I desired was sleep.

Once off the plane, I trailed behind Ella and Amie, another new teaching assistant, toward the nearest coffee shop. While others flocked to an open bar in the surprisingly bustling Doha airport, we sat on a bench, watching travellers navigate the corridors—the hurried steps, whispered conversations and fleeting glances.

Only twenty minutes later, the announcement of our second flight reverberated through the terminal. This aircraft offered slightly more space, with empty seats scattered about. Perhaps Myanmar's lesser-travelled status contributed to its relative spaciousness. I lightly snoozed, and after another eight hours, the captain signalled our descent.

By the window, I cautiously raised the small shutter. The view was mesmerising. I saw sprawling green and red fields, their patchwork quilt of colours blending seamlessly into the horizon. Rivers wound gracefully through the landscape, their sinuous curves reflecting in the morning light. Clusters of quaint thatched houses nestled together like protective huddles, their roofs catching glimmers of sun.

It was bright and lost in the hazy fog of semi-consciousness, I couldn't discern the time or the seamless transition from night to day.

The unnatural sensation of flying tugged at my senses. My stomach somersaulted, and my palms grew damp with unease. As the plane's wheels unlatched with a jittering motion, my heart began to race. With a sudden thud, we made contact with the tarmac, prompting a collective unbuckling of seat belts and a flurry of passengers retrieving their belongings. With hesitant limbs, I stretched my tired body and heaved a weary sigh. The adventure was about to begin.

Chapter 6. Four Walls

Myanmar had some of the strictest COVID-19 regulations in the world, contributing to its low case numbers. As a foreigner, I was wary of the potential stigmatisation and distrust from the locals, fearing accusations of importing the disease.

Before flying, I'd read an article detailing the stringent pandemic restrictions enforced in Eritrea, a small African country. These restrictions were even more extreme than those in Myanmar, including a complete cessation of public transportation and a ban on private cars from December 2020. While hopeful for a more flexible situation in Myanmar, I felt uneasy as we touched down in our new home.

As we disembarked, I was struck by the stark contrast between the scorching heat outside and the plane's chilly interior. Despite the cramped conditions onboard, strict adherence to the two-metre distancing rule was enforced. After descending the steps, we were ushered into a designated area teeming with expat teachers from various international schools in the city. An hour passed before a school representative announced the arrival of buses to transport us to the quarantine hotel, allowing us to clear customs.

As I joined and shuffled forward in the queue, my ears caught a snippet of conversation—an officer sternly informing a visibly worried British traveller that a signed COVID-negative certificate was mandatory. The NHS text message they had relied on? Dismissed. Shit. What if my test results didn't arrive in time? Would I be whisked away to a government facility? Or worse, sent back to England?

Fingers trembling, I connected to the airport's Wi-Fi. Those seconds before the screen lit up felt like an eternity. Then, in a moment of triumph, my official test result finally appeared: negative. Relief washed over me as I watched the British traveller escorted away, their fate uncertain.

I presented my test to the officer, who stamped my passport and visa with finality. I had made it.

The minibus was packed and loud, and my extreme jet lag and lack of sleep increased my anxiety. All I craved was oblivion, a respite in sleep. Amid polite exchanges, my new colleagues reminisced about pre-pandemic Yangon.

"Myanmar is beautiful," they told me.

I peered out the window as we ventured beyond the airport premises. The atmosphere appeared deceptively calm until we reached the outskirts. People perched atop vans, families balanced precariously on single motorbikes. Drivers honked their horns incessantly, swerving through the chaotic traffic, disregarding any semblance of English road rules. It was precisely like Jakarta. I recalled our driver in Indonesia warning us about the unconventional traffic practices, explaining, "You'll have to get used to this," as people dangerously stuck their hands out to cross the road, "Drivers just dodge people and cars. There is no right-of-way here."

Myanmar's road laws appeared advisory—lane markers were mere suggestions, and crossroads were like fancy road decorations. However, the cityscape was not as densely built as Jakarta's; highrise buildings were scarce, and the spaces between them were measured in yards rather than inches.

Heavy traffic significantly slowed down our journey. An hour later, on the brink of dozing off, the minibus abruptly stopped. A rough shake on the shoulder woke me. "You can sleep soon," someone said. "This must be so strange for you. Moving to a completely new place in the middle of a pandemic."

I nodded, stretched, and looked ahead. A grey, box-shaped building loomed, with "NOVOTEL" emblazoned on top. Hazmat-suited figures lined the entrance. We stepped off the bus and followed a large, friendly-faced man, our designated representative. He led us into a capacious, airy hall with high ceilings adorned with grand chandeliers. Chairs dotted the space, not distanced strictly—acknowledging the shared risk if any of us carried the virus.

We lined up to sign forms that bound us to quarantine regulations. Wooden tables stretched before us, and we waited anxiously for the detailed guidelines that would govern our confinement. Each of us was handed a hotel key card, programmed to allow only a single entry and exit from our assigned rooms.

As the regulations were laid out, the gravity of the situation sank in. We'd be treated as if we were contagious, the week ahead a test of endurance against isolating solitude. If we broke the rules, then to the government facility it was. Haunting images of those facilities flashed in my mind—bleak rooms furnished with nothing more than a thin mattress, a pillow, and a blanket. Wi-Fi access was a rare luxury, and healthcare workers monitored every move through omnipresent CCTV cameras, with their directives echoing through the sterile halls via crackling loudspeakers.

Days earlier, I'd dreamt of being caught sneaking an unauthorised guest into my room. Orange-hazmat-clad figures descended on me, swiftly immobilising me with hazard tape and subjecting me to decontamination before thrusting me into a claustrophobic, solitary cell. Cold sweat, racing heart—the nightmare's realism clung to me.

Fortunately, reality diverged from that chilling nightmare, and while the rules were strict, they were manageable. The most rigid rule to digest was that no windows were allowed to be open, unless you smoked. Envy tugged—I wished I'd lied. After an exhaustive hour-long discussion of the rules, we were guided to the elevator, dragging our weary bodies to our assigned rooms. Saying goodbye to my colleagues, I lingered for a moment, knowing it would be some time before I would have human interaction again.

My fourth-floor room was spacious and airy and thoughtfully set air conditioning enveloped me. I slipped under the thick covers, adjusting my watch to Myanmar's time zone—five and a half hours ahead of the UK. Eyes closed, I succumbed to sleep almost instantly.

Sometime later, I was roused by a series of urgent knocks.

"Hello, hello, Miss!"

Groggily, I lifted my head from the pillow, momentarily disoriented. With half-closed eyes, I shuffled toward the door and swung it open, greeted by the sight of a friendly young man wearing a mask and visor, holding a tray of food on top of my suitcases.

"Lunch." He grinned, extending the tray towards me. I mumbled thanks and took the tray into my room. The aroma of the meal stimulated my senses and made me more alert. I was hungry— a day or so had passed since I'd eaten a proper meal. The tray contained a plate of chips and sausages, an odd-looking dessert, a salad, bread, and a chocolatey snack. I made a mental note to message our representative and request vegetarian meals and nibbled on some chips. I sighed and looked around my new surroundings.

Comparing our situation to the accounts I had read on travel forums about other quarantine hotels, I realised how fortunate we were. Reports of unclean rooms, damp towels, and even mould were common. Solo travellers arriving at the airport were given the choice between a one-star or five-star hotel, with no middle ground. It was either paying a hefty sum for a luxurious stay or ending up in a shithole with a high risk of gastrointestinal discomfort. We were treated generously, with an impressive array of snacks, water, and beer in each room. A welcome letter and a Myanmar SIM card with credit awaited me on the bed. The king-sized bed stood prominently, but I chose to lie only on the left-hand side after sleeping in a small single at home. I had a kettle, mini fridge, bath, shower, hairdryer, desk, sofa, and a large TV. However, my excitement dimmed as I drew back the curtains to peer out the window. It offered nothing but the drab facade of the neighbouring side of the hotel. I hoped I wasn't the only one with a less-than-ideal view; the prospect of staring at walls for a week filled me with dread, fearing monotony and a potential decline in sanity.

A few hours later, another knock signalled dinner. The food offerings were similar to the previous meal, and I doubted anybody would have an appetite after such a large lunch. After inserting my new SIM card into my phone, I discovered a WhatsApp group named 'hotel quarantine crew' had been created. Messages filled the chat, responding to the representative's question of 'How was the food today?'

'More fruit, please.'

'Requesting vegetarian, please, and more fresh vegetables.'

'It was great, but I feel myself fattening up after all the food and being stuck in a room. We need a hamster wheel.'

Some responses were comical, and after adding my response of 'vegetarian and gluten-free, please,' I was pleasantly surprised to see my meals amended instantaneously. From that point on, the stream of food deliveries seemed never-ending. I found myself accumulating leftovers in the mini fridge, determined not to let anything go to waste, even though I knew I would probably never finish it all.

A familiar knock echoed through the door three times a day. Each time, a smiling waiter appeared, placing a tray filled with fresh towels, bottles of water, and dozens of tea bags outside my room. I began to amass a small collection of mini shampoos, conditioners, tea, coffee, and earbuds. "I realised I might never need to buy these items again.

My daily routine revolved around the scheduled delivery

times of my meals. Breakfast arrived promptly at seven in the morning, lunch at midday, and dinner at six in the evening. I became alert to the sounds in the corridor, eagerly anticipating the clattering of the trolley, which indicated the arrival of my next meal. Muffled coughs and occasional footsteps from neighbouring rooms provided a distant soundtrack. The constant hum of the air conditioning, which I left day and night, brought comfort, punctuating the silence that enveloped my confined space.

Between mealtimes, I found my yoga mat useful as I scrolled through different workouts and daily yoga routines. The school also arranged several virtual welcome meetings, including a virtual pub quiz, a far cry from the in-person welcome fortnight from the previous year. Regardless, it was great to connect with my new colleagues. One of my favourite meetings was the "Top things to do in Myanmar," although most of the suggestions revolved around bars and nightclubs.

During these meetings, everybody seemed to be in good spirits, and it was amazing to witness the human spirit's adaptability. Gradually, I established a semblance of routine within the confines of my room, where I spent every hour of the day.

By the third day of quarantine, I discovered I could order food using the *Grab* app or the local supermarket. While I wasn't particularly hungry, the monotony of the days left me longing for some variety. I ordered some snacks, and the anticipation of the delivery brought a welcome diversion to my otherwise mundane routine.

On that same day, I realised I was the only one without a window that offered a view of the outside world. Feeling a tinge of disappointment, I casually mentioned it in our staff hotel quarantine chat. A lovely lady named Mina contacted me, expressing concern and checking if I was doing okay. I assured her that I was physically okay. Still, I admitted that the lack of natural light was taking a toll on my mental wellbeing.

Diary insert:

This morning, I woke up and watched another five episodes of 'Below Deck.' I also tried FaceTime with every family member, but none replied. I tried various new foods, most of which I did not like. However, the hotel staff were lovely, giving me gluten-free everything after lying that I 100% cannot eat it.

On the fifth day of isolation, we were called down for our COVID-19 tests. Everybody was thrilled, sharing our quarantine highs and lows and discussing the meals we had received, with particular emphasis on the desserts.

"Ella," I exclaimed, unable to contain my joy. "I am so happy to see you!"

"Oh my god, me too," she screeched. "I have been going insane, making my mum and friends FaceTime me for hours. This is Maeve, her room is in my corridor. She is also a new teaching assistant."

"Hey!" Maeve chimed in. "How are you holding up?"

"Going a little stir-crazy," I confessed.

"We've been having chats in our corridor with the door open or propped open," Maeve said.

"I wish I was on your floor!" I moaned, "I can't even see anyone from my door!"

"Jeez, I'm not surprised you're going crazy!"

Stepping out of the confines of our hotel rooms and into the corridor felt liberating. We strolled down the hallway, relishing the opportunity to stretch our legs. In a large conference room, chairs stood meticulously two metres apart. This time, I observed my colleagues more closely—the established cliques and friendships, weathered lines etched on older faces, and apprehension on the young ones, still uncertain about what they'd signed up for.

I tried to prolong my stay downstairs, soaking in the different surroundings and the company of others, but eventually, the moment arrived for my test. Escorted to an adjoining room, I met three men dressed in hazmat suits. One stood enclosed in a large transparent box, gloved hands reaching out to swab our noses and throats. I watched a colleague squirm before me, another man steadying her as the swab probed deeper. Fifteen agonising seconds in each nostril, ten in the back of the throat—she shouted an expletive, tears welling.

Watching my colleague squirm taught me to relax, and as the swab was pushed up my nose, I battled my automatic response of fighting back. Painful, yes, and I hoped that the testers, despite a few smirks that escaped their otherwise professional demeanour, understood the discomfort. In the waiting room, we learned the protocol if anyone tested positive: a twenty-one-day extension to our quarantine. No government facility, but the thought of potentially being the one responsible for prolonging everybody's quarantine, plus the hefty cost—around a thousand dollars a week—terrified me.

On the seventh day of our quarantine, a message broke the silence in our group WhatsApp chat, bringing hope. The results were negative—we'd "passed our quarantine." The next day wouldn't grant immediate freedom, but it promised change, a step toward normalcy.

Reflecting on my time in the hotel, surprisingly, the solitude brought a sense of calm, paired with unexpected reluctance to leave the safety of my room. The absence of human connection, first during London's lockdown and now in quarantine, left me with a lingering sense of anxiety about reintegrating. A paradoxical mix of comfort and apprehension.

On the fourth of August, we transitioned from hotel quarantine to home quarantine. Time again stretched endlessly before us. As we headed to our respective apartments in Sanchaung, the distinction between teachers and teaching assistants became apparent. We would live in different apartment blocks scattered across various parts of the city. The number of teaching assistants was limited since most were still in England. Yet, despite our small group, a bond began to form.

"This is a really nice part of town," Ivy, who was familiar with the area, commented with a smile. "It's better than where the teachers will be placed."

"It looks amazing," I replied, gazing at the bustling shops, vibrant market stalls, and the colourful array of smiling faces.

As our taxi navigated towards our new abode, Amie and Ella shouted "KFC" in unison, causing us to erupt into laughter. The road was narrow and crowded, with people going about their daily business, pushing carts filled with an assortment of meats, fish, fruits, and vegetables. Our taxi driver honked his horn several times, alerting barefoot pedestrians to move out of the way. Onlookers gazed into the car window, perhaps intrigued by our presence or simply curious about the world beyond their own.

Upon arriving at Sanchaung Garden Residence, we bid farewell to each other once again as we were led to randomly allocated apartments. Reaching my apartment, I was pleasantly surprised. It felt empty, like a blank canvas awaiting my personal touch with my few belongings. The space felt almost too large for a single person, and I suddenly felt tiny at that moment. The master bedroom was large, with an ensuite bathroom. I knew the plumbing system was delicate and could not handle toilet paper, necessitating the bin beside it. The apartment featured a spare bedroom, another sizable bathroom, a cosy lounge area, and a fully equipped kitchen.

I was pleased to find two large boxes left for me in the living room. One contained a double duvet, pillows, and sheets. The second box held essential kitchenware, including pots, pans, various utensils, mugs, and cutlery. I discovered a third box filled with food in the kitchen—a loaf of bread, baked beans, beer, potatoes, onion, milk, and cornflakes.

Soon, a new group chat titled 'Sanchaung crew' appeared, quickly filling with images and videos of each other's apartments. Maeve, the first among us to arrive at her flat, had the privilege of a tour that morning.

[Maeve] Got a tour of the pool and gym. It's very nice!
[Me] Yay! Pics of apartments, please!
[Maeve] Oh wow, that's way nicer than mine! Is it clean?
[Me] They are cleaning mine now.
[Maeve] The more I look around mine, the dirtier it is. The freezer is gross.

After a moment of silence:

[Ivy] Mine is horrible. I've asked to move.

[Amie] What is it like?

[Ivy] There's no hob, and it is so dirty. A lot worse than where I was living before.

[Me] Has anybody heard from Ella?

[Ivy] Erm, no, did she have a SIM?

[Amie] The internet isn't working. Maybe she has no SIM.

[Ivy] I've not moved from one spot. So dirty there's men's hair all over the place.

As the messages in the group chat gradually dwindled, my attention turned to the mounting pile of recycling awaiting transport to the bin on the ground floor. Despite being a chore typically dreaded in London, I felt eager to tackle it. I grabbed my mask and a cardigan, thinking it wise to cover my arms and legs, then paused at the doorstep. Suddenly overwhelmed, thoughts such as "Is this even allowed?" and "What if I end up in Myanmar jail? I wouldn't survive," raced through my mind. Just as my worries peaked, a loud knock shattered my thoughts. Shit, I had been caught.

"Hello?" I called out wearily,

"Lydia," came a shaky voice, "is that you? Please let it be you?"

Throwing the door open, I pulled Ella into a tight embrace. "I thought you were the mafia!" I blurted out, stopping short when I noticed the worry on her face.

"I'm sorry. Can I please get a hotspot from you?" she asked. "My SIM card isn't working, and I need to contact my mam."

My heart softened as I realised how brave Ella had been to fly across the world, experiencing Asia for the first time, during a pandemic. We were among the fortunate few who had made the ten-thousand-mile journey. Still, the coming weeks would be challenging as we navigated our new surroundings, repeatedly seeking hope but often falling short.

"Of course you can," I reassured Ella as I helped her connect to my hotspot and resolve her SIM card issue.

During that mid-August week, we had several work meetings and training sessions to keep ourselves occupied. Our safeguarding skills were refreshed, and I delved into the complexities of phonics—I never knew learning to read could be so complicated. In between, I continued to read my Myanmar fact book, uncovering intriguing titbits of history and culture. I learned of the sudden shift of Yangon's status as the capital city to Naypyidaw in October 2005. The clandestine construction of this new administrative hub had left government staff blindsided by the abrupt relocation of over 400km. Each fact fuelled my curiosity, instilling a growing restlessness within me as the second week of quarantine unfolded.

Unlike the windowless confines of the hotel, I was now presented with a tantalising glimpse of the outside world. Through the glass, the humidity and catching the fragrant scent of Burmese street food beckoned me. Large dark buildings loomed on one side of our apartments, their walls bearing the weathered scars of time, cloaked in a deep, murky brown hue. The concrete streets below were pocked with potholes, traversed by carts laden with hanging animal carcasses. Barefooted men and women meandered while children played with makeshift toys fashioned from discarded bottles. The scene was a tableau of chaos and noise. I loved it.

Unlike the steady stream of meals provided during our hotel

stay, our second week in home quarantine came with a limited supply of groceries, necessitating the need to order food. Thankfully, the school administration offered us a cash advance, considering our lack of local bank accounts and our inability to use foreign cards for delivery services. Armed with two hundred dollars, a sum that stretched considerably further in Yangon than in London, I was delighted to find meals similar to those I would order at home cost a mere two dollars, including delivery fees.

Venturing downstairs to the front entry gate to collect our food orders felt surreal after days of confinement.

[Maeve] I can't take it anymore. I am going to get some wine.
[Me] Wait, are we allowed to leave? Like, go to an actual shop?
"Do it," everyone replied.

With a rendezvous point quickly established by the security desk in our residence, we gathered on two long wooden benches overlooking Sanchaung Street. Awaiting daily food deliveries provided a convenient excuse for our brief escapades. Besides, with our negative COVID-19 test results in hand, the notion of enduring another week of quarantine seemed excessive. And then there was Ivy's birthday to celebrate. We all empathised with the loneliness she felt amidst the solitude of her apartment, far from her boyfriend, family, or friends. Determined to lift her spirits, we conspired to surprise her with a cake and coffee, which we enjoyed on those wooden benches, celebrating together.

"It's not long now, girls," Maeve sighed, voicing our group's collective agitation. "I've exhausted all my Sims playing."

"Same here," said Ivy. "Terminal 5 is just across the road," referring to a lively bar adjacent to our building.

"Oh, the temptation to be a little naughty is strong now," Maeve admitted with a mischievous grin. "I want to run free!"

Chapter 7. Making Home in a Foreign Land

August 2020: Six months prior to the coup

"It's the tenth of August," I sang, springing out of bed with enthusiasm as Monday dawned.

The past few days had presented us with a myriad of challenges, from Ella's bout of food poisoning to the unwelcome presence of geckos and beetles. However, as I stepped out into the lively streets of Myanmar, a sense of liberation washed over me. The sun drenched the city in its warm embrace, casting a golden glow over every corner. Today, I resolved, would be a day of indulgence—a chance to explore the neighbourhood and bask in the sun by the pool.

With my swimming bag slung over my shoulder and a towel wrapped around me, I embarked on my quest to find the rooftop pool. Navigating the maze of stairs and corridors proved challenging, but the anticipation of a refreshing swim spurred me onward. Finally, I discovered the staircase leading to the second-floor rooftop oasis. The pool shimmered under the sun's radiant gaze, its surface reflecting the golden splendour of the Shwedagon Pagoda towering in the distance.

Leaning over the balcony encircling the pool, I was captivated by the scene below. Tiny hands wrung out wet clothes, sending droplets cascading into the streets below, while the melodic chime of nearby temple bells filled the air. Unable to resist any longer, I dove into the cold water, feeling its embrace wash away my fatigue. I swam towards the pool's edge and rested my arms on the cool tiles.

As the day wore on, the sky gradually transformed into a canvas of vibrant colours. The setting sun painted the horizon with luminous reds and oranges, signalling the arrival of a new chapter. Night descended, ushering us to explore the city's nightlife. We celebrated our newfound freedom from quarantine alongside Ivy's birthday. As we made our way towards the towering Penthouse bar, the nostalgia of times in Indonesia came—the familiar smells and sounds, the clubs you could enter from age fourteen if you were Western or 'wealthy.'

As we strolled through the streets, mindful of uneven pavement slabs, I couldn't ignore the locals' curious gaze and wandering eyes. Surprisingly, the staring didn't bother me as much as I thought it would—the staring because of the colour of our skin. Young children and older men were watching, and some women too.

As we walked, I told the girls of the time my family and I visited Jakarta Zoo. The entry fee was only twenty pence, and despite mixed reviews, we decided to visit after exhausting all other half-term activities. Our expedition concluded in the Monkey Sanctuary, where, to our disappointment, all the monkeys were hiding.

"Let's go home," my father sighed.

"Let's wait a few more minutes," protested Zach. "The monkeys want to meet us."

After reluctantly accepting defeat, we turned towards the exit. However, a group of adults and children nearby caught our attention, their curious eyes fixed upon us with intense fascination. I quickly spun around, expecting to see the sudden appearance of a dozen monkeys. There was nothing to be seen. I turned back towards the group, only to find them still staring at us, their expressions deepening.

"Hello, miss," they started. "Photo, please." I assumed they wanted me to take a photo, but suddenly, a young woman placed her arm around my brother's shoulders. They swarmed around us, snapping pictures one after another.

"We should start charging per photo," my father smirked.

Eventually, the attention grew tiresome. "We are not the monkeys here," my father snapped as he hurried us away from the crowd. Afterwards, we quickly grew accustomed to the lingering stares accompanying our presence as foreigners. When asking an Indonesian friend why, she pointed at my skin and said, "You're white." It was a moment of revelation for me. The desire for fairer skin ingrained in the cultural beauty standards was evident, with skin-whitening products filling the shops. The pursuit of whiteness was seen as an aspiration for many Indonesians.

Westerners are even more uncommon in Myanmar, where immigrants comprise only 0.12% of the population, compared to 6% in neighbouring Thailand. Nevertheless, I had grown accustomed to blank stares and wandering eyes. The sensation of being a foreigner had become a thread woven into my experience.

"I don't like it," Ella expressed, her discomfort evident. "It's off-putting."

"You'll get used to it, love," Maeve reassured with a warm smile. "It's because you're so gorgeous!"

As we approached the entrance of the Penthouse, a sky bar bistro with breathtaking views of the Shwedagon, we were greeted by the thumping bass of music seeping through the doors. The venue was quiet, filled only with colleagues. Seated across from Amie at a table near the dance floor, I sensed her nervousness. I wanted to make her feel comfortable, reminding myself of how young she was at only twenty years old.

"How are you finding it here?" I asked.

"Overwhelming," Amie replied, a hint of sadness flickering in her eyes. "Everyone is lovely, though, and I'm glad you're all here too."

"It is overwhelming," I agreed.

"I miss my family. It's been a long time since I've seen them, especially after living in the UK and now in Myanmar. They are in the Philippines."

"We're all here for each other. We're like a second family, always here to support each other."

Amie smiled gratefully. "You're right. Having you all here makes this transition a little easier."

"Let's dance," I suggested, taking her arms and leading her to the dance floor. We joined Maeve, Ella, and Ivy before settling by the railings overlooking the Shwedagon.

"Isn't it beautiful?" Ivy sighed.

"It really is," Maeve agreed. "Ain't we lucky."

The next day, we took a short ten-minute walk from our apartment to see the Shwedagon pagoda up close. From afar, it appeared magnificent, but up close, the gold-plated complex was truly breathtaking. Adorned with over four thousand diamonds, the Pagoda's splendour stood in stark contrast to the nearby slums, a juxtaposition that was both striking and humbling.

"It's over two and a half thousand years old," Ivy exclaimed. "Marvellous, right?"

We learned that the Pagoda was the most sacred site for Myanmar's Buddhist population, housing relics of Gautama Buddha himself. Though we couldn't enter the Pagoda, the surrounding area was bustling with worshippers and visitors.

After our visit, we lunched at Rangoon Tea House, a charming restaurant reached by a slow taxi ride through the city's congested streets. The restaurant's cosy interior, constructed from recycled teak and bricks, was welcoming. We bonded with fellow expats over a meal of Burmese specialities, including the renowned Tea Leaf Salad, sharing stories and savouring new flavours.

Before heading home, we quickly stopped at the upscale supermarket Marketplace to restock our nearly empty fridges. Despite the higher prices, the wide variety of local and international products offered a taste of familiar comforts. Cooking elaborate meals seemed daunting, especially since, like in Indonesia, eating out was often more economical than buying ingredients and cooking at home. Also, like in Indonesia, early September brought the rainy season with it.

Myanmar's rainy season is spectacular. The country does not have a distinct winter, spring, summer, or autumn: the seasons are categorised as wet or dry. Yet the rainy season possesses its own enchantment. Each raindrop that falls brings a sense of freshness and life to the earth, nourishing both plants and animals—a time of renewal.

At night, the sounds of torrential rainfall were comforting. The rhythmic tapping of raindrops against windows and the gentle patter on the roof was meditative. The warmth of the rain left behind dense, humid air, rendering raincoats and umbrellas ineffective against the deluge. The sticky residue clung to our skin, leaving it clammy and soft, while hair rebelled against the moisture, frizzing up in protest.

Initially envied for the perpetual warmth, life in tropical paradise revealed its complexities beyond sunshine and sangria. Arriving in August, the rainy season was in full swing and would continue until the end of October. While the lush vegetation thrived under the rain's nourishment, its continuous downpour proved relentless.

Heavy clouds loomed overhead, shrouding the once-clear blue skies in a hazy, grey veil. Mosquitos emerged, eager to partake in the rain-soaked dance. The pitter-patter of rain momentarily hushed the once-vibrant streets, their worn pavements now slick with moisture. Roads transformed into rushing rivers. The incessant drumming echoed through the night as the city grappled with the consequences of the downpour. Flooding became inevitable, impacting both affluent and less privileged areas alike.

The monsoon season reminded me of an even more

dramatic event in Indonesia in 2014, one that highlighted the fragility of developing countries. One evening in Jakarta, as another hot, sticky day came to an end, I was resting in the top part of our family bungalow. Our home, located near a river, faced a severe storm. At first, the sounds of rainfall were hypnotic, but they soon turned menacing, flooding our home.

Water seeped through tightly closed doors, turning the swimming pool into a churning reservoir of green. The house soon filled with shouting and directions, and voices barking orders and rallying everyone to action. Frantic, I rushed down to the lower level to check the state of my bedroom.

The lower flower was a flurry of activity. Buckets were strategically placed to catch leaks from above, and mops moved in rhythmic motion to battle the invading water, a stealthy intruder intent on claiming its territory. For four gruelling hours, we mopped tirelessly, with no end in sight. The rain had become unyielding in its assault, and our living space had become submerged.

As the rain momentarily eased its intensity, we visited the rooftop to assess the damage. We stood on the rain-soaked surface, our eyes faintly discerning the graveyard beside us. The graves, too, were now submerged.

"We see the damage in the morning," our houseboy, Adoel, concluded.

"Where will you sleep? I'm so sorry," I said, my eyes opening to the state of Yanti, the cook, and Adoel's belongings. Their bedrooms, bedding, and clothes were all drenched, the deluge sparing no corner of the living space. We quickly laid duvets in the living room, making makeshift beds for them to finally rest their heads, anxious to see what sunrise would reveal.

The following day, Adoel yelled, "Look at all the fish in the pool, mister!" My father hurried to the pool, and I followed, rubbing the sleep from my eyes. The once pristine, crystal-clean swimming pool had transformed into a brown, murky fishpond, and a dozen koi swam amidst the cloudy waters.

Our once spotless floors were now covered in a thick layer of indistinguishable muck, and the driveway was full of water. Adoel bravely waded out to test the depth, which rose to his waist.

School was cancelled, and we worked to restore our home. The following morning, a boat emerged, and Zach and I gently lowered ourselves, clutching our school bags tightly. Pushing off from the safety of our gates, we ventured onto the water-laden road, where the school bus awaited us.

The Jakarta floods of early 2014 claimed lives and left tens of thousands homeless, highlighting the city's vulnerability to rising waters. While there was little chance of my new home in Yangon being flooded, the rain reminded me of the challenges faced in Southeast Asian countries.

Chapter 8. Henry's Village

August 2020: Six months prior to the coup

"I want to do something adventurous," Ivy declared, her boredom evident in her voice. She stood by the window in her apartment, gazing out at the streets below. "I'm bored of staying in Yangon."

Unlike Ivy, I was not bored. With a week left to explore before the school year started, I revelled in the streets surrounding our apartment complex. Each step immersed me deeper into my new home's diverse population and rich spiritual heritage. Monks draped in saffron robes glided gracefully, their shaved heads bowed, bare feet against the warm pavement. Hidden treasures nestled in narrow alleyways, and intricately designed pagodas dotted the city, their golden spires reaching skyward.

Observing men—mostly taxi drivers—spitting red saliva onto the pavement piqued my curiosity. I turned to Ivy, our go-to Myanmar guide, seeking answers. She explained that many men chewed betel nuts, also known as areca nuts, which caused their crimson spit. These nuts, consumed for their stimulating properties during long shifts, contained a psychoactive substance called arecoline, similar to nicotine. Sold in parcels with tobacco, lime, and spices, they balanced out the bitter taste. I watched as a man expertly folded the concoction into a small parcel and placed it between his teeth, his lips stained a deep crimson. "So that's why their teeth are red," I reflected.

"I am always up for an adventure," I mused, lounging in the comfort of Ivy's stylish flat. Adorned with unique furniture and decorations collected before the COVID-19 pandemic, her home was an enviable sanctuary.

Pointing to a large rattan hanging basket, I said, "I want one of those."

"I got it in a village." Ivy smiled, eyes glimmering with fond memories.

"Which village?" Maeve asked,

Ivy's smile widened. "Do you want to go?" Her tone was mischievous.

Days later, a plan was set to visit "Henry's village." A private bus collected the five of us and twelve other teachers at six in the morning the following Sunday. Tired and groggy from waking early, half of us dozed off during the two-hour bus ride to the outskirts of Yangon. Unable to sleep, I focused my gaze on the surrounding scenery as we edged further and further away from the condensed city and into the neighbouring countryside.

Concrete buildings and tangled wires were replaced by endless expanses of emerald-green rice paddies glistening with morning dew. The majestic mountains on the horizon marred the sky above. As miles passed, the air changed—it became fresher, infused with the scent of earth and blossoms.

Upon our arrival, the village greeted us with open arms. The ground was soft underfoot, a patchwork of moss and fallen leaves, and beautiful flowers and palm trees bloomed outwards. It felt like a hidden oasis.

Children paused in their play to wave at us, their faces lighting up with unabashed curiosity and joy.

"Welcome, welcome!" Henry, our host, greeted us. His cheeks were ruddy, and his eyes crinkled at the corners. "Where are you from?"

"We are all from the United Kingdom," Ivy replied, noting that we were among the fortunate few teachers who had secured a flight.

"How long have you been here?" he inquired further. "You flew this year?"

"Yes, in July," I responded. "Just a few weeks ago."

"What about your family? Boyfriends?" he pressed.

"Just us," we chuckled. "We escaped them."

"Family is very important here," Henry remarked, casting a fond glance at his two young children playing nearby.

Our day unfolded with trekking along untouched trails, our footsteps sinking into the damp earth. We canoed and paddled in Ngamoeyake Creek, navigating the waterways, raindrops dancing on the surface. For the return journey to Henry's home, we clambered into the back of an open truck. The vehicle jolted into life, and we held on tightly as it bounced along the rugged, muddy tracks. Puddles splashed up, coating us in layers of mud. The wind whipped through our hair, and our collective laughed filled the air.

"This is better than any theme park ride!" one of our colleagues shouted over the roar of the engine.

Back at Henry's, we were greeted by a feast of authentic Mon cuisine. We sat cross-legged, passing dishes between us. There was fragrant Thingyan rice, delicate Shan noodles, Burmese fish, vegetable curry, warm mohinga, and a delicious tea leaf salad. I savoured every bite.

As dusk descended and the sun dipped behind the mountains, we climbed a ladder onto a netted cocoon woven from ropes and sticks. Pillows and blankets were dotted around, cradling our tired bodies. The air, crisp and untainted, contrasted with Yangon's pollution-choked atmosphere. The sky transformed into a canvas painted with a spectrum of oranges, pinks, and purples. In the distance, we heard the sounds of crickets and frogs.

When the time came for us to leave, our gratitude swelled. Henry and his family had welcomed us with open hearts. We'd glimpsed their richness in simplicity, community, and local culture. As we departed, I realised I was in love with my new home.

"Please come back anytime," Henry said warmly. "You are always welcome here."

Six months later, the world around us would shift dramatically with the onset of the coup. But in that moment, the future was a distant concept. I was exactly where I was meant to be.

Chapter 9. Do Not Believe the Rumours

August–September 2020: Five months prior to the coup

The twenty-first of August arrived, marking our first day at work. It served as a preview of our year ahead—one filled with unforeseen challenges. Just the day before, I had read an amusing quote: "*And just like that, nobody ever asked why teachers need a fall break, spring break or the entire summer off again.*" Little did I know how prophetic those words would prove.

As the first term commenced, it became evident that parents were eager for respite, a break from their children's incessant demands. Yet, on this eagerly anticipated "first day of school," children remained absent from the familiar school premises. The Myanmar government, cautious in the face of a global pandemic, had withheld permission for schools to open fully, especially private institutions like ours. Resolute in their assurances, the managerial team vowed that reopening was imminent. With that promise, our task for our first workday was straightforward: prepare and sanitise all classrooms thoroughly—a Herculean endeavour.

Alexa, the class teacher, and I spent hours organising, chatting, and devising lesson plans. The scent of cleaning solutions mingled with the faint aroma of chalk and paper. We rummaged through toy boxes, prepared displays, and organised supplies.

Only ten days after this initial visit to the school, news of an impending lockdown reached us. When I first arrived in Yangon, COVID-19 cases were remarkably low. From February to August 2020, there had been only three hundred and fifty registered cases—an impressive statistic compared to the United Kingdom. However, as borders gradually opened, cases surged, surpassing a thousand. The rising numbers sparked concerns about the virus's spread within the country.

As foreigners, we began to sense a subtle shift in how we were perceived. Hostile stares lingered a moment too long, and shopkeepers' once-warm smiles faded behind wary eyes. Every outing brought scrutiny, and we feared saying the wrong thing.

"Do you feel it, too?" Maeve asked one afternoon as we navigated the narrow aisles of the supermarket.

I nodded, keeping my voice low. "It's like we're walking around with a target on our backs," I murmured. "I understand their fear, but it's unsettling."

It made sense. A significant outbreak, comparable to those in England, would devastate Myanmar. The country lacked the safety nets of an NHS or furlough schemes. Locals feared not just missing social gatherings but the prospect of not being able to feed their children or facing homelessness.

In an effort to stem the tide, the government enforced strict health protocols. Nearby townships faced draconian stay-at-home orders, sealing off entire areas. Unlike in England, leisurely sixty-minute walks were prohibited—everything was off-limits. Once-bustling parks now lay barricaded with red tape bearing a clear message of NO ENTRY.

The news of lockdowns in neighbouring townships reached Sanchaung, sparking fears of stringent measures. One afternoon, weary from work, I headed to the pool area for a refreshing swim, only to find it deserted and blocked off. The gym, too, stood dark and padlocked. My heart sank as I realised they were also closed.

Leaning against the door, I felt a pang of longing for the normalcy the pandemic had disrupted. The water was my safe space—the rhythmic strokes and weightlessness of being submerged in it had been my refuge from the chaos of the outside world.

Within our residence, an undercurrent of worry prevailed. The allure of exploring beautiful locales suddenly felt out of reach. At the same time, the school's eerie silence—devoid of children's laughter echoing through the halls, classrooms, and playgrounds—amplified the sense of unease. However, it was better than working alone in my apartment.

DO NOT BELIEVE THE RUMOURS AT ALL

Our concerns materialised into reality in mid-September when a sweeping 'stay at home order' was declared across all townships. From my window, I observed a paradox—the streets below were still alive with locals going about their day, their laughter and animated conversations drifting upward as if in defiance of the restrictions.

With the language barrier, deciphering the lockdown rules

became a puzzle. According to the government, we were permitted to attend work, but other ventures or excursions were strictly forbidden. The school, however, still arranged weekly shopping trips to the mall, blurring the lines of compliance. I was torn between a desire to adhere to the rules in a foreign land and an inclination to follow the locals' lead.

A day after the decree, we returned to our apartments, greeted by a gigantic 'disinfection chamber.' Intended for our safety, it demanded passage upon entry and doused us and our belongings in a pungent mist. A shrill alarm marked each person's journey through the sanitising ordeal while security personnel meticulously recorded the details of everyone's ID and barred guests from entering.

That night, the confines of my apartment felt particularly stifling. The weekends, once a cherished time, had become something to endure rather than enjoy. The knowledge that the city's wonders lay just beyond reach was a constant tease.

"Did you hear that pools are still open in other townships?" Ivy said one day.

"Seriously? It feels like we're under house arrest!"

A nagging thought began to gnaw at the recesses of my mind, relentlessly reminding me that I had travelled all the way to Myanmar only to find myself confined to an apartment, teaching virtually. I tried to find the positives: at least there would be no squabbles over the television remote, like back home. I had ample space to roam freely, naked, through the rooms of my apartment. I could dance and sing, finding ways to entertain myself for an unforeseen stretch of time.

And, of course, I could still go to work.

Whether or not children were physically present, our virtual sessions provided a sense of connection and socialisation. Our small cohort of colleagues formed a close-knit group, embracing the new norm of teaching through screens. Amid speculations of continued closure until the next academic year in June 2021, I remained focused on creating engaging lessons for my reception class. The thought of my thirteen students, who had been deprived of the presence of their friends for so long, fuelled my dedication. Whenever Alexa and I were at the school, we transformed our lessons into comedic productions, using a green screen, props, and the invaluable assistance of our Burmese teaching assistants.

"Maybe we'll go viral," Alexa joked one afternoon as we reviewed footage from our latest escapades, both of us clad in mismatched costumes and absurd props as we trekked through a makeshift jungle.

"At this point, I'd settle for a 'like' from one of the parents," I quipped, grinning.

Time, strange and fluid, slipped on. "Time is a circus, always packing up and moving away," Ben Hecht once wrote. It was a sentiment that resonated as we found ourselves at the cusp of the first half-term holiday.

Sadly, the virus thwarted any plans we had for a holiday. The opportunity to step outside, even briefly, became a precious gift.

During this time, Maeve had scheduled a visit to the small foreign medical clinic to receive the final dose of her typhoid vaccinations. The rest of us had been diligently getting our rabies vaccines due to the sadly large number of stray dogs in Myanmar.

However, that morning, I awoke to a deep ache in my stomach, a bloated discomfort that made each movement a chore, accompanied by debilitating fatigue. Desperate for the alleviation of my symptoms, I travelled with Maeve to seek medical attention for myself. With each visit to the clinic, our temperatures would be scanned before we could cross into the entrance. On this occasion, my only slightly elevated temperature of 37.8 degrees Celsius prompted concern. In response, the clinic staff dramatically whisked me away to a separate room, concerned about the possibility of contagion. My temperature remained elevated, prompting a battery of tests to determine the underlying cause of my symptoms. I was not allowed to leave the room until deemed safe, and the language barrier with the nurses added to my anxiety.

"I have bloody typhoid," I grumbled to my mother over the phone after waiting hours for a diagnosis.

"It's probably all the fruit and vegetables you eat," she said pointedly. "What's the plan?"

"I have to have intravenous antibiotics over the next few days," I said with a sigh, relaying the details I had received. "They've also scheduled an ultrasound of my stomach and further bloods for tomorrow."

Having been in Myanmar for almost two months by that point without needing medical attention, I considered myself lucky. So, I resolved to take it in stride and embraced the idea of spending an hour peacefully reading while hooked up to an IV line for the next five days. However, soon after the doctor's appointment, the school delivered a bombshell: we no longer had the option to work in person. Effective immediately, we were all required to work from home, without exception. The once familiar camaraderie and social interactions between colleagues during the hours of seven in the morning to four in the afternoon would be replaced by solitude. The structured routine that had provided a sense of purpose was shattered. We were also instructed to carry our Form C^2 information at all times when outside our apartments. The sudden change in rules was frustrating, and Alexa and I felt ill-prepared, as we had limited resources at home.

Initially, the prospect of an extra hour of sleep each morning seemed like a welcome respite from the early mornings and the rush to prepare for the day ahead. However, that initial excitement soon gave way to the all-too-familiar sense of despondency. I regretted not choosing to work at the school the week before when we had been given the option. A hastily circulated email informed us that we could take a taxi to the school and gather as many supplies as possible within twenty minutes.

As the only teaching assistant from the early years department present, I hurried through five classrooms, collecting games, whiteboards, and posters, and stuffing them into a large bin bag. Little information was provided regarding the duration of the lockdown, which could be a week or two or perhaps a month at most.

The children in my class were very perceptive. "Where are you, Miss Goldman?" they'd ask, their voices filled with uncertainty. Their parents shared their concerns, hoping to have their children back in school soon. Weeks prior, they had received an update that

---

[2] A Form C is legal paperwork for foreigners, stating their residential address and visa details.

the government would soon be inspecting the school, raising the hope of reopening. But then, the possibility of the school reopening in 2020 seemed increasingly slim, if not non-existent.

Chapter 10. Typhoid, a Massage, and Power Cuts

October 2020: Four months prior to the coup
By mid-October, memories of Henry's village seemed like distant dreams. To stave off the encroaching sense of insanity, Alexa organised a weekly virtual pub quiz, offering a brief reprieve from the monotonous days. As the gym remained closed, online workouts also made a strong comeback.

Every day, I stood on my balcony, observing the outside world and hoping for movement. Outside activity gradually increased, fuelled once again by the ambiguity surrounding the rules. However, despite the declining number of cases, the prospect of the lockdown's end seemed to drift further and further away with each government announcement of its extension.

To make matters worse, power cuts became frequent, making it increasingly challenging to fulfil our job responsibilities.

[Maeve] There are loads of people in People's Park. We have been

missing a trick.

[Ivy] No way. Are we allowed to do that?

[Maeve] Apparently so. A friend has been riding her bike, so I came to look. People are walking, cycling, and running with their kids.

[Ivy] Game changer.

The conversation continued as we gathered in Maeve's apartment. Perched on her newly acquired beanbags in her transformed flat, brimming with decorations and beautiful plants, we discussed our next steps.

"People weren't even wearing masks!" Maeve exclaimed. "I feel like we've been fed exaggerated information about the lockdown."

"Maybe," I muttered.

"I've spoken to other Westerners, and they're still hanging out with their friends," Maeve continued. "Our mental health is suffering. Let's get outside and enjoy this beautiful city we are trapped in!"

People's Park, adjacent to the Shwedagon Pagoda, matched its renowned reputation. With its picturesque landscapes, colourful flowers, and harmonious blend of Burmese tradition and modernity, the park teemed with life. The no-entry signs had vanished. Maeve's observations proved true. After enduring numerous IVs and a cocktail of medications, my body was finally recovering from its relentless battle with typhoid, and the open park and my improving health called for celebration. We roamed, smiling, hopeful for an end to the restrictions.

Ella chuckled. "As soon as I can get back to Penthouse and have a bloody drink, I'll be happy. When this is all over, we are having a massive party!"

"We absolutely need one," I agreed. "Let's make this a daily ritual because I don't know about you guys, but I can't stay inside one bit longer."

"Agreed," the girls chorused.

The next day, the parks were closed. Desperate for any semblance of normalcy, we resorted to writing impassioned pleas to the condo management, begging them to reopen the gym and pool. Nothing worked.

Then, my typhoid resurfaced, necessitating a four-day hospitalisation. It was frightening, made worse by the communication barrier with the non-English speaking nurses. My assigned room was austere and cold, with bugs crawling up the walls.

Before my hospital admission, I had to negotiate with the staff to return home and pack some belongings briefly, having arrived empty-handed. Thirty minutes of explanations later, I finally conveyed that I wasn't a flight risk. The emergency room attendant even proposed a chaperone or issuing a formal order to ensure my return. Eventually, they relented, allowing me to quickly gather my belongings before returning to the stifling confines of the hospital room.

I grappled with my constant complaints, plagued by the guilt of knowing I was privileged to have shelter while others had none. Still, I couldn't suppress my discontent. The bed was uncomfortably hard, and the incessant ICU alarms made sleep elusive. Despite this, the treatments proved effective, revitalising my body despite the lingering fatigue. Finally, release day arrived.

A week later, we stumbled upon a hidden gem—access to

local hotel amenities by purchasing a day pass for their pool and gym. It felt like uncovering a secret treasure, though the staff warned us of its questionable legitimacy, cautioning us not to post about our presence on social media. If anybody asked, we were simply guests of the hotel. By November 3rd, our workplace reopened its doors, operating on a bi-weekly rotational schedule between Groups A and B. Maeve and I had to say goodbye to Ella, Amie, and Ivy.

The atmosphere at work was subdued, marked by an eerie quietude, as many colleagues opted to stay at home or come in on irregular days. Compared to early August, the once lively workplace felt like a hollow shell.

Nevertheless, it was good to be back in some context—even if it was a modified version of normalcy. It was also exhausting; a day filled with in-person exchanges took getting used to. Sadly, all other social interactions remained prohibited. There was no dining out, no shopping, and no leisurely walks in the parks. Our world was reduced to the narrow boundaries of our workplaces and apartments, and with each day, my mental health suffered a gradual decline. The monotony and isolation became unbearable, and I craved something, anything, to help me relax.

Throughout the stay-at-home order, one thought kept me going: the anticipation of indulging in an hour-long deep-tissue massage. There was a spa conveniently located just a few streets away from our place in Sanchaung, and it was one of the first outings I had planned for the group when we arrived. I was surprised to learn that Ella had never experienced a massage before, and despite our attempts to persuade her, she remained reluctant. Nonetheless, some other girls were eager to try an authentic Asian massage experience, so I made the reservation.

"Masaaaaage?" echoed the masseuses' calls as we stumbled upon the parlour's entrance. We must have looked like bedraggled, lost puppies as a man hurriedly approached with towels while we dabbed and wrung out our soaked T-shirts. Moments later, a peculiar-smelling tea was placed before us.

"You booked an oil massage?" the boss-lady asked,

"Yes, three oil massages," I confirmed.

"Can only do two oils, one Thai."

'Why?' I asked, puzzled.

'That is available, okay?' she responded matter-of-factly.

Without any choice, we accepted the situation, but a decision had to be made on who would brave the Thai massage known for its more rigorous techniques. Despite my reluctance, it was unanimously decided that I would be the one to experience it. As our towels were whisked away, we followed a male masseuse and two female therapists upstairs, entering a corridor adorned with velvet curtains and beds.

"Please take off your clothes," the ladies told Amie and Maeve. "Then I will come."

As I entered my own massage room, I was handed a strange sumo-like garment. Uncertain of the protocol, I debated whether to keep my clothes on underneath or strip naked. Opting for the latter, I slipped into the scratchy attire. Giggles echoed behind the curtain, indicating my friends' presence in the neighbouring room. The sound of beds creaking suggested that my friends had already settled in for the massages, so I followed suit and reclined on the mat on the floor.

Time seemed to stretch endlessly until I felt the weight of my masseuse as he suddenly leapt onto my back, his rough toes digging into my skin while his hands manipulated my spine. I buried my forehead into the slightly musty-smelling pillow as my body resonated with the cracking of bones along my spine. The experience, though not entirely unpleasant, brought back memories of my first-ever massage in Indonesia. Back then, the idea of a stranger touching and manipulating my body for money had somewhat unsettled me. Yet, curiosity drove me to try it. During our first visit to the Gili Islands, my family arranged for a masseuse to visit our villa. Just ten minutes after dialling an advertised number in the villa handbook, a short, squat woman arrived at our doorstep, carrying a bundle of towels and a bottle of oil.

"Who is first?" she barked, causing me to retreat into the background. When it was my turn in the queue, I removed my clothes, leaving only my bikini, and made my way to the makeshift wooden hut she had set up as her "salon."

"Bikini top off," she demanded, and I nodded in compliance before she turned her back and departed the room. I slipped off my top and quickly lay on the worn-out mattress on the floor. The room was filled with the scent of a potent, sweet-smelling incense stick.

The masseuse re-entered the room and firmly grasped my ankles, pulling herself onto my body until she straddled my hips. Her hands, slick with oil, glided across my spine and shoulders.

This was not the relaxing massage I had anticipated.

"I do gently," she had stated, but her touch was anything but gentle. I could feel every bone and muscle in my body being manhandled. I forced my eyes shut and willed my body to relax, but it was challenging. Her hands roamed over every inch of my body, and the frenzied bum massage was mortifying.

Midway through, she flipped me onto my back, exposing my naked form. Embarrassed, I instinctively clutched at my body. She chuckled and gently urged me to let go and close my eyes again. She positioned herself across from me and resumed her rough hands on my shoulders, scalp, and collarbones. To my surprise, she quickly moved to massage my breasts, leaving me startled and my mind desperate for this experience to be over. I knew there were plenty of 'happy ending' massage parlours in Asia, but all I wanted was a soothing therapeutic massage to alleviate my chronic back pain.

Fortunately, the Thai massage in Myanmar was less uncomfortable, and after enduring the sixty-long minutes, I felt some relief in my muscles.

During the stay-at-home order, spas were presumed closed, leaving spa owners and masseuses in a dire situation without government support. To make ends meet, they secretly contacted loyal customers through messages, offering enticing discounts and promotions for their services.

As my patience for staying indoors wore thin, the temptation of a rejuvenating massage became irresistible. Longing for the soothing touch of skilled hands and the release of tension from my weary body, I embarked on a clandestine journey with Maeve to a nearby neighbourhood spa.

"Are you sure they're open?" Maeve questioned as we stood in front of the seemingly closed spa.

"This feels a bit eerie," I whispered, my eyes darting towards the nearby presence of the police, who were now eyeing us disconcertingly. Just as we hesitated, movement caught our attention at the lower-right window of the small salon. A discreet gesture from a man signalled us to follow him through a hidden gate.

"Next time you message," he whispered, nodding toward the police.

Entering the hidden oasis, the spa's facade successfully masked its existence, providing a sense of secrecy and tranquillity.

"Thank you so much for coming," a lady said, shaking our hands with gloves on hers.

Chapter 11. Winter in the Sun

November 2020: Three months prior to the coup

As much as I loved spending time with Ella, Maeve, Ivy, and Amie, I needed to expand my social horizons and explore new connections. This was especially true as the COVID-19 situation improved and restrictions began to loosen by late November. In the hope of finding new friends and purpose, I delved into research, seeking out charitable organisations that would welcome foreign volunteers despite my inability to speak Burmese.

After scouring the internet, I stumbled upon a volunteer group called Hope Haven, which is dedicated to aiding those affected by poverty and conflict. Intrigued by their mission, I contacted the founder, Meg, to express my interest in volunteering. With her unmistakably fair complexion and dimpled smile, she intrigued me. I clicked on the message page and wrote, *"Hello, are you looking for or have any space for new volunteers in Yangon?"*

A few hours later, a response appeared:

[Meg] *Hi there! We always have room for enthusiastic volunteers! Thanks for your interest. Currently, we are working on many online projects, as volunteers are worried about leaving their homes.*

Meg, half-Scottish, half-something-else, was currently abroad, serving as an army medic in Syria. Fellow volunteers later spoke highly of Meg. They shared stories of her selflessness and tireless dedication, determined to fit as much as she could into a twenty-four-hour day.

[Meg] *A donation is being organised for this Sunday. Can you make it?*

Filled with a newfound sense of confidence, I said yes. That weekend, I navigated Yangon's streets in sweltering heat, questioning my outfit choice: long black trousers and a long-sleeved T-shirt. Surprisingly, the traffic was light, and I arrived at the designated location early. Meg had told me that I would notice my fellow volunteers as they would be wearing the charity T-shirt. I paid the taxi driver and settled on a bench, nervously scanning the surroundings. The curious gaze of passersby made me slightly self-conscious, and I wondered how long I would have to wait, soon learning that the Burmese were never on time.

The peaceful square was soon graced by Buddhist monks, their orange-coloured robes and freshly shaved heads shimmering in the sunlight as they carried alms bowls under their arms. Intrigued, I observed their silent footsteps as they traversed the square, extending their arms humbly, seeking alms from passersby.

Having learned about Myanmar's deep-rooted Buddhist traditions, I understood the significance of this ritual. Almost ninety per cent of the population practices Buddhism, with around half a million monks residing in the country. Their shaven heads symbolise simplicity and renunciation, embodying their pursuit of spiritual enlightenment in accordance with the teachings of the Buddha.

The daily sustenance of these dedicated monks and the functioning of monasteries rely heavily on the public's generosity. Donations of food and money from the community are vital in supporting their ascetic lifestyles. Hence, it was a familiar scene to witness the glint of silver alms bowls, awaiting the charitable contributions of those who recognised the nobility of their calling.

Soon, my contemplation was interrupted by the arrival of a group of young men and women, some of them wearing the T-shirts as Meg had described. Feeling nervous in the unfamiliar park, I was relieved to encounter Nilar and Kyi, the two kind-hearted and soft-spoken girls who would later become my closest friends.

In the months that followed, Kyi and Nilar often fondly recounted our first meeting, teasingly sharing how they had found my people-watching habits and seemingly intense gaze amusing. With their genuine kindness, they took me under their wings, and their impeccable English skills put my extremely minimal knowledge of Burmese to shame.

Moments later, a foreign lady appeared with a car overflowing with food.

"Are you Lydia?" she asked, startling me with her strong British accent. "I'm Lenny."

"Yes," I replied. "I'm so happy to find another Brit here. I was worried about the language barrier."

She smiled. "Nah, don't worry, love, the volunteers are brilliant."

I returned the smile and noticed two other young British volunteers emerging behind her: Maya and India, both nurses from the UK. We quickly found common ground as we shared our experiences working in international schools in Yangon. It soon became apparent that Lenny held a prominent role within the charity, second only to Meg. Her wealth of knowledge and warm demeanour made it easy to gravitate toward her.

Before long, dozens of donation-filled bags appeared before us. With around twenty volunteers, we swiftly helped pack the bags into the trunk of Lenny's car. She informed us we would visit several hospitals, including a COVID-19 ward and a children's clinic. At the same time, other teams would head to a nearby orphanage. I felt slightly on edge at the prospect of visiting the wards, but I knew it was necessary.

As we entered the nearby public hospital's COVID-19 ward, I felt a heavy sense of unease. The scene before us was a raw portrayal of the grim reality faced by a healthcare system ill-equipped to battle the relentless onslaught of the pandemic. The ward was dimly lit, filled with a beat of coughs and moans echoing off the stark, bare walls. The air hung thick with the unmistakable scent of sickness. Instead of the expected rows of neatly arranged beds equipped with modern medical equipment, we were met with patients lying on makeshift mattresses strewn across the floor, their faces etched with exhaustion and fear.

A sense of urgency permeated the atmosphere, palpable in the hurried movements of the healthcare workers, clad in worn-out protective gear, as they tended to the suffering patients. The scarcity of ventilators was glaringly evident, with patients struggling to draw breath, their desperate gasps filling the room.

"They only have one ventilator," Kyi translated, her voice trembling with emotion.

Speaking with one of the overburdened nurses, we learned firsthand of the dire circumstances—insufficient equipment and an overwhelming surge of patients stretching the hospital's capacity beyond its limits. We felt helpless, knowing that our donations of food and blankets, offered with gloved hands and masked faces, could only do so much.

"I'll never take the NHS for granted again," Maya murmured.

"That was heart-breaking," I whispered.

After thorough disinfection, we made our way to the nearby children's clinic. The young patients, battling various illnesses, from cancer to malnutrition, occupied rows of beds. In the dark rooms, we saw the weary faces of parents, who lay on the floor beside their ailing children. The clinic, too, desperately lacked resources.

In the centre of an adjacent room lay Mya, a young girl bedridden for weeks with an undiagnosed condition due to lack of funds for specialist tests. Despite her illness, her eyes sparkled with a happy curiosity as we waved hello.

Before saying our goodbyes, we distributed care packages filled with toys, food, and comforting items to each child. The excitement and gratefulness in their parents' eyes were tangible as their children unwrapped their gifts and began eating the food.

That initial donation marked the first of many, and my friendship with Kyi and Nilar grew. Volunteering alongside them gave me invaluable insight into the daily lives of those in the country, from their personal stories to the impact of the pandemic on their lives and community. The girls transformed my perception of Myanmar, and I came to appreciate the Burmese's resilience and kindness, wanting to learn more and more.

Aside from bouts of volunteering, November dragged on, and I found solace in the hope of a Christmas escape to London. Though Christmas isn't traditionally celebrated in Myanmar, traces of Christmas could still be found in certain pockets of the country.

Chin state, home to many Christians, embraces the spirit fervently. Streets glowed with twinkling lights, and churches donned elaborate decorations. Nativity scenes depicted the birth of Jesus, with snowmen standing tall in the sunny climate of Myanmar and baby Jesus nestled in a crib in the centre of the town. As Christmas Eve approached, the joyful sounds of carols filled the air. Bundled in their winter attire despite the tropical climate, children went from house to house, singing traditional songs. Santa Claus even appeared in some communities, carrying a sack filled with sweets and delicious sticky rice packed in banana leaves.

Yet, in Yangon, Christmas felt like a distant echo, reduced to a shopping opportunity in malls and hotels. It wasn't like home. I could almost taste the tantalising scents of holiday food and the invigorating smell of pine filling the air. I daydreamed of cosy evenings spent playing board games and watching Christmas movies while an elegant table groaned under the weight of delectable delights. Imagining succulent turkey, salmon, vegetables, and the colossal Yorkshire puddings watered in thick Bisto gravy made my mouth water.

All of us at Sanchaung Gardens longed to fly home for Christmas, but our hopes were dashed by an email from the headmaster on November 20th. We were bluntly denied permission to leave, without reprieve from the mandatory quarantine upon return. While the email acknowledged our mental strain, it offered little consolation, leaving us yearning for more proactive support—perhaps a tiny Christmas gathering or, on the other hand, a counselling session where we could collectively vent our frustrations and shed tears over the absence of Yorkshire puddings.

When we realised that our Christmas plans were no longer possible, we gathered to dispel our feelings of depression and disappointment. My heart ached for Ella and Amie, knowing how much they longed to be with their families for the holidays. They were terribly homesick, and with both being so young, I could only imagine how difficult the past few months had been. The weeks leading up to Christmas felt sluggish, burdened with a sense of letdown and simmering anger. Yet, amidst my frustration, guilt crept in again—I felt undeserving of my discontent.

Friends and family would say, "You're so lucky. Christmas in the sun sounds wonderful." Yet, I couldn't help but long for the cherished family traditions.

Ultimately, Boris Johnson's announcement of cancelling Christmas in the UK seemed serendipitous, as I hadn't booked a flight home. Deep down, I knew even if I had, it wouldn't have been the grand gathering I'd envisioned.

In brighter news, hope flickered when word spread that some teachers from the UK might fly over in late December or early January. It had been months since any flights had been granted entry into Yangon, with the flight we had arrived on being the last one. The prospect of new arrivals excited us. Perhaps my friend Sophie would be among them, infusing our small circle in Sanchaung Gardens with fresh energy.

By some miracle, Ivy's boyfriend, Matt, secured a seat on the upcoming flight, thanks to his previous position at a Burmese company expediting his visa. This was a relief, especially to Ivy, who had hinted at returning to England if Matt couldn't join her. We couldn't lose her. Even so, I understood that the strain of a long-distance relationship had taken its toll. Witnessing Ivy's longing for Matt made me miss my own boyfriend, Daniel, even more.

Daniel and I faced similar hurdles due to the time difference that separated us, requiring us to carve out virtual date nights intentionally. Months of lockdown taught us to adjust to each other's schedules, and communication through FaceTime and Skype became second nature. During one call, Daniel broached the concept of an open relationship, catching me off guard. After I initially ended the call in shock, Daniel persisted in explaining the potential benefits of how it would only strengthen our partnership. After several conversations, I relented.

Matt's flight proceeded as planned, and he successfully completed his hotel quarantine just in time for Christmas Eve. Seeing him reunite with Ivy warmed my heart, and his presence brought a much-needed balance to our sometimes-temperamental female energy.

Restaurants in Yangon reopened just in time for Christmas and New Year's Eve celebrations. Choosing a venue for our special day proved challenging as we scoured the menus of each hotel.

Eventually, we booked a table for brunch at a nearby hotel, although my attendance remained uncertain.

The day before, I managed to compose myself. It was Christmas, and I couldn't spend the day cooped up in my flat, longing to be elsewhere. Sadly, Amie chose not to join us, weighed down by homesickness and wanting to be alone. Despite our attempts to persuade her, Ella, Matt, Ivy, Maeve, and I transformed our lethargy and disappointment into the joy of the Christmas spirit.

The day was sweltering, and we congregated around a glistening pool, embracing the blistering sun. Laughter and joy filled the air as families, couples, locals, and foreigners sat round tables, drinking cocktails and exchanging gifts. Champagne flowed as we indulged in non-traditional Christmas fare.

After the meal, and as the sun's warmth enveloped me, I found myself in a festive scene unlike any I'd experienced before. For me, Christmas has always been associated with snow, cold weather, and rainy days. Yet here I was, experiencing my first "winter" abroad, surrounded by the gang at a poolside brunch. We laughed about the peculiarity of the situation, sharing tales of our unique Christmas traditions.

"Christmas Eve pyjamas and a book," I began, reminiscing. "Brunch the next morning, Christmas Walk, dinner and presents!"

"Presents after dinner?" Maeve exclaimed, shocked.

"Presents as soon as we wake up," Ella chimed in. "Always."

It was fun, and for a few hours, I smiled and joined in with the others. But as the drinks flowed, the delicate balance of my fragile mental state began to crumble under the burden of my suppressed emotions. Hiding my sadness became increasingly difficult.

By around four in the afternoon, I had fabricated an excuse, mentioning a family Skype session I needed to get home for. While somewhat true, the underlying source of my anguish was my family's complete lack of communication throughout the day.

Each time a phone rang, not mine, my emotions intensified. I watched the girls and Matt receive messages and calls from their parents, friends, and partners. Ella's mother even woke up at four in the morning to chat with her while she got ready for the day. They exchanged gifts, and though I didn't want to focus on material things, the absence of even an e-card really upset me.

Just the day before, I had tearfully poured my heart out to my mother, sharing my low spirits and sadness at not being able to spend the day with her. She had comforted me, assuring me that everything would be okay. The contrast between her reassurance and the complete silence the next day hurt.

I ordered a taxi, tears streaming down my face as my "happy" playlist played in the background. As soon as I reached my apartment, I let my emotions flood out, changing into thick pyjamas and cranking up the air conditioning, trying to recreate the chill of London. The family Skype call that evening was brief. Everyone seemed busy preparing their elaborate meals, leaving me to feign composure for a mere twenty minutes. My conversation was mostly indirect, aimed at my older brother, Ben, and his new girlfriend. That night, I sought solace in two sleeping pills, tears lulling me into a fitful sleep.

The day after Christmas brought not just a hangover from the festivities but also from my emotions. I withdrew, cutting off communication with my parents for several days. Trapped in a state of depression, I felt betrayed and unloved. The six days leading up to New Year's blurred together as I barely left my apartment, feeling the world around me come to a standstill. With my awareness of my privilege, guilt gnawed at me, knowing that most people in Yangon had far less than I did.

Chapter 12. It's All Falling into Place

My winter blues ended on New Year's Eve. Determined to shake off the melancholy that had enveloped me during the days of isolation in my apartment, I decided to embrace the upcoming year with open arms. Besides, I couldn't bear the thought of wasting the money I had spent on a pre-booked overnight stay at the Chatrium Hotel.

Despite the technicalities and rules against hotel stays, the Chatrium Hotel discreetly opened its doors and presented itself as a "quarantine" location, clandestinely opening its doors to expatriates searching for a getaway or vibrant party atmosphere. The girls and I loved spending our weekends here, lounging by the pool, eating delicious sushi, and drinking intoxicating cocktails. Fondly referred to as 'Le Chat' among us, the hotel became our secret retreat. We had already visited three times and were longing for another weekend getaway. The irresistible allure of the hotel's perpetual promotion, which offered a weekend stay complete with meals and beverages for a mere ninety-nine dollars, was too good to resist.

On New Year's Eve, the Chatrium outdid itself by arranging an extravagant buffet and party for its guests. The atmosphere was electric, and a tapestry of twinkling lights and festive decorations transformed the hotel into a wonderland. Expats we had met before mingled, forming a close-knit community of like-minded individuals seeking connection.

We arrived early, wanting to soak up the sun with cocktails around the pool.

"This is bliss," Ivy murmured, cuddling next to Matt on a sun lounger. "I love day drinking."

Once again, Amie was absent, leaving Ivy and Tom as a pair while Maeve, Ella and I formed our usual trio. Maeve playfully nudged me, her grin mischievous. "Look who's here," she said, nodding towards Tomos and Liam.

Returning the wink, I replied, "Right next to yours," acknowledging the connection between Maeve and Tomos.

"See you later, guys," I said, leaping into the pool and swimming over to Liam. The celebration continued into the early hours of the morning, the atmosphere electric. I felt alive, and as midnight approached and we clinked our champagne glasses to the fireworks, I felt excited for 2021.

Exhilarated, I darted from one hotel room to another, each door opening to a different scene—a karaoke session in one, a group engaged in a lively game in another, soft melodies and whispered confidences behind the next. The night was exactly what we all needed.

Chapter 13. 16th Street

January 2021: One month prior to the coup

16th Street was crowded. It was a Saturday morning, and I was exploring the town with Nilar and Kyi. The air was thick with the tantalising scents of street food, enticing passersby with sizzling meat skewers and steaming bowls of noodles. Colourful tapestries adorned the roadside, their intricate designs catching the sunlight. Nearby, women sold fresh vegetables from overflowing baskets, their voices blending into a melodic chorus as they interacted with customers.

Downtown Yangon revealed a captivating blend of old and new. Ancient pagodas gracefully emerged amidst modern high-rises, their golden spires reaching skyward. The glistening sun accentuated the intricate architectural details of the buildings dating back to the colonial era.

As we weaved through the narrow streets, our eyes were drawn to the vibrant street murals, which painted a vivid picture of the city's artistic scene. In the heart of downtown Yangon, the iconic Sule Pagoda stood tall, a sacred sanctuary amidst the urban chaos.

"It's so manic," I exclaimed with a contented sigh. "I love it."

Kyi smirked mischievously and glanced at Nilar, anticipating our next adventure. "Just wait until we catch the bus," she teased, aware of the mixed reputation of public transportation in Yangon.

As foreigners, we'd heard warnings about the drawbacks of public transport—tales of filth, danger, and restless drivers. However, we were also cautioned about taxis, with which I'd had no issues thus far. "It'll be fine," Nilar said, sensing my fear. "Just stick with us."

We waited at the bus stop for what felt like an eternity until I asked, "How do you know when the bus is coming? What number are we looking for?"

"What do you mean? How do you know when it's coming?" Nilar replied, looking slightly perplexed. "You just wait."

I chuckled at the response's simplicity. The concept of real-time updates and precise schedules seemed foreign to them.

I explained the technological conveniences I was accustomed to back home, which intrigued both girls. "You have mobile apps for buses?" Kyi asked. "Are you serious? And do you know which bus is which?"

"Yes, of course," I replied. "How do you know which bus to get?"

"You ask the driver when the bus arrives," she replied matter-of-factly. "And you ask to make a stop where you want to get off. They will tell you 'Yes or no'."

The bus soon came, and the journey exceeded my expectations. It was slightly bumpy but ultimately safe. After disembarking, we headed to our first stop: the Secretariat—a Victorian colonial masterpiece deeply intertwined with Myanmar's history and struggle for independence. Finished in 1905 under British rule, it served as the administrative hub of the British colonial government in Burma. In 1948, it saw the transfer of the British colonial administration to an independent government. However, in 1947, General Aung San and six of his cabinet members were assassinated within its walls. Today, the Secretariat stands as an important cultural landmark. As we explored the building, I was captivated by its distinctive red-brick facade and intricate detailing. We were transported to a different era, where the echoes of history lingered within its walls.

"It's beautiful," I reflected. "It doesn't feel like we're in Yangon at all."

Next, we walked down Pansodan Street, a mile-long stretch lined with colonial-era buildings, street vendors, and government offices. Named after Pansadon, a Burmese prince who served as the Commissioner of British Burma in the 19th century, the street has a rich history.

As we walked, we were immersed in the bustle around us. Antique stores, art galleries, and bookshops lined the pavements. Our journey led us to Maha Bandula, a public square adjacent to Yangon City Hall. The square was teeming with life as locals shopped at markets or relaxed in tea shops on a busy Saturday.

The girls shared that the square was named in honour of General Maha Bandula, a Burmese national hero who fought against

British colonial forces in the First Anglo-Burmese War. We paused by the bronze sculpture, taking a moment to rest and absorb the surroundings.

"Many people protest here," Nilar told me. "If you see protests here, it will get rough."

"Thanks for the warning!" I laughed.

A few weeks later, Kyi and Nilar visited my home for the first time. They brought thanaka with them. The white paste-like substance was traditionally smeared on the cheeks and foreheads of women and girls, acting as a sunscreen to protect skin from the harsh tropical climate. Unique to the Burmese natives, it was impossible to leave your home without spotting a sweet young girl daubed with thanaka, or an elderly lady with intricate designs on her face. With grins on their faces, the girls applied the thanaka to my cheeks, laughing as they took photos.

"It suits you." Kyi smiled, admiring their handiwork.

"Are you hungry?" Nilar asked. "We bought noodles."

"Good." I laughed. "My cupboards are empty."

As they boiled water for their instant pot noodles, the spicy aroma soon filled the air. Seated on cushions on my living room floor, the girls took the opportunity to quiz me about my culture.

"So, Lydia, tell us about being British. What's it like?"

"Well…" I began softly. "Being British means having a love-hate relationship with the weather. And we are obsessed with tea and queuing!"

"Yes, what do you queue for? The bus, like we saw you do today?" Kyi mocked.

"Oh, absolutely," I nodded, a smile playing on my lips. "We

take queuing very seriously."

"And tea?" Nilar asked, "Is it like Burmese tea?"

"Very different." I chuckled. "We have our own tea-drinking rituals, often with milk and sometimes biscuits. We need tea every day."

Kyi, pretending to be taken aback, feigned shock. "So, you can't function without it?"

"Yes, but let me tell you a secret," I laughed. "I hate tea. What I do like, though, is gin."

"Me too," Nilar said, her eyes lighting up as she quickly grabbed a bottle we had found stashed in my cupboard. She poured a generous amount of gin into our glasses and mixed it with juice.

"Cheers," I smiled, raising my glass.

As the evening progressed, our conversation flowed effortlessly, punctuated by laughter that seemed to make time disappear. However, I began to notice signs of discomfort in Kyi and Nilar. Kyi swayed slightly, her movements unsteady, while Nilar wore a queasy expression.

"How much did you drink?" I asked, shocked, assuming they had consumed the same amount as me.

"Just one glass," Nilar laughed, her words slurring as she reclined with her head back on the ground.

"I feel sick," Kyi moaned.

"Just one glass?" I sighed, realising their tolerance levels were minimal.

"We don't really drink."

"Why didn't you say so?" I asked, irritated.

Nilar burst into laughter, her gaze fixed on me intently. "We wanted to fit in with the British."

Kyi's moans grew more urgent. "Where's the toilet?"

Reacting quickly, I jumped up from the floor and grabbed Kyi's hand, leading her hastily to the bathroom. The sound of running water followed as I stood outside, concerned.

Stretching out on my bed, I asked, "Are you okay?" hoping to provide some comfort.

"I'm fine," came the weak response. "Just leave me for a bit."

Nilar entered my bedroom with a smile. "Hi, Liddi."

"You don't feel sick, do you?" I asked.

"No," she reassured me, her laughter lingering. "I just feel a bit funny."

With a playful slump, Nilar joined me on the bed, her gaze intensifying. "You are so beautiful."

Caught off guard by her unexpected advance, I hesitated in response, sensing something wasn't quite right. Gently, I placed a hand on her shoulder, halting her advance. "Nilar, I think you do feel funny."

She reddened, pleading softly, "Please, Liddi. Don't tell anyone."

"Of course, I won't," I assured with a smile. "But I think I need to get you both home."

When Kyi felt better, I helped clean them up and guided them downstairs. I ordered a taxi and added a generous tip, urging the driver to ensure their safe journey home. Though they could have stayed over, I knew Kyi would face even greater consequences if she didn't return home that night.

Watching the car fade into the distance felt unsettling.

Nilar's actions hinted at a deeper truth she had been concealing. In Myanmar's social and cultural landscape, same-sex relationships were not widely accepted, and the repercussions could be severe. However, as much as I wanted to offer support and understanding and explain that these feelings and actions are completely normal in other parts of the world, I didn't want to push her.

Chapter 14. Emerging from Lockdown

11th January 2021: Twenty days prior to the coup
My birthday fell on a school day that year. My homesickness had dissipated, and I was glad to be living in Yangon. The recent easing of restrictions had brought a sense of newfound freedom and liberation.

With restaurants reopening, the chance to celebrate birthdays was a possibility again. I reserved a table for our group of six at a restaurant I'd wanted to visit for months. Though some restrictions still lingered across the city, there was a sense that things were gradually returning to normal.

The preceding four-month lockdown had been a test of endurance, with some of the strictest measures worldwide. With parks closed, I longed for the familiar green spaces of South-East London. The simple freedom to walk and exercise outdoors felt like a fundamental right unjustly stripped away. We all grappled with the effects of prolonged restrictions, resulting in strained friendships and heightened tensions.

However, on the 11th of January, my birthday, everything changed. The celebratory meal with my friends was just the beginning, as we soon found ourselves booking more staycations. Alongside the Chatrium, Inya Lake Hotel had become a firm favourite, which held historical significance as the former home of Aung San Suu Kyi during her twenty years of house arrest. The delicious and endless buffet-style breakfasts of fruit, fluffy pancakes, juices, and noodles were exemplary. The coffee, however, was subpar. Our complex pool and gym had also re-opened a few days after my birthday. Things were on the up.

In addition to our memorable weekend getaways, we booked a series of adventures to explore areas beyond central Yangon. One such outing took us to Thanlyin, an important seaport connected to Yangon by one of Myanmar's longest bridges. Ivy, Matt, and I set off on a bike tour accompanied by our guide, Sam, a young Burmese man who had recently joined the bike company Uncharted Horizons.

We pedalled through quaint villages and along the lakeside, where children joyfully played in the waters while their mothers washed clothes nearby. Our journey eventually led us to a unique monastery. As we parked our bikes outside, Sam ventured into the quiet, dimly lit building, and we hurriedly followed him.

Inside, a soft voice greeted us. "Shoes off."

The atmosphere was serene and mysterious. Our curiosity was piqued as we noticed the presence of an unlikely duo—a pet snake and a monkey—adding to the monastery's distinctive charm. Following Sam into the depths of the sacred space, we encountered a short, bald monk who greeted us with a polite bow. Reciprocating the gesture, we smiled and removed our shoes and socks. The floor beneath our feet was a patchwork of misshapen tiles and hardened mud, creating an uneven surface. We followed the monk cautiously, guided by Sam's translations of the monk's sparse words.

"We will see the snake now," Sam told us, leading us into a half-open building where the majestic creature awaited. Coiled in all its glory, a seventeen-foot-long Burmese python lay at the centre. Its movements were captivating and mesmerising as it glided gracefully within its secure enclosure.

We stood in awe, watching the snake's every twist and turn. Its presence commanded respect and held us captive, awestruck. Eventually, our attention shifted to the outside, where the famous monkey resided. Leaping with boundless energy, the monkey traversed a vast man-made playground structure, tethered by a long chain as it swung from ropes in the surrounding trees.

The contrast between the snake's tranquil elegance and the monkey's playful antics created a fascinating juxtaposition.

Our visit to the monastery ignited a sense of adventure, leading to a month of further excursions. We explored an abandoned theme park, went canoeing and even dared to walk along the Yangon pipeline.

The Yangon Pipeline, a testament to engineering marvel, became a central point of exploration. It stretched over seventy kilometres and had stood tall for eighty-five years. On a sunny day, we gathered at a section of the pipeline located in a small town. As we approached, we were greeted by children from the neighbourhood—dressed in their school uniforms—playing and laughing on top of the pipeline. My heart skipped a beat as I watched them, nervous for their safety, wishing I could shout out a warning to be careful.

We carefully climbed onto the rusty pipeline, its metal surface cool against our palms. Ducking under bridges and traversing heights that reached up to eight feet above the ground; it was exhilarating. It felt like walking on a pedestrian highway rather than atop a metal tube carrying water.

As we followed the pipeline's winding path, scenes of everyday life unfolded around us. Women laid out clothes to dry, their vibrant fabrics fluttering in the breeze. Others rested on the sturdy structure after a day's work, their laughter echoing across the metal expanse. We respectfully sought permission to cross their paths, acknowledging the pipeline's role as a symbol of community for the locals.

Continuing our journey, we passed tiny, thatched houses and slums. Life revealed itself in raw glimpses: children playing football in narrow alleys, men leisurely smoking and chewing betel nuts.

The pipeline, constructed by the British in 1935 during the colonial period, had evolved from a mere conduit for water transportation to a lifeline for four and a half million people. Stretching from the Yankin Township in Yangon, it connected communities along its path, opening doors for developing a micro-economy and offering prospects for growth.

But eventually, we reached our limits. We stepped off the pipeline and back onto solid ground.

Stray dogs roamed freely that day, their scruffy coats

blending with the cityscape. They found solace in the busy streets, temple courtyards, and even small shops.

"Oh my goodness," I cried after climbing down. "Look at the poor puppy."

I grabbed Alexa's arm and guided her toward the small, trembling puppy hiding behind a black vehicle. The puppy's painfully skinny body revealed protruding ribs. Naively, I extended my hand for it to sniff.

"I need to do something," I moaned to Alexa,

"Leave it here," she affirmed. "Its mother will probably come back for it."

"Are you sure? What if she doesn't?"

"There are so many street dogs in Yangon," Alexa said. "It's very sad, but we can't rescue them. This isn't our country."

As we walked away from the puppy, we wished there was more we could do to alleviate its suffering. The city's lack of stray dog management programs left these poor animals to fend for themselves.

And then, in late January, the long-awaited news arrived—the potential reopening of our school. Excitement and anticipation buzzed among students, parents, and teachers. After months of remote learning and virtual interactions, the prospect of returning to the physical campus and finally meeting the children I had grown to love was met with relief.

The school administration worked tirelessly to ensure all necessary safety measures were in place. Once again, guidelines from the Ministry of Health were meticulously followed, and protocols were implemented. The return of us teachers to the classrooms was a glimmer of hope. Our video feeds showed us back on school property several days a week, reassuring parents. Eleven long months had passed since students last set foot inside the school.

In conversations with my teacher friends in England, their struggles with managing pupils who had been off school for just three months paled in comparison. Our approach to education had transformed drastically during those eleven months, leaving me pondering how the children and I would navigate the unfamiliar terrain ahead. If the school could fully open after the Thingyan holidays (Easter holiday equivalent), we'd have at least one term of physical school before the summer break. We longed to breathe life back into the school halls. The children and I craved interaction.

The year, so far, hadn't unfolded as I'd imagined, but perhaps that was the essence of adventure—to embrace the unexpected, even when teaching from halfway across the world.

PART TWO

Chapter 15. First of February, 2021

If the term coup d'état translates to the government being overthrown by the military, how could a whole government be overthrown? Why has no one stopped it?

Monday 1st February 2021

It happened this morning. I woke up at six o'clock, feeling groggy and still half-asleep. The weekend had been busy, spent socialising at one of the many newly opened restaurants and bars. After nearly a year of lockdown, the sudden surge of social opportunities had overwhelmed me, leaving me questioning my newfound sociability. This evening, we had plans to meet at Atlas, a local bar, but with my energy reserves depleted, I wasn't sure if I wanted to go—not that it mattered anymore.

My daily ritual began—a bracing cold shower. Shivers chased each droplet as I dried off, half-naked, and shuffled to the small kitchen to prepare some coffee. But dismay awaited: electricity, gone. Another bloody power cut. Over the past month, we'd had at least four power cuts, one stretching a gruelling ten hours. Although not uncommon, it was frustrating and made teaching near impossible.

Resigned to a caffeine-less morning, I checked my laptop to see if I had charged it overnight. Thankfully, I had. I would have to rely on my mobile hotspot for my class starting in an hour. I headed back to my room to fetch my phone, but as I glanced at the top right corner of the screen, I noticed no signal bars or 3G signs. Power cuts were usual. However, internet blackouts were not. I was worried; how would I conduct my classes without internet access? Believing I was the only one facing this issue, I hurriedly prepared to run down to my friend's apartment before the school day began.

Just as I slipped into my flip-flops, ready to step out, a sudden eruption echoed through the building—shouting, clapping. Eerie and unsettling. Curiosity nudged me into the corridor. To my surprise, a crowd of people rushed past me, their faces filled with a mix of worry and uncertainty. I'd heard the clapping, but why did everyone appear so troubled?

Unease drove me back into my apartment. I slammed the door shut and pulled open the long curtains that covered the glass doors leading to my balcony and stepped outside. High-rise apartments spilled upward, their balconies hanging out like precarious ledges. People leaned over railings, their expressions a fractured mosaic of excitement, fear and apprehension. The streets below teemed with figures standing on cars. Pots banged; rhythms clashed.

And there, amidst the chaos, I stood—half-dressed, coffee-less, and bewildered. The morning had taken a sharp turn. As I waited there, reality sank in. The coup d'état—the very thing the Tatmadaw military had denied would ever happen—was unfolding before my eyes. Subtle signs along the way had hinted at what was to come, but I'd dismissed them as mere anomalies.

Yesterday, I met Nilar and Kyi in a trendy bubble tea cafe near my apartment. Their cautious explanations of a military takeover carried an underlying gravity that I had failed to grasp at the time. "What does that mean, a coup?" I asked, curious and somewhat naive about the implications of such a term.

Nilar and Kyi exchanged cautious glances, aware of the sensitivity of the topic. Lowering their voices, they explained, "A coup. It's a military takeover."

"The military takes over what, exactly?" I pressed, my mind struggling to comprehend. "The government, or us too?"

"If the military takes over, they take over everything." Kyi nodded solemnly.

"It will not be good," Nilar added, her expression mirroring her concern. Her eyes clouded with worry. "Not good at all."

The girls spoke in hushed tones, warning me of the potential consequences. I began to sense the underlying tension that permeated the town—the fear that had become a constant companion for its residents. Unlike anything I had experienced before, this was their daily reality.

"I can't imagine what that must be like," I murmured, feeling the stark contrast between my world and theirs. Nilar reached across the table, her hand resting on mine. "It's okay," she reassured, sensing my confusion and privilege. "It's understandable. The situation seems strange to you. I am sure it would not happen in England."

Her statement highlighted the freedoms I often took for granted—the luxury of living in a (mostly) stable democracy. I couldn't fully comprehend the fear and uncertainty that loomed over Kyi and Nilar.

After meeting with Nilar and Kyi, I returned to the comfort of my flat. My thoughts were swirling, and I emailed the school for guidance on whether we should proceed with our planned visit to the orphanage.

The subject line was simple: "Orphanage Visit: Proceed or pause?" I hesitated for a moment, then began typing. The school library is overflowing with donations—clothes and toys for the children—all collected over a month as part of our donation drive. The idea originated from a conversation I'd had with the head teacher before the Christmas holidays, in which I expressed my concern for the children living in orphanages and slums, especially during the challenging times of the ongoing pandemic.

To my surprise, my proposal had been approved, and weeks had been dedicated to organising logistics, creating colourful posters, and sending out reminders during assembly. Our students and their parents responded eagerly, and their generosity was heart-warming. Their drivers delivered the donated items to the school, filling the library shelves.

Yet, yesterday's response echoed caution. The email read, "Yes, we need to be cautious and evaluate the situation day by day. Let's see how things unfold in the next few days first."

Then, last night, as the clock struck midnight, marking the

transition from 31st January to 1st February, an email arrived from our employer. It delivered an unexpected announcement: instructing all staff members to work from home today due to the unfolding political situation. Typically, I would have been fast asleep at that hour, but the prevailing tension had overridden my need for rest.

Grateful for the unexpected reprieve, I adjusted my alarm, allowing myself to sleep a bit longer—if sleep would come. I read and reread the email several times, each time questioning its implications. Reluctantly, I began to acknowledge the possibility of significant change, of the coup that Nilar and Kyi had hinted at that morning.

Still, I clung to the hope. Perhaps the school was merely exercising caution, and the day off was to avoid potential traffic disruptions. After all, we couldn't afford to be late for our first lesson, could we?

Today, the first day of the coup has engulfed me in an unexpected whirlwind of emotions—simultaneously exhilarating and paralysing. It feels as if the world is in a chaotic stillness.

This morning, our access to the internet has been erratic, flickering on and off unpredictably. Now, it has returned, yet who knows for how long? I haven't been able to reach my parents. The time difference of five and a half hours between Myanmar and England taunts me, exacerbating my frustration with the unreliable lifeline of the internet. My attempts to call have thus far been futile. It is early morning UK time; however, I don't know when and if the internet will be shut off forever.

Chapter 16. Rumblings of Rebellion

Tuesday 2nd February 2021

Dear Diary,

Today, I find myself feeling more numb than I did yesterday. The weight of my emotions has dulled, leaving me in a state of detachment and apathy. I am glad I was able to reach my parents yesterday afternoon, even if I had to awaken them from their blissful slumber. After countless futile attempts to establish a connection, the monotonous ringtone of the WhatsApp call persisted until I finally stumbled upon a source of communication through my mother's best friend, Sally. In a desperate quest for contact, I mindlessly scrolled through Facebook; it was there that I came across a post shared by Sally, unveiling the shocking news of the coup. I quickly messaged her.

[Me] Hi Sally, do you have our home number?

[Sally] Yes.

[Me] Can you please call home? I know it's late. I can't get *through via WhatsApp and want to speak to Mum before all our Wi-Fi gets cut.*

> *[Sally] Are you okay?*
> *[Me] I think it's pretty bad here.*
> *[Sally] You want me to call her now?*
> *[Me] If you can, I can't call home, and their mobiles are off.*
> *[Sally] Okay.*
> *[Me] They may not wake up.*

I had almost lost hope when Sally's reply came. She told me that she had reached my father, who promised they would turn their mobiles on.

Shortly after ending my conversation with Sally, my phone emitted a resonant buzz. With trembling hands, I answered the call, and the weariness and grogginess of my mother's voice seeped through the speaker. The sound of her voice, heavy with fatigue and concern, reached my ears, and at that moment, I felt the walls of strength I had built around me begin to crumble. Though our conversation was brief, I reassured her of my safety, even if silence fell upon my end. In the background, my father's murmurs attempted to downplay the situation, assuring my mother that such occurrences were routine in Asia. But for me, it felt far from ordinary.

With a quivering voice, I asked my parents to inform others about my limited internet access if they asked. Then, I said bye, apologising for the disturbance our early morning conversation had caused.

Today, internet access has remained volatile, appearing and disappearing at random moments. Whenever we manage to establish a connection, we are instructed to carry out our lessons and teach as usual. However, maintaining the flow of lessons has become increasingly challenging as children, unsurprisingly, vanish from our virtual classrooms, leaving a sense of frustration and a lingering two-minute void. In the background, I catch glimpses of frantic parents, their faces etched with anxiety and urgency. Teaching virtually for the past eight months has already proven to be a challenge. Our sessions are limited to only twenty-five minutes, as managing the boundless energy of four and five-year-olds through a computer screen feels like corralling a pack of energetic kittens.

"Myat, please sit down." Alexa asserts, her tone growing stern with each repetition.

Every lesson begins with a cheery "Good morning, class!" only for half of the children to immediately spring up from their seats, their tiny bodies bouncing enthusiastically. I quickly learned the art of distraction and perfected my "teacher voice" to rein them in. We established ground rules: hands in your lap, listening ears on. Of course, technology has its own sense of humour, often freezing us on the screen with bizarre facial expressions. My favourite virtual session is snack time. Each child brings a snack, or three, to our optional virtual meeting. We chat about their days, and I love listening to their rambles and questions: "Miss, what are you eating?" or "Why do you look like that?" I hope we continue our snack lessons, if not for the children's sake, then for mine.

As if the technological challenges weren't enough, the language barrier adds another layer of complexity. While a few of the children can communicate in English, the majority only speak Burmese, often accompanied by their Burmese-speaking nannies. In the initial weeks of school, we quickly adapted, resorting to sign language and relying on facial expressions to bridge the gap of understanding.

Some of the children's parents hold positions in the embassy and the United Nations or have affiliations with the military. Their knowledge and insights far surpass my own limited understanding, fuelling my desperate need for information. As I tried to maintain focus on my lessons this morning, attempting to mask my trembling body with a professional and friendly demeanour, my thoughts inevitably veered towards the safety of my Burmese friends and the children.

Earlier, I contacted my Burmese friends, hoping to glean any morsels of insight I could. I scoured the Hope Haven group chat and scrolled through hundreds of messages, trying to piece together the fragments of truth in this chaotic puzzle. Yet, no one has been able to provide answers, whether due to a lack of willingness or a genuine lack of knowledge. I sincerely hope it's the latter.

While the present remains uncertain, I've gained some clarity on the events of yesterday morning and the preceding months. The recent election, held on November 8th, is still vivid in everyone's minds. It was a hugely significant moment, echoing the historic 2015 elections that ignited a flame of hope and optimism across the county.

Over five years have passed since that transformative November when the National League for Democracy (NLD) emerged as the dominant political party, securing an overwhelming victory. However, General Min Aung Hlaing, the formidable leader of the Tatmadaw military, defiantly contested the election results despite his party having secured only a meagre thirty-three seats. Clinging to allegations of electoral fraud, he cast a shadow of doubt over the resolute will of the people.

Led by the charismatic Aung San Suu Kyi, a figure drumming with charisma and determination, the NLD had captured the hearts and aspirations of the people, winning an astonishing eighty-six per cent of seats in the Assembly of the Union. It was an unprecedented feat, a watershed moment that shattered political stagnation, breathing life into a nation yearning for freedom and democracy. For the first time since 1960, Myanmar witnessed the exhilaration of a free and fair general election.

Aung San Suu Kyi, the youngest daughter of Aung San, had walked a path fraught with intellectual prowess and dedication. As a young scholar, she graced the halls of the University of Delhi and St Hugh's College in Oxford before dedicating three years to the United Nations. In 1988, she returned to her homeland and emerged as a founding member and the General Secretary of the NLD. However, her unyielding resolve posed a threat to the military rulers, who swiftly moved to suppress her dissent by placing her under house arrest in 1989 under the guise of martial law.

The chains of confinement had bound her for years, stripping away her liberty and casting a shadow over her pursuit of justice. Yet, even behind the walls of captivity, Aung San Suu Kyi remained a beacon of resistance, inspiring a nation yearning for change. "*Whatever they do to me, I can take it*," she declared, finding solace in writing her book '*Freedom from Fear*,' which she sold alongside her furniture to afford fresh food. She lived sparsely, without internet access and minimal contact with the outside world.

Her days were consumed by household chores, exercise, and the sound of BBC Radio and the Voice of America.

Tragedy struck in 1999 with the passing of her husband. Before this, the authorities callously denied her husband's request for a final visit with his wife. After his passing, thousands congregated outside Aung San Suu Kyi's home for a religious ceremony to honour her husband. Yet, amidst this sacred gathering, she became the target of relentless physical and emotional attacks.

Despite enduring multiple re-arrests and years of imprisonment, Aung San Suu Kyi's spirit remained unbroken. The world watched, their hearts heavy with empathy, as she endured fifteen long years confined under her house arrest. Her eventual release in 2010 marked a moment of hope, propelling her onto the global stage as an icon of resilience. The NLD's resounding success in the 2015 elections further emboldened the nation's hunger for political change, with Aung San Suu Kyi hailed as a champion of democracy and human rights.

Celebrations continued for days, sweeping through the streets, and the news gained international recognition. However, a bitter reality loomed. The re-drafted constitution in 2009, implemented by the military junta, posed a significant obstacle to her rightful ascendancy to presidency. Crafted with calculated precision, it barred those with foreign spouses from Myanmar's top office. Unfettered, she assumed the role of State Counsellor.

The re-drafted constitution also ensured a quarter of parliamentary seats were reserved for the Tatmadaw. This strategic provision, along with the requirement that any constitutional amendment receive over three-quarters of all votes, effectively entrenched power dynamics and thwarted meaningful revisions.

Conversations among friends and colleagues were rampant in the lead-up to the highly anticipated 2020 elections. The collective pulse of the nation quickened, fuelled by a potent mixture of excitement, uncertainty, and hope for a brighter democratic future. Campaign posters splashed vibrant hues across street corners. At the same time, balconies proudly displayed crimson flags, declaring unwavering support for their favoured political party.

"The military expects to win the election," a voice had cautioned. "They will be furious if they lose."

As Election Day neared, an undercurrent of trepidation, mingled with the electrifying energy, cast a shadow of uncertainty over the nation's future political landscape. Concerns regarding the Rohingya Muslim community's exclusion from the electoral process had surfaced, casting doubt on the fairness and inclusivity of the entire process. Reports hinted at measures implemented by the NLD government that prevent the Rohingya from voting or standing for election, a stark contradiction to Myanmar's democratic aspirations.

Mindful of the underlying tensions, we were instructed to exercise prudence and remain vigilant on Election Day and the following days. We were advised against leaving our apartments and to avoid venturing into potentially volatile or crowded areas. Discussions regarding the election results were to be held in the strictest confidence, and sharing views on social media or elsewhere would invite unwanted consequences.

During the monotony of the COVID-19 lockdown, it felt exciting. Group chats became a hub of activity. Burmese members proudly displayed their voting experiences, sharing selfies of purple-ink-stained fingers. Yet, alongside the excitement, the stories and perspectives from locals highlighted concerns about the Rohingya exclusion, tempering the euphoria with a sobering reality.

As Election Day passed and night fell, the country collectively held its breath, eagerly awaiting the gradual emergence of results. It was a time of heightened emotions, where hopes and fears danced on a tightrope, poised to be either shattered or realised. And then, as the curtain slowly drew back, the outcome was revealed: the NLD emerged victorious once again. The news sparked waves of celebration and contemplation, culminating in the final tally on 13th November, showcasing the NLD's triumph with a landslide victory with 346 seats out of 412.

However, despite this win, the issue of Rohingya representation in the electoral process remains a sensitive topic. The NLD did not select any Muslim candidates in the 2015 election, and of the one thousand candidates, only two Muslim candidates were included five years later. And the Tatmadaw were angry.

Yesterday morning, while we were sleeping peacefully in our beds, Aung San Suu Kyi and her compatriots were forcibly taken during a pre-dawn raid. Around four hundred elected Members of Parliament found themselves under house arrest. At precisely three in the morning, internet and phone lines were severed, a meticulously orchestrated move intended to delay the dissemination of this chilling news until daylight. Yet, even now, the full gravity of these events escapes me.

Late last night, we received a text message from the British Embassy:

> *The Foreign, Commonwealth & Development Office (FCDO) advises against all but essential travel across Myanmar based on recent political events and the current assessment of the COVID-19 risk.*
>
> *As of 1ˢᵗ February, the Myanmar Military has declared a state of emergency and assumed control. There are reports that the military has detained figures in the Civilian Government and civil society. The British Embassy is following the situation carefully and will continue to update the travel advice. There may be disruptions to the internet, phone networks and ATMs. You are advised to stay home and stay safe.*

While these words offer a modicum of comfort, the escalating turmoil threatens to overshadow any sense of reassurance. I question whether the Embassy is even aware of the number of British citizens present in the country. Surely, given the limited number of us here, they must. They will keep us safe and vigilantly monitor our whereabouts.

Today, our email inboxes have been flooded with a flurry of security alerts, keeping us informed of the unfolding events. The latest communication came only minutes ago, soon after I returned from visiting the bank with Alexa. Wrapping up our lessons by mid-afternoon, Alexa expressed her intent to withdraw all her funds and urged me to do the same. Confused, I asked, "Why would you need to take all of your money out?"

Her hurried explanation left me reeling. The last time there was even a hint of a possible coup, the military seized all bank funds.

There was no guarantee that we would ever see that money again. Sensible or overly cautious? I wasn't sure, but I decided to follow suit. My one thousand dollars—January's wages—were too precious to risk.

The bank queue stretched endlessly, defying any semblance of social distancing, and I felt queasy at the sight. COVID-19 had become a forgotten concern, overshadowed by the urgency of the moment. With a $100 withdrawal limit, the process dragged on. Nausea gnawed at my insides, and sweat trickled down my back. I watched a Westerner insert a dozen credit cards ahead of us, muttering, "For my friends."

When my turn finally came, the world spun. Without breakfast or sleep, dizziness overwhelmed me. Faces blurred, and the intensity of the stares from those behind only added to my disorientation. I collapsed momentarily, Alexa's worried gaze mirroring my own concern. Standing and summoning every ounce of strength, I withdrew my money and stumbled down the steps.

"Can we sit for a moment?" I pleaded weakly. "I'm sorry."

Alexa's smile was small but reassuring. "Don't apologise. You look really faint. Are you okay? Are you worried?"

"No," I whimpered. "I just feel sick. It's probably another infection."

Minutes later, with my head between my legs, I regained some composure. The queue had tripled in length, a serpent-like line weaving through the anxious crowd. Two of the three banks across the road had closed, their doors shut tight, and their cash reserves depleted. People vented frustration, and Westerners argued heatedly with bank staff.

"I came earlier," one shouted. "But the power cut prevented me from withdrawing my money. I need my money."

"Sorry, Sir," a helpless bank employee responded, clearly distressed.

"This is awful," I muttered to Alexa. "Good job we came early."

"Yes," she agreed. "Now, keep your money safe."

We walked in heavy silence, our eyes darting around, trying to absorb the kaleidoscope of sights and sounds of a city in turmoil. Rhythmic chants echoed off walls, flags fluttered like desperate prayers, and the faces—oh, the faces—carried the weight of fear and sorrow.

"Our poor students," I lamented. "They were so excited to come to school. Do you think they understand what is happening?"

Alexa nodded heavily, her eyes tracing the jagged skyline. She loves the children—their laughter, their curiosity. Their young lives hung in the balance, suspended between innocence and harsh reality.

"Their lives have been so shaken," she said softly. "The fear they will see on their parents' faces, the confusion at the protests. We will have to find a way to talk to them about their fears, but also to make school a safe space."

I am lying in bed, hoping to fall asleep soon.

Chapter 17. Bitter Truths

Wednesday 3rd February 2021

Today, I had to remind myself that I am not alone in this. I didn't come here alone, and I am not alone now. There are five of us: Ella and Amie on the fourth and fifth floors, Maeve on the first floor, and Ivy on the eighth. We're a mismatched band, thrown together by circumstance. I first met Ella in the queue at the Myanmar Embassy in London, a memory now tinged with nostalgia. It was early July, and the city basked in summer's golden glow. Walking through St James' Park on my way to the embassy, I felt love for my hometown. London—the cracks in its pavements, the graffiti tags, the memories of first dates and internships—would always be my home.

Outside the embassy's cool confines, Ella appeared, flustered and nervous. Her Welsh accent tumbled out as she introduced herself.

"Hi," I smiled warmly. "Are you also new?"

"Yes, hi, I'm Ella," she spluttered. "God, I'm sorry, I am so bloody nervous."

I laughed warmly, knowing the feeling all too well. "Don't worry. We're in this together. How stressful, hey?"

"God, it truly is. We drove all the way from Wales this morning. Dad promised McDonald's, so that's the reason I came."

"I hear there's no McDonalds in Myanmar," I teased.

"You're joking," she gasped. "I will have to load up today and at the airport."

Now, I worry about Ella. She's only twenty-one, far from home. I imagine her mother's panic—their usual daily phone calls disrupted by an unthinkable situation unfolding thousands of miles away.

This morning, as the sun's rays touched the city on the third day of the coup, I packed my grab bag. The concept of a grab bag was foreign to me until I glimpsed the internet during one of its brief windows. Emergency items—first aid kit, whistle, batteries, and a torch—were essential. I have none of them, save for a solitary Triple-A battery unearthed from the depths of my wardrobe. Another search emphasised underwear, medication, and small snacks. Frantically, I scoured my apartment, stuffing available supplies into my trusty school rucksack, now sitting forebodingly by my front door.

I also learned this morning that the British Embassy in Yangon has no official record of our existence. This news hits me like a punch to the gut—disbelief and frustration mingling in a bitter cocktail. How can they not know? We'd meticulously navigated the labyrinth of bureaucracy before our move: exhaustive details, visa checks, and the promise of a year-long stay. Yet here we are.

Yesterday's relief has quickly soured into anger. My phone continues to buzz incessantly, each message a warning: Avoid rallies, stay quiet, and do not post anything. Our emotions, fears, and dissent are to be locked away. We are to be pigeons, not eagles—huddled, cautious, and silent.

Beyond the occasional updates from the embassy, silence envelops my apartment and the empty streets outside. It's a far cry from the fictional chaos portrayed in the movie "No Escape," the film I had convinced Maeve, Amie, Ivy, and Ella to watch at Christmas. Huddled in my flat a few days before Christmas Eve, it was my turn to choose the film for our weekly movie night.

"Let's watch No Escape," I pleaded. "It stars Owen Wilson and Pierce Brosnan."

"What's it about?" Amie asked.

"I can't remember all the details," I admitted, "but it involves a family of expats who move to Southeast Asia and find themselves trapped in political unrest. It's super interesting, a bit of a thriller, but not too graphic."

"Fine," the girls responded. "It better be good."

With popcorn ready and the air conditioning cranked up to counteract the tropical heat, we squeezed onto the sofas, cocooning our shivering bodies in blankets. The film was fast-paced, a heart-pounding thriller that exceeded my recollection of its balance between suspense and drama.

"Shit," Maeve muttered, her voice filled with disbelief and apprehension. "Imagine if this happened."

"I mean…" I started. "A coup could happen here. We need

an escape plan, like they did in the movie."

I gleefully danced around the house, blissfully unaware, as if mocking the impending darkness that would soon unfold.

"The balcony," I yelped. "We would get a rope."

"No," Ivy interjected. "We could go to my flat. Eighth floor, or we can climb onto the roof."

"Perfect." I laughed.

"That was horrific," Amie moaned. "You are never picking the film again!"

I laughed ironically, reassuring Amie that it would never happen to us, especially not like the chaos depicted in 'No Escape."

Yet, just five weeks after watching the film, we find ourselves in an eerie calm. I'm overreacting, surely—things are very different here. For now.

Despite the quietness, whispers of fear swirl around us. Over the past twenty-four hours, rumours have taken root. I've heard that the military has released over twenty thousand prisoners—an attempt to induce fear, no doubt. But the most chilling rumour is about bribes—money exchanged for poison, a sinister plot to taint citizens' water.

I turned to Kyi and Nilar, hoping they could dispel the unsettling tales. Yet, hope proved to be a fragile shield against the harsh realities of the coup.

"I don't know, Liddi," Nilar said. "I think it's true."

"Life is shit," Kyi sighed, her words heavy with resignation.

Their bitter truths hung heavy. I lay on the cold floor of my bedroom, unsure of what to do and how to act. I didn't want to see the Sanchaung girls at that moment, imagining them all in their own states of despair. I rang my mother.

"You need to do something to distract yourself," she said.

"Like what?" I snapped, my anger misplaced. "What can I do?"

She paused momentarily, sensing my frustration. "Is the pool open? Or the gym?" she asked, knowing that exercise helped calm me. Go there, even if just for a little while."

***

This afternoon, I visited the pool with Alexa, seeking refuge in the cooling waters. As we sat submerged, a captivating melody floated through the air. Beautiful voices carried a song that reduced me to tears. I need to find out what it is called—a reminder to ask Nilar and Kyi tomorrow.

As evening descended, another sound took me by surprise: an hour-long symphony of pots and pans. I was initially bewildered, uncertain of its significance of either hope or warning. Stepping onto my balcony, I observed torches blazing, candles flickering, and makeshift instruments striking in perfect rhythm. The eager audience spurred them on as car horns blared and cyclists rang their bells while the streets of Yangon echoed with cheers and cries of solidarity. I recorded the scene before me, the darkness concealing its true beauty.

Once the internet returns, I'll share the video with my parents, and Sophie and Megan. A few hours ago, the girls messaged me to ask me about the situation in the country. Their well-meaning messages felt empty, assuring me that everything was fine and that they'd experienced worse.

Similarly, the school's stance mirrors Sophie and Megan's

viewpoint, telling us that everything will be "okay" with no reason to panic. Yet, our first all-agency meeting since February 1ˢ left us with hollow words and dismissive assurances from a leadership team absent from the country. Acts of violence hadn't occurred, they reminded us, treating such situations as not uncommon in Southeast Asia. Despite the return of intermittent internet access supporting their narrative of an improving situation, deep down, we knew the truth—the complexity, the uncertainty. The constant barrage of shouting and unnatural noises made it impossible to ignore.

During the call, a colleague bravely voiced our concerns. "What if we feel unsafe and want to leave the country?" they asked.

"Then you will be resigning," came the cold, dismissive response.

Minutes after the call ended, the Sanchaung chat erupted with anger and frustration.

[Maeve] How dare they decide whether we feel safe or unsafe.

[Amie] It's ridiculous. I can't afford to lose my job.

[Ella] Maybe they are right, however. It's only been three days.

[Maeve] Fair enough. Maybe we are overreacting, haha.

[Ivy] If anything happens, let's go into Karen mode. I might go back home anyway. Screw this.

Shortly after Matt's return to Yangon in mid-January, Ivy began expressing her longing to leave once more. The yearning for England shimmered in her eyes, and her disillusionment with the situation grew more tangible. During New Years, we believed she would stay and work the remainder of the school year. However, her desire to depart has resurfaced, making me contemplate leaving home. On the one hand, there's the pull of returning to the familiarity and comfort of London. On the other hand, there's the attachment I've developed for the country I now call home.

Though it's still early in this ordeal, the realisation that opting to go back home means losing our jobs is a bitter pill to swallow. It feels unfair that the teachers who aren't currently in Myanmar, like Sophie and Megan, will remain unaffected by this decision.

Chapter 18. The Weight of Uncertainty

Thursday 4th February 2021

Dear Diary,

Earlier, I managed to call my mother, eager for news from England.

"It's very Myanmar-heavy," she'd exclaimed. "The video of the exercise instructor dancing is everywhere!"

The video in question has caused quite a stir. It features an exercise instructor energetically dancing in Naypyidaw, dressed in vibrant yellow attire. Unbeknownst to her, the instructor unintentionally became a witness to history. As she danced, tanks and black SUVs silently rolled in the background, enroute to a security checkpoint. What started as a simple dance, originally intended for an aerobic dance competition, has now become an unexpected window into the early moments of the military coup. She has unknowingly become an overnight internet sensation. Her video has taken on a deeper meaning, symbolising the unsuspecting nature of the unfolding events. According to my mother, her image has transcended boundaries, capturing the attention of a global audience.

Beyond the video, my mother had nothing further to report, so I filled her in on whatever I could. Yesterday was a pivotal moment in the unfolding drama gripping Myanmar. Dozens of medical staff, including doctors, made a resounding statement by walking out of Yangon General Hospital. It marked the first of the protests—a collective act of defiance after the people of Myanmar realised that banging pots and pans was not enough.

Today, the VPN I had purchased on the first day of the coup proved to be a lifeline as the military unleashed its latest assault on our freedom—a temporary blockade of social media. Who knows how long it will last, but the use of Facebook, Instagram, and WhatsApp were now forbidden, in an attempt to curb calls for protest. News had also spread of the first street protests being held, organised in the city of Mandalay, with those marching raising signs with slogans of: "Our arrested leaders: release now, release now." I've also seen pictures of protestors raising their hands in a three-finger salute.

The military had responded swiftly, deploying forces to quell any signs of unrest and extinguish the flames of resistance before they can ignite a larger conflagration. However, acts of defiance had already sown seeds, and a Civil Disobedience Movement (CDM) had begun. Healthcare professionals refused to work under the military; instead, they provided essential services to those in need, using makeshift hospitals, cars, or motorbikes to travel to patients' homes.

Kyi has told me that the state-run MRTV channel is being

used to threaten Burmese citizens, as it plays every night and echoes warnings of arrests of those who partake in the CDM. Medical licences hang in the balance and teachers who protest face arrest. I'm even more glad now that I withdrew my money from the bank after Kyi also told me that the military had begun to address the citizens' high demands for physical cash, threatening to arrest those who took out money and kept it at home.

The military, attempting to regain control of the narrative, released an official statement claiming that Aung San Suu Kyi was in good health, as kindly translated by Kyi. Yet, the veracity of their words remains in question. Without firsthand confirmation of their leader's wellbeing, the people are angry, further fuelling their determination.

I had finished teaching now. The children seemed calmer, mirroring the uneventfulness outside. When I think about it, I never wanted to be a teacher. When I was younger, I excelled academically, yet school was an intricate environment to navigate. I carried a perpetual sense of inadequacy, always holding myself to impossibly high standards. It wasn't that our parents exerted undue pressure on us; we were fortunate enough to have never been subjected to the demands of after-school tuition or the scrutiny that often accompanies underwhelming grades. My torment only intensified in sixth form, and my relentless inner critic would cast a shadow each time I did not achieve what I, or my teachers, wanted. School became a battleground for my insecurities, so it came as a surprise, even to me, when I became interested in working as a teaching assistant at a school in Myanmar. Perhaps I yearned to be the empathetic and understanding teacher that seemed almost non-existent during my schooling. Or maybe I longed to confront the deeply ingrained fears that had taken residence in my subconscious.

Teaching has been quite a different experience than I anticipated. Of course, the pandemic shattered all my preconceptions, but regardless of my initial apprehension, one thing has remained constant: the pure joy the children bring into my life each day.

Alexa has taught me a lot. Ever since our first day at school last year, she has been a lifeline, my muse and mentor. Back then, we were full of hope that the school would reopen soon. The existing teachers at the school had been rapidly evacuated following the outbreak of the pandemic in March. Entering our newly assigned classroom, Alexa and I couldn't help but release a sigh. An atmosphere of disarray greeted us: toys were strewn across the floor, and papers were stacked high on our desks. The challenge before us seemed daunting. Fortunately, the rest of the school was in a relatively decent state and teams of cleaners had begun to sanitise every room, diligently setting up sanitisation stations and social distancing markers as mandated by the Government.

That first day also surprised me in another way. Being physically present in the school reminded me of my first day at the British International School in Jakarta when I was sixteen years old. There were so many similarities—the guarded checkpoints, mandatory storm and lightning, and intruder practice drills, and diverse cultural displays.

When teaching commenced the next day, I scanned my virtual classroom filled with Burmese children and noticed a lone British child among them. A few months after the school year started, his father rightly relocated the family back to London, where he joined a state school. I wondered how he might have felt being the only non-Burmese student.

As an expat, I've learned not to be lazy. I realised that relying solely on English would not suffice in a foreign country, despite its status as a universal language. I had to be proactive and put in the effort to learn and communicate in different languages. However, I also learned that being a foreigner or an expatriate was not always a seamless experience. In the Netherlands, I had to blend in, conceal my Britishness, adapt my accent, and strive to fit in with the local children. One afternoon, Zach and I visited the park, still clad in our school uniforms. Students in the Netherlands did not wear school uniforms, meaning we stuck out sorely. It proved to be a magnet for some neighbourhood children, who quickly seized the opportunity to taunt us. They jeered, snatching my brother's new bike and callously tossing it to the ground while labelling us as "Dom Engels" (stupid English) or "lelijk" (ugly).

Determined not to be victimised, I summoned the courage to showcase my honed Dutch language skills. Standing tall, aged ten, I confidently warned them, "ik ga de politie bellen" (I will call the police). To my surprise, they scattered like frightened rabbits, their bravado evaporating instantly. It was a small but significant victory, illustrating that language could be both a shield and a weapon.

Again, when I was twelve, I had trial days at two new schools in England after leaving the Netherlands. During one of those days, I found myself in a random class's morning registration. The teacher, somewhat unexpectedly, asked me to share my experiences at an international school. However, instead of questions like 'Do you learn similar things?' and 'How is it different to here?', she directed her attention to Jerome, the only black student in the class.

"How many black kids were there?" she asked, her gaze fixed on Jerome. "Jerome is our only one."

"Erm," I mumbled, not giving much thought to my previous school's racial composition. "Maybe six or seven."

"Oh wow," the teacher exclaimed, her mouth hanging open in astonishment. "How does that make you feel, Jerome?"

I watched as Jerome shifted uncomfortably in his seat, his expression a mixture of surprise and unease. The teacher's question had clearly put him on the spot, drawing attention to his race in a way that felt isolating and uncomfortable. I wondered if her question was out of ignorance or pure curiosity. I endeavoured to ensure that all children in my class felt included and loved.

I miss the routine we quickly developed in our initial months. Each morning, the school transport arrived promptly at 6.45 am to collect my colleagues and me. The departure time was strict; if you weren't punctual, the bus would unapologetically leave without you. Adjusting to the early start was a challenge, and occasionally, someone had to rely on a taxi and arrived at school slightly late. Despite the early mornings, the bus rides were enjoyable. They provided an opportunity for us to bond if we weren't too tired, and we shared stories and discovered the motivations behind our bold decisions to uproot our lives. I also learned about the children in their classes, with Ivy and Amie teaching year six, Ella year four, and Maeve year two. The lingering sense of loneliness I had experienced during the lockdown was gradually fading away, replaced by a growing sense of connection and friendship with my new fellow teaching assistants.

Our workdays ended at four in the afternoon, and when we commuted, we typically reached home at five. The highlight of our workdays was the delicious Burmese food we were granted each lunchtime and our much-needed one-hour break in the staff room at midday—of course, we do not have either of these luxuries anymore. At home, we would take a dip in the cooling waters of the swimming pool.

This morning, before lessons commenced, I went back to the swimming pool. My release in the cooling waters was soon interrupted when my every breaststroke was met with the intense scrutiny of two young Burmese teenagers. I tried to ignore the stares, yet it was so painstakingly obvious,

I said, "Hello."

"Hello," one of the girls said, her face immediately flushing red, "where are you from?"

"England," I said hesitatingly. "London," hoping the answer would resonate.

The girl continued her line of questioning, her English slightly broken but understandable, while her friend stood grinning by her side.

"Why are you here?" she inquired—the question on every Burmese's mind—a curiosity about why foreigners like us had chosen to be in their country. Perhaps we were seen as an anomaly, or maybe they possessed knowledge or insights that we did not.

"I am working as a teacher," I explained,

"Wow, I do not see many foreigners," she replied with

genuine awe.

Her ability to converse in English was impressive. I commended her language skills, saying, "Your English is excellent. Where did you learn it?"

She told me that she was in grade eleven and had English lessons as part of her curriculum. As we spoke further, she shared that they had been staring because they didn't know how to swim. They wanted to learn and were intrigued by anyone who could navigate the waters confidently.

"I will help you swim. It will give me something to do." I smiled. "If you teach me Burmese."

"Deal," she smiled back.

Chapter 19. Ruminations

Friday 5th February 2021

Today, all I am craving is company. In my boredom, I've turned to re-watching YouTube videos I made with Zach during the first lockdown. We captured everything—the lockdown diaries. I re-watched the tensions that had surfaced, the raw emotions laid bare.

We captured the weekly NHS clap, which united us every Thursday evening at 8 p.m. We would rush to our front gardens, banging pots and pans as loudly as possible. The initial claps brought tears to my eyes—a heartfelt tribute to our tireless NHS staff. But over time, they began to anger me. Claps could never be equated to a monetary value, to the sacrifices made by those on the frontlines.

In Yangon, the COVID-19 pandemic was just as bad, if not worse. Myanmar shares a border with China, and in March 2020, there were no confirmed cases of the virus nationwide. Fake news spread like wildfire throughout the country—claims that hot water could ward off infection or that eating ice cream could lead to contracting the disease. We had to mask up outside our homes, even in the parks, as people were so scared.

Now, masks were non-existent, and the protests were surely a breeding ground for the spread of the disease—not that anyone cared anymore.

Even so, the lockdown was worrying for the locals, and it soon turned into a draconian stay-at-home order. The fear of facing prosecution or hefty fines loomed over us if we dared to venture out without a valid reason, like a medical appointment or grocery shopping. As foreigners, we couldn't afford to take any unnecessary risks. So, like a ritual, I adapted. Daily, I purchased minimal food supplies, justifying my daily shopping trips, selecting stores slightly further away each time. Carrying shopping bags became my shield, a semblance of legitimacy against potential encounters with the police.

I was unsure whether to leave my apartment and go to the shop at all. An air of unrest brews beyond these walls, and I remained in the dark about unfolding events. Nilar rung me earlier, forewarning of impending action by the restless citizens. She might be right, as the clamour of pots and pans was more fervent tonight. It lasted for a full thirty minutes, bringing me to tears yet again.

As I lay in bed, hoping for an early night, I was filled with dread about the approaching weekend. Teaching has been a welcome distraction, but I was worried about how I would cope with nothing to occupy my mind for two whole days.

I hoped sleep would come soon.

Lydia

Chapter 20. Fifty Things to Do in an Internet Blackout

Saturday 6th February 2021

Dear Diary,

Six days have passed since the turmoil began, and just when it seemed like the situation might be improving, a sudden and complete internet blackout has engulfed the city. Aside from a plane journey or when I was too young for a phone, I can't remember not having access to the outside world and social media for more than eight hours. Fortunately, or unfortunately, the blackout occurred on a weekend, sparing me from the challenges of teaching classes. Parents will be home with their children, as well as their nannies, providing care and entertainment.

During our first seven months in the country, we were fortunate enough to encounter only intermittent power cuts. Although these interruptions were frustrating, particularly when they occurred at inconvenient times like during a lesson or while using the treadmill, they paled in comparison to the complete absence of the internet.

I am trying to reframe the blackout as a "blessing in disguise." I recall reading a journal article about the potential effects of the internet on our cognition, including changes in memory, concentration, and real-world social interactions. As we approach the one-year mark of a global pandemic, it is no surprise that I, like many others, have become heavily reliant on the internet. Yet, not being able to search for information about Myanmar online means being shielded from potentially biased portrayals of the country from afar.

This morning, I embarked on a futile quest in my apartment, scouring every nook and cranny for a hint of internet connectivity. When my fears were confirmed that there was no connection to be found, be it WIFI or 3G, a wave of helplessness washed over me. Unsure if I would succumb to a meltdown or find serenity, I found myself sprawled on the floor, starfished and staring at the ceiling. It was neither a meltdown nor a rush of calm that enveloped me but rather a state of numbness. I felt the coolness of the tiled floor, grounding myself as my muscles twitched. Gradually, my racing thoughts began to slow, and I made the decision to trudge down to Maeve's flat. It was conveniently located on the first floor, where the swimming pool and gym were also situated, accessible to all residents. I knocked on her door. It swung open to reveal her bewildered expression. I was not surprised to find Saffie sitting on Maeve's floor, casually sipping beer at eleven in the morning.

Saffie is an interesting woman; someone I haven't quite figured out yet. Our previous encounter was brief, a chance meeting when we discovered she was Ivy's neighbour on the eighth floor. After that, she extended an invitation for a film night at her home, a welcome break from the monotony of lockdown evenings. We happily gathered with drinks and nibbles, overjoyed with the opportunity to mingle with new people. Her apartment was homely, filled with things that clearly belonged to someone who had lived there a while. The atmosphere was awkward, with Saffie's attention primarily focused on Maeve, leaving the rest of us somewhat on the sidelines, with Ivy somewhere in between. Saffie's watchful eyes scanning the room left an unsettling feeling. As we sipped our drinks and engaged in conversation about the lockdown, Yangon, our school experiences and travels, it always circled back to Saffie. She reminded me of the type of girl I steered clear of in secondary school—quick to pass judgment, targeting others for being too loud or too quiet, too bright, or too stupid. I remained silent, avoiding her gaze, and relaxed only when the movie began, and the lights dimmed. Perhaps I had jumped to conclusions too quickly, as Maeve clearly sees something in her that I don't.

As I found myself sharing a room with Saffie once again, her evident disdain for me was palpable. Fortunately, it was only a short time until the remaining Sanchaung crew joined us. Ella entered first, with a look of alarm plastered on her face, "Is it just me, or is there no internet?" she asked.

I sighed. "Unfortunately, it's not just you."

"It's fine," Saffie interjected. "It won't last long, I'm sure."

Moments later, Amie and Ivy burst into the room together, "Here you are!" Ivy said gratefully. "We should have known you were here!"

Ivy slouched comfily into Maeve's giant green beanbag and lolled her head back, releasing a big sigh.

"Where's Matt?" Ella inquired.

"He's out cycling," Ivy said. "I begged him not to be out long. I have heard that there are tanks out there!"

"It's all rumours," Saffie moaned. "Everything will be fine. I may go out for dinner later."

"Are you sure?" I asked wearily, looking to Maeve for support in my concern.

"Yes, and stop fear mongering," Saffie responded.

"I haven't said anything," I retorted. "I'm just thinking it may not be a good idea. That's all."

Ella pondered, "I'm sure everything will be fine, but things can change in an instant."

"It'll be fine," Saffie insisted.

Changing the subject swiftly, Ivy smiled and asked, "What is everyone planning to do today? Let's enjoy the sunshine. Since there's no internet, we might as well sunbathe and swim, right?"

A plan was soothing, and I was grateful for it. Before going our separate ways, we agreed to meet at designated times throughout the day if the blackout persisted.

The day has passed slowly, and I'm mentally and physically exhausted. The imposition of the blackout has left me in a state of both frustration and curiosity. Without any updates, the day has stretched out before me like an expanse of uncharted territory.

I have discovered little ways to keep myself entertained. Earlier, I retrieved my collection of paints and canvases, a remnant from the time when the girls and I attended a "paint and sip" session.

I even filmed a YouTube video titled "50 things to do in an internet blackout." Yes, that's how bored I was. Engaging in art and creation has slightly repressed the whirling thoughts. I used to enjoy painting, and I am glad I have decided to pick up a paintbrush again.

In the afternoon, I found that I no longer needed to find ways to entertain myself as large streams of people soon gathered outside my building. I remain unaware of the specific events unfolding, yet the sight spoke volumes. The growing crowd, carrying signs, flags, and loudspeakers, was unmistakably a protest. The purpose behind this huge internet blackout suddenly became clear—it was being used as a desperate measure to deter the burgeoning masses that now flooded the streets of Yangon. From my vantage point on my balcony, I observed the sea of red shirts worn by most protestors. Children held red balloons and waved small NLD flags, their innocence intertwined with the spirit of resistance.

The crowd's voices echoed through the city, chanting, "Are we united? Yes, we are!"

Captivated by the energy, I moved my canvas to the balcony, painting there for the rest of the day. Despite the size of the gathering, the protest appeared to be peaceful. Police officers attempted to maintain control of the situation but to no avail. In the afternoon, demonstrators sat and smoked cigarettes with the police and offered them refreshments to get them onside. I cannot imagine what the police officers would have felt, torn between risking persecution from either the military or the public by choosing one side over the other.

The CDM movement is gaining momentum, as is the battle against it: over one hundred and sixty arrests have been made and counting. The cutting of internet access serves as a cloak, obscuring these distressing developments from the wider world. Phone lines have also been severed. This is not the first time that internet access, or the media's ability to operate, has been restricted in Myanmar, whether through repressive laws or censorship. "Controversial" films addressing themes such as LGBT or ethnic minority rights are unlikely to be broadcast. Television channels and radio stations are predominantly owned by the Tatmadaw or ex-generals, leaving limited scope for progressive thinking. Before 2011, Myanmar had banned websites of political opposition groups, and any keywords or phrases deemed suspicious, such as "government," "democracy," and "8888," were closely monitored. Access to popular platforms like Facebook, MSN Mail, Gmail, and Twitter, among many others, were sporadically blocked. Internet access slightly improved after the transfer of leadership to the NLD in 2015, and censorship slowly declined until February 1st, when it took a significant step backwards. To the people of Myanmar, it must feel as if the country has suddenly regressed twenty years.

Although today was not as bad as I initially thought it would be, I really hope the connection returns tomorrow. It has only been one day, but I miss speaking to my mum. I want to tell them about the protests, the protests that gave me goosebumps as I sat and watched for hours.

Chapter 21. Privilege and Protest

Sunday 7th February 2021

The internet did not return this morning as I'd hoped. However, today is passing by more quickly, and I am starting to enjoy the temporary disconnection. It's giving me the chance to reconnect with my hobbies. I'm also realising that my anxiety, driven by the incessant streams of messages and updates, has found a temporary reprieve. Still, I continue to watch the protests. Today marked the largest of them so far, with thousands taking to the streets for the second day in a row. By mid-morning, protestors were marching all over Yangon, in Mandalay and central Myanmar. Hundreds more camped outside a police station in Karen state, where local NLD politicians had reportedly been arrested.

In between protest-watching, I've managed to carve out some time for reading. It is a welcome respite. In all honesty, I'll gladly take any chance to escape my own mind for a little bit. It's a shame

I don't have any psychedelics; George Orwell will have to suffice. His *Burmese Days* has been sitting on my bedside table for months, but today, I am proud to say I'm almost finished with it.

As I read, I learned about the backdrop of British colonisation in Burma, and it's shedding light on themes of gender, racism, and discrimination. Despite being set in the 1920s, it's painfully evident that many of the prejudices depicted still persist today. This struck a chord, having always been passionate about equality, human rights, and global health equity. However, I can't ignore the privilege that comes from growing up in a middle-class white family. It's easy to say that I'm passionate when I come from a culture where children aren't shot playing in the street, where wife beating is not an accepted social standard, and where children aren't forcibly recruited into the armed forces.

As a teen, I participated in a Community Action Service module for my IB Diploma in Jakarta. The program aimed to instil empathy and social responsibility among students attending the thirteen thousand dollars-a-year fee-paying international school. Choosing to volunteer at Sekolah Bisa, dubbed the 'jungle school,' I was introduced to the United Nations Child's Rights initiative established by the British School of Jakarta. The school provided education to children in the nearby Bulakan shanty, amidst Jakarta's towering malls and luxurious mansions.

Trapped in a vicious cycle of destitution, many children from these slums or shanties scavenged for recyclables and valuables from as young as eight. Their days were spent scouring the town, combing through landfills, and rummaging through rubbish bins, searching for raw materials and items to sell. Education remained an unattainable dream for many of them as they battled persistent illnesses caused by unsanitary conditions and faced an uncertain future.

Arriving at Sekolah Bisa, I encountered a small, bamboo-framed school where children aged seven to sixteen learned together in a single classroom. I watched as older students huddled in a corner, poring over textbooks. Some were preparing to transition to vocational college, perhaps, or jobs that would help lift them from the mire of poverty. But it was the younger ones who captured my heart. A blind girl traced her fingers over raised braille letters, guided by a classmate who patiently whispered explanations. Nearby, a boy with severe mental challenges clung to his worn-out teddy bear, his smile radiant as he listened to a story.

Sekolah Bisa wasn't just about education; it was a lifeline. The programme provided more than lessons—it offered sustenance and medical and dental care. The children's laughter echoed through the bamboo walls, drowning out their hardships beyond these safe confines.

As the school day ended, I wondered what awaited them at home. Did they return to shanties with leaky roofs and empty stomachs? Or did their families share in their dreams, clinging to hope like friable threads?

Sharing our home in Jakarta with household staff also highlighted the reality of living in a developing country. In the bustling city, where wealth and poverty collided like tectonic plates, I navigated a new reality that blurred the lines between privilege and necessity. It was strange, not to my father, who had lived in India for a few years before, but to my mother, Zach and me. It felt wrong for somebody to make me breakfast and fold my clothes. But we were told that those who could afford their wages, of only one hundred dollars a month, had a social responsibility to hire staff. Still, I grappled with questions. Was this a necessity or exploitation? Respect or convenience?

Our Jakarta home was a hive of activity. Yanti, our cheerful cook, moved through the kitchen like a maestro, orchestrating flavours that danced on our tongues. Adoel, the houseboy, was a quiet and peaceful presence, his thin frame always in motion. Guards stood sentinel, their eyes always scanning our surroundings. And then there was Pak Rasimin, our driver, and Ibu Sodiyah, our tireless cleaner—a married couple with three young children of their own, whom they returned to every evening.

Our dog revelled in the attention, her tail wagging as hands reached down to throw her ball or stroke her ears.

Yet, within those walls, hierarchies emerged. Yanti assumed the role of the boss, her authority unquestioned. Complex dynamics played out—the unspoken tensions, the silent divisions. Adoel, tall and lean, with stories etched into his skin, became my confidante. He had worked since the age of eleven while his own family lived far away in the countryside. We teased him with English food, but he politely declined, rooted in his culinary traditions.

During our second year, Adoel welcomed a baby girl. His wife moved hours away to live with her family, and Adoel chose to stay and work, sending money back to them. Eventually, he relocated to Singapore for work, leaving behind memories and a piece of his heart.

In my Yangon home, there are no household staff. Yet, I

imagine the dynamics are similar—the delicate balance of dependence and camaraderie. And as the military coup shadows over lives, I wonder about the significance of hiring domestic help. Perhaps it isn't just about convenience; perhaps it's a thread woven into the fabric of survival—a way to stimulate an economy frayed at the edges.

This morning, I went to visit Ivy and Matt. I met Ivy long before the other girls when I first came to Yangon to visit Sophie and Megan. She is intuitive, not in the way of fortune tellers or mystics, but in how she listens. When Ivy looks at you, it's as if she sees your soul laid bare.

Today, though, something was different. Ivy's usually serene face was etched with worry. Her hands trembled, and her gaze darted toward the window often, which scared me. Our current situation is an odd one, but Yangon remains calm. There is no immediate violence or imminent threat, but it's the uncertainty that lies ahead.

"We react," she said, "as if danger lurks around every corner."

Let's see what tomorrow brings.

Chapter 22. Broken Promises and Deceptive Hopes

Monday 8th February 2021

Dear Diary,

Last night was a turning point—the kind that etches itself into memory, leaving scars that never entirely fade. It revealed the depths of depravity to which the military is willing to sink. We gathered at our usual spot downstairs to buy snacks. The shopkeeper, with kind eyes, handed us our crisps and beer, and we watched another movie saved from our dwindling list.

The film played—a grainy classic, its colours muted. We made a pact to be there for each other. We vowed to speak up when fear or anxiety threatens to take hold. Our friendship had become a lifeline in these difficult times, knowing we can rely on one another to avoid brewing isolation and a spiral into the anxiety and depression that we were all too familiar with.

Over the past few months, it had felt like we were always in each other's footsteps. The speed at which our bond had grown seemed almost unreal, yet there we were—five strangers turned confidantes. They had seen the best and worst of me, and I, of them.

As the movie played, the usual clatter of pots and pans outside Ivy's flat pulled our focus. The metallic sound—a protest in its rawest form—drowned out the dialogue on-screen.

We drank, laughter bubbling up but laced with bitterness. Rumours swirled: the reports of the military's escalating atrocities; whispered accounts of disappearances, and tales of midnight raids. Conversations shifted to escape plans—routes, safe houses, contingency plans.

In the late hours, the phone lines flickered back to life, offering a fleeting connection to those within the country. Messages trickled in. Updates from Kyi and Nilar promised a brief window when the internet might return. Hopefully soon.

By 11 p.m., exhaustion had taken its toll. I descended the winding staircase to my fourth-floor apartment, hoping to call my boyfriend before bed, though I already knew it wouldn't work. His voice echoed in my mind. Watching Matt and Ivy together only deepens my ache for closeness—the touch of a hand, the warmth of shared breath. Daniel wants me to return to England, eager for us to see each other again. It's a small silver lining in the possibility of having to leave.

The dim glow of my bedroom lights welcomed me as I slipped into bed. The day's weariness clung to my bones, and the cool pillow was a relief against my cheek. Just as I began to drift off, a sudden eruption of clapping shattered the silence.

This time, it was different. Last week's claps had been desperate, defiant. But tonight, the applause was positive, like a melody rewritten in a major key. There were cheers, too.

I leapt out of bed and peered through the curtains of my bedroom to catch a glimpse. It wasn't enough. I hurried to the balcony in the living room for a cleared view. The scene below took my breath away. Torches and phone lights pierced the darkness. Families spilled into the streets, their faces alight with joy. Babies were twirled in the air, their squeals joining the chorus of celebration.

I didn't need to know the reason. The air itself buzzed with an energy that was impossible to ignore. I joined in, clapping with the others. My hands met the night, a rhythm of shared joy that transcended words, language and fear.

I rushed back to my bedroom to grab my phone, which was buzzing with messages from the volunteering chat and Kyi. She urged me to switch on the military news channel—the sole flicker of biased information in our disconnected world. I hesitated, knowing I wouldn't understand the words, but she insisted, "Watch it."

The television flickered to life. A man in a crisp suit sat in the studio, clutching papers. His broad smile radiated through the screen. Images of Aung San Suu Kyi flashed across the broadcast. My chest tightened as I strained to piece together the meaning behind the visuals.

I quickly called Kyi and begged her to explain. Her voice cracked with emotion. "They have released Aung San Suu Kyi," she said. We will be okay tomorrow. Everything will be normal."

Bewilderment washed over me. Shock, followed by a surge

of happiness. Just a week after Aung San Suu Kyi's abduction, news of her imminent release felt almost too good to be true. My mind raced with questions. Would she resume her role as president? Would the other democratic leaders be freed as well? But I forced myself to quiet the noise. For once, I let the joy stand on its own. It was a gift.

After wishing Kyi a good night, I lingered on the balcony, basking in the jubilation and joy. Miraculously, the internet had also returned, though limited to 3G. It felt like a sign that things were improving, even if just temporarily. Not wanting to waste the moment, I quickly called my mum and boyfriend to share the good news.

"I knew it would be fine," my father's voice rang out with a cheerful certainty.

When the call ended, I glanced at the time: one in the morning. I crawled back into bed, hoping to find sleep. But my mind refused to quiet, a tempest of unanswered questions. The hum of the air conditioning couldn't drown out the cheers still echoing through the night. No matter how I shifted, no position felt comfortable.

An hour later, just as my eyes began to close, my phone buzzed—a single message.

Weary-eyed, I reached for it.

Lydia

Yes, I replied.

It was fake.

Fake?

The military staged the announcement. Aung San Suu Kyi is still in captivity...

Why?

They are animals.

The words hit me like a physical blow.

Today, I am heartbroken. Broken for the country, for my friends, for Myanmar and its people. The weight of this betrayal is crushing, unveiling their true corruptness. The military had exploited the internet blackout with chilling precision, fabricating hope only to weaponise it. They are holding the entire country under their firm control.

With the return of the internet, further rumours have circulated. The latest is that the military had orchestrated the staged release of Aung San Suu Kyi as a diversionary tactic, allowing them to evacuate their own children safely. While the nation rejoiced at the supposed freedom of their beloved State Counsellor, little did we know what a sinister plan may have been at play behind the scenes.

The culmination of both the military's lies, and the rumours has sparked an unyielding defiance. Something feels different today. The Hope Haven chat has warned me to be extra vigilant about posting anything on social media. Many of the volunteers have been issued warnings of arrest; section 505(a) of the penal code—criminalising comments that "cause fear," spread "false news, or agitate directly or indirectly a criminal offence against a Government employee."

Today marked the first nationwide strike day, and protests continued to escalate. The CDM has disrupted deliveries and internet access, and only a minority of individuals are still going to work. "We will return to work only after power is handed back to the democratically elected government," most say.

From the window in my makeshift office and spare room, I can hear the resounding chants echoing through the streets. Groups of students march together, offering support and rallying each other along the way. I notice a girl towards the back of a line, visibly exhausted. Her friend immediately steps in, wrapping an arm around her shoulders in a quiet, compassionate embrace. The message is clear: they are in this together, now and in the days to come.

The people of Myanmar stand united, transcending divides of religion, ethnicity, age, and occupation. In a country where LGBT rights are often met with discrimination and prosecution, the unity is nothing short of admirable. Myanmar's diverse population is genuinely remarkable. Today, I saw Muslims, Christians, drag queens, doctors, nurses, adults, and children standing side by side. My favourite image remains from a protest last week: a group of LGBT activists adorned in dazzling drag, holding a sign that defiantly declared: "Gays for Democracy."

Once again, I observed the protesters' hands forming the symbol of resistance popularised by the *Hunger Games* trilogy—a raised trio of fingers. The military's response to the growing protests and the CDM has been swift and harsh. In Yangon and Mandalay, gatherings of more than five people on roads or parks are now illegal. These measures are an attempt to tighten their grip and quell the unrest spreading like wildfire.

As I sit and write on my balcony, the night air feels heavier and thicker with tension. Minutes ago, Senior General Min Aung Hlaing addressed the country for the first time since the coup, a moment that must have sent ripples of anticipation and unease through every household. I can almost picture families gathered together, eyes fixed on screens—televisions, iPhones, laptops–each one a portal to this pivotal moment.

When the screens flickered to life, I imagined silence descending in these homes. Children likely jostled for the best view of the man whose actions had irrevocably changed their lives. The atmosphere would have been electric, weighed with expectation—a delicate balance between hope and fear.

As the General spoke, waves of emotion must have swept over his audience: anger at the usurpation of power, fear of an uncertain future, and an unyielding longing for the restoration of democracy.

Kyi's firm and resolute words echoed in my mind: "We cannot give up. If the military has power, we will end. This cannot be allowed to happen."

I became angrier when we received a single email informing us that regular school would proceed as planned, instructing us to prepare offline work in case of unpredictability. They are obviously oblivious to the chaos unfolding. There has been no inquiry about our wellbeing. The email's lack of empathy has incited a wave of backlash, a collective expression of frustration at the disconnect between the reality in Yangon and the apathy demonstrated by those in positions of authority, safe in their home countries.

***

As much as I am angry at how the school is handling the situation, I only have to think of Kyi and Nilar and how they must be feeling. They are acting oddly, unsurprisingly. However, it is frustrating when their anger is directed at me. "I don't understand," and I do not pretend to. However, I am trying.

Tonight, I visited Maeve. She's strong and fiercely independent—the kind of person I hoped could lend me a bit of her courage. We have had a love-hate relationship, with several heated arguments and debates since we arrived in the country. But beneath it all, I know she is a gentle soul, perhaps with underlying anxieties that force her to put on a front.

We spent the evening watching the final episode of a TV series we'd been following together over the past few weeks. It was nice, and I'm glad I went.

We haven't heard much from Amie. I will check on her tomorrow.

Chapter 23. "Miss, it's so loud."

Tuesday 9th February 2021

In addition to the ban on gatherings of more than five people, we're now under a general curfew from 8 p.m. to 4 a.m. I'm unsure of the repercussions of breaking these limits or curfews, but I'm hesitant to find out. These new regulations will likely make protests more boisterous, fueling determination and further anger and possibly leading to more arrests. The military claims the measures are in response to the increased protests over the weekend and alleged threats of force from certain groups.

Kyi told me this morning, only after the fact, that she had been protesting. This worried me, of course. However, I know there is little I can do to stop her from taking action. It pains me to think that if our situations were reversed, if my country, home, and life were at stake, I, too, would be driven to protest. I have pleaded with her to be cautious. I don't know what I would do if anything happened to her.

Since the weekend, the uncompromising internet blackouts have persisted, leaving us in darkness and cutting off our means of communication. From the early morning hours, from 1 a.m. to 9 a.m., we cannot access Wi-Fi, 3G, or 4G. As if these restrictions weren't enough, the regime had also now permanently banned all social media platforms. This further isolated us, preventing us from connecting with the outside world and the Burmese people to share their stories.

The school schedule had been adjusted accordingly, pushing the start of lessons back by an hour. What was once a quarter past eight in the morning start had now become a quarter past nine one. When the internet was restored at nine this morning, I hurried to prepare for my first lesson, logging onto the portal and setting up for our Zoom class. It felt like a rush, overwhelming even. The regime's grip has extended to every aspect of our students' lives, dictating even the most minor details of daily routines. The children have been asking difficult questions. I am unable to respond.

This morning, I didn't know which children would be attending class. It was entirely unpredictable. The classroom hummed with uncertainty. Faces—some wide-eyed, others furrowed—stared back at Alexa, their young minds grappling with a world turned upside down. The morning sun filtered through the windows, casting shadows across my screen.

"Good morning, children," Alexa's voice cut through the tension. "I hope you are all safe and well."

Soe, bright-eyed and curious, raised her hand. "Miss Alexa," she said, her voice barely audible. "What will happen? It's so loud!"

The chorus of agreement followed. "Yes. So noisy. All day."

Alexa's gaze softened. "We can hope," she said, choosing her words carefully, "that things will get better soon. But for now, let's focus on class. Shall we sing a song?"

Another voice chimed in, this time Sebastian, from Singapore. "But, Miss Alexa, what if the soldiers come to our homes?"

"Don't worry. You have lots of adults looking after you. We look out for one another."

And so, in that small virtual classroom, the children clung to hope.

But beyond those screens, my lifeline stretched across oceans. Ben, my older brother, lives in Tokyo, only two and a half hours ahead of Yangon. Unlike Zach, whose bond with me had been forged in Jakarta's heat and laughter, Ben and I share a quieter connection.

When I called Ben on February 1st, he answered immediately. Our video call bridged the gap, and he listened as I poured out my fears.

"It will be okay," he reassured me. "Has there been any violence?"

"Not yet," I wavered. "Not that I know of."

"Is the embassy helping you?"

"Not yet."

"Is the school helping you?"

"Not really."

"I am going to call you every few hours," he promised.

"Thank you," I whispered. "If you can't reach me, the Wi-Fi has been cut again."

And then there was Zach, my childhood partner in crime, who had faded into the chaos of Myanmar.

Lost in my thoughts, I noticed a group of children playing on the balcony opposite mine. Their youthful laughter floated through the air. Their playful fighting—slapping each other's arms in jest—reminded me of Zach, and I longed for his infectious laughter to fill the void between us. But now, as Myanmar teetered on the edge, our connection felt tenuous, like a radio signal drowned in static. Why hadn't he checked in?

Disappointment settles, a fine layer of dust dulling the once-vivid memories of dressing him up in pink frilly fairy outfits and midnight McDonald's runs.

Reflective, I traced the contours of uncertainty. Perhaps it was here, in this moment, that I wondered whether some connections were meant to fray, no matter how tightly they were once woven.

Following the backlash from yesterday's email from the school, another message arrived later in the evening. This one seemed more attuned to the gravity of the situation.

"I understand that the situation in Yangon has been very stressful, especially over the weekend. We will review it at the end of the day and decide based on advice from embassies and official security organisations. Should it come to that, we have plans for all eventualities, including repatriation. Currently, demonstrations had been raucous in places but not dangerous, so all official guidance was still, 'Stay at home.'"

As the internet blackouts persist, my primary concern is how to reach my family. This afternoon, I experienced a glimmer of relief:

we were asked to provide emergency contact details.

However, the instruction to hand this information to the school administration seems pointless.

Like me, the Burmese staff also remained in Myanmar. If I, with the advantage of an English SIM card, struggled to establish a connection with my family from within Yangon, how would they fare? Could we truly trust the school management, shielded from firsthand experiences, to act in our best interests if the time called for it? I wasn't so sure.

The email also offered a one-off counselling session scheduled for tomorrow afternoon. The mental toll of isolation weighed heavily. The ceaseless barrage of "what ifs" and nervous thoughts had begun to affect everyone mentally. Stress manifested physically—an ache that refused to relent. Sleep, elusive as a wisp of smoke, slipped through our fingers.

Friendships frayed. Differing viewpoints, conspiracy theories—friction and closeness danced a delicate tango. But we clung to each other, even as uncertainty pulled us apart.

Some dismissed the possibility of worsening conditions as far-fetched, but I see it differently: things could only deteriorate. Through my voluntary work, I had built connections—a web of contacts leading to the UN, the ousted government, and even elements within the military. Every day, group chats inundated us with grim imagery: lifeless bodies, gunshot wounds, grieving families in all corners of Myanmar. Each message offered a painful window into the nightmare unravelling across the country.

Arrests were inevitable now. Warning gunshots echoed through the streets, an attempt to enforce compliance. Yet the protestors stood undeterred, their resolve unwavering.

Today, Kyi's Facebook account was blocked despite her use of a VPN. The military sent her a cautionary message. I urged her to be careful, but she had already created a new profile—a digital chameleon. Meanwhile, Maya, one of the British volunteers, left our chat—the Hope Haven group—fearing the soldiers could infiltrate it. Her caution was warranted; if the military gained access to our communications, it would put us all in danger.

Maya advised me also to leave the chat, but I hesitated. It was a lifeline—daily intelligence, and without it, I'd be lost in a sea of nonsensical information.

I wondered what tomorrow would bring.

Lydia

Chapter 24. Finding Courage in the Chaos

Wednesday 10th February 2021

Dear Diary,

This morning, I discovered that the beautiful melody we often hear in the evenings is called "Kabar Ma Kyay Bu," the revolutionary anthem of the 1998 pro-democracy movement. The haunting melody and poignant lyrics evoke tears whenever I hear it. It's so beautiful, you should listen. The words remind me of the sacrifice and the unwavering courage of those who fought—and continue to fight—for democracy: "*The Strong Revolution. Oh, the brave heroes died for democracy. Our country, Myanmar, is a place built with Martyrs. There is no pardon for you till the end of the world. Cause that's the bloody record written by people's lives.*"

I heard the song again while cycling around town this morning. My trusty steed was only purchased last month. I had been eager to explore Yangon's winding streets and discover hidden gems. Yet, despite my bike's brief lifespan, I am unsure if I will ever be able to ride it again after today's events.

In early January, I mustered the courage to navigate the treacherous roads and cycle to work. I needed a new form of exercise, and I was excited by the thrill of cycling in the unknown. Initially, I embarked on the journey alongside Alexa, who often travelled by this mode of transport. Her bike was nicer and more expensive than mine, with adequately functioning gears and a cushioned seat. At the time, she lived in a different apartment complex, approximately a ten-minute cycle ride from my home and enroute to the school. In my gym clothes, I would leave my complex at quarter to seven in the morning, storing my work clothes in the bike basket I had purchased. Alexa and I would meet outside her complex, occasionally joined by other colleagues, as we continued our journey.

In some areas, the traffic was heavy and fast-moving, with poorly marked or absent bike lanes. Not that I expected any different. In other parts of the journey, the traffic was agonisingly slow. I saved minutes weaving through congested cars. My heart was pounding relentlessly the entire trip, refusing to ease even after repeating the journey several times over the month. I soon learned to watch out for the potholes, memorising where they were along the route. Buses became objects of caution as I narrowly avoided being cut off by their sudden manoeuvres, and cars tended to pull out without looking. The roads were wide and accommodated multiple vehicles in a single lane. Cycling on the pavement was discouraged as pedestrians would dart out unpredictably or spit red saliva onto the streets. Cycling through the city became more than just a hobby but an act of bravery. Yet, I loved the adventure.

I soon yearned to explore further afield, beyond the city

limit—to taste the untamed air, to feel the pulse of Myanmar's heartland. And so, two cycle rides with Uncharted Horizons allowed me to do this.

Mandalay, beaches, Bagan—the names shimmered like distant stars. But the pandemic and coup had clipped our wings, grounding us. The Lonely Planet guide, once my trusted companion, had gathered dust. The countryside and rural villages remained elusive—except when I sat atop my bicycle.

After purchasing my bike, one of my first rides took me back to Dala—a small town I had first visited on a cycle tour.

Perched on the southern bank of the Yangon River, Dala was like a quaint fishing village frozen in time. Its streets held ancient secrets, revealing glimpses of "simple Burmese village life." Here, tradition danced with the present—a delicate waltz that tourists rarely witnessed.

In other corners of the world, cultural tourism was rife in these small villages. Villagers donned costumes, performed rehearsed dances, and brewed medicinal concoctions made from leaves and herbs. Visitors marvelled, snapped photos, and savoured the illusion. But when the tourists departed, the facade crumbled. Smartphones emerged, revealing modern lives beneath the surface.

Dala appeared to remain untouched—a hidden gem, authentic, and its people unguarded. To reach the village, we had to cross the Yangon River by taking a ten-minute ferry ride, setting off from Pansodan Pier, a brief cycle ride from the downtown bike shop. The river was the city's primary access route and port of call for ships entering the Ayeyarwady Delta. It was lined with docks filled with large oceangoing vessels. Our ferry, filled to capacity with commuters travelling from Dala to Yangon for work, arrived promptly. Following our guide, Dedan, we boarded the ferry and left our bikes unlocked on the lower deck before ascending to the upper deck for a better view. The locals had brought their motorbikes, food stalls, and livestock aboard, all left unattended. Fruit, mirrors, cigarettes, and eggs were being sold, and everyone was smiling and conversing.

As we sailed, Dedan shared tales of Dala's ongoing transformation, focusing on the contentious construction of a bridge connecting Yangon, the commercial capital, with the impoverished Dala township. The project sparked heated debate. The river poses risks and has a history of disasters, as evidenced by the long-tail boats that serve as a primary mode of transportation alongside the ferry. During one return journey from Dala, we opted to travel in one of these boats, offering me a firsthand understanding of the perilous nature of the river. As we navigated the waters, I witnessed another boat dragging a lifeless, unclothed body. This image would haunt my thoughts and reappear at the most unexpected times. The body, once with light brown skin, now bore discoloured hues of blue and green, while its vacant, piercing eyes left an eerie impression. It marked my first encounter with a dead body, and the lack of reaction or shock from others seemed so peculiar to me. No police were called, and no detectives arrived. Instead, the body was quietly untied from the boat and covered with a blanket.

Such tragic deaths, not uncommon along the river, fuelled the lobbying efforts of Dala locals and their representatives in parliament for the construction of the bridge. However, opposition from operators of privately operated ports, citing concerns that the bridge's proposed height and width would obstruct large ships, presented significant hurdles. Nevertheless, the bridge was due to be completed in 2025, and despite the loss of income for long-tail boat and ferry operators, deaths would be drastically reduced.

Arriving at Dala port for the first time, we were met with a delighted spectacle of organised chaos. The road teemed with trishaws, motorbike taxis, and furry companions. Cycling thirty kilometres, we meandered past fish markets, tiny tea shops, and farm animals. As we pedalled on, boys and girls alike dashed towards us, their outstretched hands eager for a high-five. I reciprocated every gesture. Amidst the rustic charm of the fishing village, where houses stood tall on stilts above the river, women leaned over to tend to their daily chores, washing clothes in the gentle currents.

At every corner, more children filled the streets, their innocent curiosity piqued by our presence. We had to swerve abruptly at times to avoid the children and dogs who would suddenly dart across our path. Despite the backdrop of poverty, everyone seemed content, their spirits un-dampened by their modest circumstances.

I had my first taste of Myanmar tea that day, a beverage that took me by surprise in terms of its appearance and flavour. As I took my first sip, the unexpected taste almost caused me to spit it out involuntarily. Afterwards, I learned that Myanmar tea, laphet, was a blend of black tea and sweetened condensed milk. Its reddish-brown hue and overly sweet taste were not to my liking. The kind shop owners, noticing my reaction, very kindly prepared a new cup for me, which was still very sweet yet bearable. I sipped it slowly, much to the delight of the locals. Our guide told us about the symbolism of tea shops, explaining that they served as gathering places for the community.

In contrast to Yangon, where cafes and tea shops were restricted during the pandemic, these had remained open as the government knew it was their only business. I also learned that there were twenty variations of laphet tea, each differing in colour and sweetness. The Cho Seint tea, for example, was a syrup-sweet concoction that the locals enjoyed dipping their naan bread into. I thought I might progress onto that one day.

After our tea break, we cycled past a monastery where children played outside with sticks and chalk, enjoying their midday break.

"This is a special monastery," Dedan told us. "It is for children who have been abandoned. Kumakasid Monastery."

"Like an orphanage?"

"Yes," he said. "Some children still have parents here, but they were left here in hopes of a better life. Also, some lost their parents during Cyclone Nargis in 2008."

The cyclone robbed the lives of over 80,000 people, destroying the Ayeyarwady Delta region with devastating outcomes. At the time, Myanmar was under military junta rule, which initially hindered foreign aid and relief efforts. It took six days of limited assistance before the United Nations were allowed to send supplies. However, even then, harsh restrictions were imposed, allowing only basic supplies such as food and medicine to enter the country. It wasn't until three weeks after the cyclone struck that relief workers were finally granted access.

Dedan further explained that the monks we often saw

begging for food most mornings were doing so to feed the children in the orphanage. They would travel to Yangon to source supplies and provisions.

Ten days into the coup, I have continued to cycle, but it has been too dangerous to travel as far as Dala. Instead, I pedalled down the now familiar streets.

"Please be careful," my mother's voice echoed in my mind. "Always wear your helmet."

This morning, as I cycled through the city again, my grip on the handlebars was firm, and my senses were on high alert. Each pedal stroke propelled me forward, my body in sync with the rhythm of the wheels. I navigated the city streets with caution, attuned to every pothole and bump along the way that threatened to disrupt my balance. I avoided the busy city areas, knowing protests would be in full swing. Instead, I sought solace in the winding back lanes.

A gentle breeze whispered through the air, carrying distant echoes of discontent and unrest. My AirPods nestled snugly in my ears, and music played softly, an attempt to create a bubble of temporary respite from the unsettling atmosphere.

As the sweltering sun descended, casting long, stretching shadows across the cityscape, I realised it was time to make my way home. Nearing downtown, the city's pulsating heart, the streets gradually transformed from quieter back alleys to busy roads. I felt my own heart begin to quicken its pace.

Suddenly, a patrol of soldiers emerged, their presence commanding and dominant. Clad in the Tatmadaw military's unmistakable green uniforms, they held their AK47s with a firm grip. Time seemed to stand still as my body froze. Ivy had been right when she mentioned that tanks are roaming the streets.

Armoured vehicles rumbled down the roads with an intimidating force. Swiftly, I reached for my phone, silencing the melodies that had offered me solace moments ago. The gravity of the situation demanded my full attention. The soldiers stood as sentinels, their watchful eyes scanning the surroundings, their presence both intimidating and unsettling. Nearby, stern-faced police officers stood guard, their stoic expressions mirroring the tension that permeated the muggy air. Military propaganda had told us that they were present for our protection. However, every instinct within me screamed to retreat, to seek an alternative route home. Yet, a reckless curiosity pushed me forward, combined with wanting to choose the shortest route possible. I clenched my teeth, my palms sweating as I pedalled forward.

I rode past the soldiers and their tanks. Their watchful eyes drilled into me, their mere presence a reminder of the perilous tightrope I find myself walking on. My breath, shallow and strained, mingled with the oppressive silence of the streets. Beads of sweat glistened on my brow, trickling down my temples as I propelled myself forward.

I carelessly swerved between cars and motorbikes on the road. The world around me blurred in a frenzy of motion.

Finally, I reached Sanchaung Gardens, and a wave of relief washed over me, temporarily numbing the exhaustion coursing through my tired limbs. My bike trembled beneath me as I dismounted, and my legs threatened to give way after the adrenaline-fuelled sprint.

After locking the bike securely in the garage, I leaned against the wall, catching my breath. A vow formed in my mind, clear and resolute: I would never cycle the streets of Yangon again.

Our scheduled one-off counselling session was going to take place virtually over Teams that afternoon. It was timely, as I found myself going ever so slightly insane. The session had only been arranged in response to our pleas and concerns voiced over the escalating protest and our mounting anxieties. It was like they were gaslighting us, making us feel like idiots for being afraid or worried. My mind was constantly racing, and I couldn't get it to switch off. It was so noisy outside, which didn't help. Ever since Monday, the protests had been massive, and the banging of pans had been louder.

Lydia

Chapter 25. Red Moons

Thursday 11th February 2021

I carry a secret that eludes Nilar and Kyi, either by their choice or blissful ignorance. With each passing day, the possibility of me having to leave, either forcibly by the British government or the military, is increasing. It is a silent storm brewing, threatening to shatter the delicate balance of our friendship.

Their kindness, expressed through small gestures like buying me bubble tea or coffee, despite my protests, only deepens my resolve. I cannot bear the guilt of knowing I may soon abandon them. Farewells are not our forte; the pain is woven into every interaction.

The girls have shared stories of other foreigners they have lost touch with, recounting how they are "always left behind." I feel trapped between a rock and a hard place—I don't want to lose our friendship, but I also can't bear the burden of being held responsible for circumstances beyond my control.

I worry for the girls' safety. While I live in a secure complex, their independent apartments leave them vulnerable. They are not in gated buildings. Their front doors lead onto the busy roads. It would be all too easy for the junta to break in.

Nilar lives with flatmates, keeping her family at a distance for hidden reasons. The enigmatic shadows of her estrangement dance in the corners of her eyes, revealing pieces of a story that she is not yet ready to share. I don't push her. Meanwhile, Kyi lives with her aunt, far from her hometown in Rakhine, due to Yangon's better job opportunities. But her aunt's strict curfew, implemented long before the coup and mandating her return by six every evening, casts a veil of confinement over her world. Initially shocked by the curfew, I was glad it had been enforced, knowing it added an extra layer of protection for Kyi.

"Young women never live alone in Myanmar," the girls had told me. "It's not normal. Not until they are married."

Through conversations in coffee shops or over the phone, we ventured into uncharted territories of debate, discussing having partners. They were shocked when I spoke of premarital sex, a notion foreign to their cultural norms. They were even more surprised when we discussed the possibility of a single woman becoming pregnant.

Often, the conversational flow was awkward and broken. The currents of language and cultural differences created gentle ripples in our catchups. I struggled to grasp the nuances of Burmese, while they, despite their commendable English skills, occasionally found themselves grappling to understand my expressions. We always had fun, though, as I taught them the idiosyncrasies of British slang, and they taught me basic Burmese.

As the coup continued its relentless march, tightening its grip on the nation and amplifying the restrictions, I was feeling an overwhelming sense of helplessness in my ability to support my new friends. Their desperation reverberated in their words as they expressed the belief that life under the military regime had lost value. My heart ached to offer them an escape, to secure jobs for them in the safety of the United Kingdom and whisk them away in my suitcase. However, the parameters that constrained me, both practical and emotional, limited my capacity to assist. The pandemic had cast its suffocating veil upon the world, making escape from the country an arduous task, even for British nationals.

Last night, when I eventually broached the subject of my potential departure, the conversation proved more complex than the act of leaving itself. Emotions flared within them, a tempest of anger and hatred mingling with their relief at the thought of me reaching safety. Yet, this relief was fleeting, giving way to rage again, their frustration saturating their emotions. The deteriorating state of their mental health manifested in cruel acts of fabrication, weaving tales of injury and the imminent danger they faced.

In our counselling session yesterday, we had the opportunity to open up and share our concerns. It was a group session with six participants, including Nigel, the Global Head of Risk Advisory at Special Contingency Risks. Although conducted online, there was a noticeable initial awkwardness as we adjusted to the virtual setting. Despite the initial discomfort, the session was validating and cathartic.

Nigel spoke softly. "It is okay to feel scared, angry, excited, or whatever in between. It is unsettling and scary."

As educators and mentors, our main responsibility is to support the children in our care and continue delivering lessons despite the disruptive noises and uncertainties. We'd had to learn to put our own concerns aside—to hide them. However, this session provided us with the space to express our own worries openly.

Nigel, an impartial figure, understood our desperate need for understanding. Throughout his long career, he had encountered similar situations. He acknowledged the potential volatility of the current circumstances, although they may have felt peaceful at the moment. It was agreed that a plan needed to be put in place urgently, including provisions for leaving the country if we felt unsafe. It was reassuring to know that we were being heard.

"What are you concerned about?" he asked, indicating that we should respond individually.

"My biggest concern is a financial one," Maeve began, her voice quivering with an unmistakable vulnerability. "The cost of arranging a relief flight and a separate flight back to London, along with two rounds of COVID-19 tests, will set me back massively. I have been saving for my teaching qualification, and having those funds ripped away from me due to circumstances beyond my control is devastating."

"I am worried about being unable to contact my family," Amie followed. "The thought of being cut off from them in such uncertain times is unsettling. I am also concerned about losing my job if I return home. I help fund my brother's education, adding another layer of worry and responsibility."

"I am just terrified," Ella confessed, her words barely audible. "I have never been in this situation. I don't even know what to think."

Moved by the honesty and vulnerability of the group, I expressed my fears. "I am worried about our mental health. After months of pandemic isolation and quarantine, and now not being able to leave our homes again, the effect it is having on us is scary. I am also terrified for my Burmese friends. I find myself torn, unable to advise against their protests, yet consumed by the constant worry for their safety."

I opened up about my feelings of guilt, which resonated with others in the group, and physical symptoms of muscle aches, headaches, and fatigue from the lack of sleep. As the session drew to a close, Nigel expressed his intention to provide further counselling sessions.

A mixture of emotions followed the session. On the one hand, I felt a sense of relief and release after expressing my thoughts. But on the other side, it had exacerbated my emotional state. Being an empath, I tended to absorb the emotions of others. As a result, the session had left me feeling emotionally exhausted, weary-eyed and drained of energy. But, despite the fatigue, I held onto a glimmer of hope. I hoped further counselling would be available, providing a safe space for us all. Three years of therapy had taught me the natural ebb and flow of emotions and the significance of having someone to confide in during this challenging period.

That day, I learnt that in Myanmar, if you wanted to drive evil from your home, you banged pots and pans. The nightly ritual made sense now.

Goodnight

Chapter 26. One Cockroach Too Many

Friday 12th February 2021

Dear Diary,

My emotions swing like a pendulum between fleeting moments of calm and intense waves of anger. Today, anger dominates. Hopes for additional counselling sessions have been dashed. This morning, we learned that we'd only receive a fifty per cent discount on the session fees, meaning they'd now be $250 an hour. That is a quarter of my monthly wage.

The protests against the coup are gaining momentum, with marginalised groups rallying to demand democracy and justice. The coup has been met with concern by wary ethnic armies in Myanmar, who have long been fighting for autonomy within the country.

In the years preceding the military coup, Myanmar made significant strides towards peace by establishing the National

Reconciliation and Peace Centre (NRPC) in 2016. Aung San Suu Kyi led the NRPC to facilitate peace talks between the National League for Democracy (NLD) and various armed ethnic groups. By involving representatives from different ethnic armed organisations in the government, the NRPC aimed to resolve long-standing conflicts and ensure inclusivity.

During this time, unilateral ceasefire agreements were signed, including a nationwide National Ceasefire agreement in 2015 endorsed by ten ethnic armies. However, challenges persisted, as evidenced by a 2018 UN report documenting widespread violations of the agreement by the Tatmadaw in three ethnic states.[3] This raised concerns about the military's commitment to peace efforts.

Following the NLD's victory in the November 2020 elections, there was hope for renewed dedication to the peace process. Of course, this all changed twelve days ago when the Tatmadaw dismantled the NRPC and replaced it with a team of their own to directly engage with armed groups. This abrupt move rendered previously established ceasefires ineffective, undermining any progress made. The Tatmadaw's actions faced strong opposition from many ethnic organisations, who demanded the release of arrested leaders and the restoration of democracy.

Prominent ethnic armed organisations in Myanmar, such as the Karen National Union, the United Wa State Army, and the Kachin Independence Army, pose a potential threat to military

---

[3] Human Rights Council (2018). *Report of the detailed findings of the Independent International Fact-Finding Mission on Myanmar.*

control. On 7th February, the Tatmadaw convinced the Mon Unity Party (MUP) to join their newly formed State Administration Council (SAC) to prevent collaboration among these groups. However, some representatives clarified that "no one accepts the military dictatorship." Instead, they are merely seeking a place at the 'political table.'

With one ethnic armed organisation on its side, the military aimed to strengthen its position and influence. Following intense conflict between the Arakan Army and the Tatmadaw, attention turned to the Arakanese people. On 2nd February, the military lifted internet restrictions in Rakhine, which had first been imposed back in June 2019 and released political prisoners from the Arakanese community ten days later. This led to the Arakan Army, too, joining the SAC.

Many ethnic armed organisations have expressed support for the protestors and condemned the military's actions in response to the coup. Yesterday, thousands of protestors took to traditional fishing boats on Inle Lake in Shan State, using the waterways as a platform to express their resistance. Simultaneously, thousands of ethnic Karen marked their National Day in Yangon, adding their voices to the ongoing protests.

The fight for democracy and peace in Myanmar is deeply intertwined with the struggles of ethnic minority groups. The ongoing protests, fuelled by voices from diverse backgrounds, have the potential to bring transformative change to the country's political landscape and the aspirations and rights of all individuals in Myanmar. It's fascinating to learn about.

***

Lately, I have found myself becoming unexpectedly emotional, with even the slightest trigger bringing me to tears. A fleeting memory, a stomachache, or a simple mistake when teaching—anything seems to unleash a torrent of emotions. The weight of my feelings is sometimes overwhelming, and this morning, the sight of a cockroach in my home had me in hysterics.

This wasn't the first time I'd encountered such unwelcome intruders in my apartment. Left empty for however long, various critters had made themselves at home, turning my first few weeks into a constant battle against them.

The incessant buzzing of mosquitoes accompanied me wherever I went, ants scurried around for crumbs, and then there were the formidable cockroaches, robust and most definitely unwelcome.

Today, seeing that cockroach scurrying across the floor triggered an avalanche of feelings. It wasn't merely the insect's presence but rather the culmination of all the frustrations, anxieties, and uncertainties that had been built up. Feeling irrationally helpless, I leapt onto my coffee table and screamed down the phone to my mother, begging for her help.

"I wish you were here," I cried desperately. "What do I do?"

"Don't be silly, Liddi." She chuckled. "You're a lot bigger than the cockroach. Remember Jakarta? We dealt with them just fine."

Still standing on the coffee table, I stared at the cockroach scurrying across the floor. This tiny, resilient and unyielding creature seemed to mock my feelings of helplessness. Summoning my courage, I found my dustpan and brush and swept it onto the balcony. My mother was right about Jakarta, and I thought back to our first encounter with pesky cockroaches.

"Oh, my goodness, did you see that cockroach run over the conveyor belt!" my mum had shrieked during our first supermarket trip. We were in Carrefour, stocking up for the new house. Expecting some semblance of familiarity from our experiences at Carrefours in France, we were taken aback by the blunt differences: chickens with purplish-yellow skins, strange smells permeating down every aisle, and unidentifiable vegetables. Yanti, who had come with us, nonchalantly flicked away the cockroach as if such encounters were part of her everyday routine.

"They are good ones," she'd said with a smile. I wondered what the "bad" ones were like, as these cockroaches were disgustingly giant, flopping about on their backs and causing a commotion throughout the supermarket.

In Jakarta, we learned to be meticulous about everything. Sterilising all food was a time-consuming process; the sink had to be filled with water and bleach, the vegetables immersed, and then a second soak in pure, clean water for half an hour was required to ensure there was no bleach residue. The vegetables always tasted slightly strange, with a lingering hint of disinfectant.

In addition to the cockroaches, our home had become a haven for various other creatures, including lizards and the occasional snake. The lizards were beautiful, their colourful scales catching the light, and we often spotted a massive monitor lizard in our garden. We got used to applying mosquito repellent every morning and watching our steps when outside, always on alert for potential dangers.

Snakes terrified me, especially after my brother's pet corn snake devoured my hamster. Adoel's antics of dangling baby snakes in front of me only worsened my fear. How could he be so sure that this seemingly harmless snake wouldn't slither into our room and unleash its venomous fangs upon us in the dead of night? It felt like a miracle that we never got bitten or contracted diseases like dengue or malaria.

Similar worries persisted in Yangon, such as the fear of drinking tap water and contracting water-borne illnesses. We had to be careful with ice cubes and avoid accidentally brushing our teeth with tap water. Of course, I still fell ill from a few slip-ups. Even the seemingly inviting swimming pool at Sanchaung was unsafe.

"Did you get rid of the cockroach, Liddi?" my mother asked, bringing me back to reality.

"Yes, it's gone," I sighed. "Sorry for overreacting."

"It's fine," she replied. "What are you going to do now? What are the other girls doing?"

"I don't know," I mused. "I just want to be alone, though."

Today had been quiet, and so had the chat. Everyone was in their own flats, and now that the school day was over, I was not sure what to do. Fridays were always quieter, with fewer lessons as we wound down for the weekend. I felt I should check on Amie. She had been far too quiet lately.

Chapter 27. Hiding in Plain Sight

Saturday 13th February 2021

I am seeing with anger, the rage threatening to shatter the thin grip I have on my self-control. It all began last night when Kyi confided that she had defied the imposed curfew, venturing out late despite the imminent danger of the military junta nearby. As the clock ticked closer to the forbidden hour of 9 p.m.—a time when echoes of warning shots and raids taint the air—my anxiety spiralled out of control. I desperately reached out to Meg, the head of the charity, only to learn that Kyi had lied to me. Meg explained that the girls often resorted to such manipulation as a coping mechanism, seeking emotional support.

Every day, loud and huge protests marched past my apartment. From my window, I witnessed scenes of arrests—sudden eruptions of noise, banging, and shouting, followed by a flurry of people running in a particular direction, indicating yet another one. It felt like an endless loop, a real-life rendition of the 1993

Groundhog Day. The film's premise of repeatedly reliving the same day mirrors the unnerving repetition I witness outside my window.

As the month unfolded, the military faced an overwhelming number of people mobilising to support those arrested. In many instances, they were forced to let the detainees go due to the sheer magnitude of the crowd. A painting of disgust and disappointment married the faces of the authorities, perhaps aware of the scrutiny of watchful eyes or devices capturing their actions. They wanted to appear innocent. The potential arrests almost always turned into releases, and the people who had rallied around those individuals erupted into cheers, celebrating the small victory. Yet sometimes, the military overpowered the people, and the detainment won.

There was one such arrest yesterday:

[Ivy] What is happening on the street next to ours? Everyone is going crazy and running down the road towards it.

[Ella]: They reckon someone is being arrested. They agree that if cops come to someone's house to arrest someone, everyone will go outside to try to stop it.

[Ivy]: Horrendous.

[Maeve]: In places, they've been blocking the roads so the police cars can't get out. It is confirmed. It's a doctor.

[Ella]: They are arresting firefighters. They aren't going to work because of CDM.

[Me]: I keep seeing loads of people running away from my window.

[Ivy]: The people chased the police, and they let him go!

[Maeve]: Yeah, the security guards are saying they aren't sure, but they all ran off in their uniforms. I told them Myanmar is very brave,

and they said, 'You too.'

Arrests were more common now that the Civil Disobedience Movement (CDM) was growing in strength. They were a regular occurrence. The country relied on essential professionals to keep the economy, healthcare, and military functioning. Everyone understood this fact. Tens of thousands of individuals from various fields joined the movement daily, including bankers, lawyers, teachers, engineers, doctors, and nurses. They demanded the return of the elected government. Only then would they return to work. The power of numbers was crucial in their efforts, and the people seemed unfazed by the military's threats.

Signal group chats, a secure private messaging app with end-to-end encryption, had been created to share lists of military-owned products, restaurants, and shops to boycott. Funds had also begun to be established to support those participating in the CDM, as the lack of benefits and furlough meant that protestors had no income to support their families or pay their rent. Considering that a quarter of the population lived below the poverty line, the bravery displayed by those on strike for their country was colossal. Businesses knew they would likely accumulate significant debts, and individuals who had worked hard to escape poverty understood that their progress might falter.

As the movement gained traction, the military was responding by making examples out of healthcare professionals, conducting these arrests in broad daylight, and subjecting them to torment in videos circulating on social media. Despite all this, the streets did not appear to be dangerous for those who "follow the rules." However, an underlying sense of unease and anxiety permeated. Ivy and Matt, recognising the growing tension, had rescheduled their flight from the end of February to the 18th.

Our everyday activities had transformed into vigilant observations from our respective windows. We eagerly shared updates in the group chat. It had become a race among us to be the first to report any significant developments. We watched intently, scanning the streets for any signs of movement or gatherings, ready to relay the information to the group.

[Ivy] There's a group of about twenty people. They are discussing something in the little square.

[Ivy] There's more joining. It looks like they are plotting!

[Maeve] I am watching the 'Vanishing at the Cecil Hotel' now, too, as if I need to be more triggered...

[Ivy] We saw one of our security guards legging it down the street earlier as well.

[Maeve] Yes, I was there! I was chatting with them, and three out of four pegged it. I was so confused. I was like, no worries, guys, trot on. I'll hold the fort.

Tomorrow, we have plans to visit our favourite Burmese restaurant, a farewell to Ivy and Matt. With our departure time set for four in the afternoon, we should have ample time to reach the restaurant, eat, and return before dusk settles upon the city. However, the mounting unrest and deteriorating situation has me feeling uncertain, torn between my desire for normalcy and the growing concerns about our safety. Is it wise to venture outside at all, curfew or not?

I miss wandering the streets of Sanchaung. There is still plenty to learn about my new home. Experience has taught me many lessons, such as how strict the Burmese are with money. Even a slight crease in a US dollar bill renders it useless, so I carefully keep my notes in an envelope instead of a purse.

Walking through the streets of Myanmar feels like traversing a bygone area, where pavements are scarce and produce, or meats are sold along the roadside while families display their laundry out front. The streets are lined with small food stalls, emitting enticing aromas that fill the air. My nostrils tingle at the unfamiliar scents as I catch whiffs of spices and herbs. The food looks delicious, and I would be tempted to try some if it weren't for the flies swarming around and on the food. The country has minimal food safety regulations on food storage or refrigeration.

Everything is different, from the sights and sounds to the customs and way of life. I like the hum of the air conditioning when I try to sleep. I appreciate the gentleness of the Burmese and the scorching heat. I enjoy dodging the traffic and laugh when Ella stares at me in shock as I fearlessly stick my hand out and dive into the stream of passing cars and motorbikes.

However, adapting to our new way of life wasn't always easy and in my initial weeks, I clung to my Britishness as a security blanket. My new neighbourhood's peculiar smells and humidity soon became intoxicating, and I began to feel trapped. I missed hopping on a bus and knowing exactly where I was heading. Cultural nuances frequently puzzled me, and I had to navigate the language barrier challenges. As I transitioned from a fully-fledged third-culture kid to an independent expat adult, the exhilaration mingled with moments of self-doubt. I could no longer hide behind moving overseas because of my dad's job. This time, I had chosen to come to Myanmar, fully aware that I would be an outsider, a foreigner. I found myself bowing my head as I walked, attempting to convince myself that no one was staring at me, though the weight of their gazes was palpable.

These feelings of homesickness and disorientation settled in, casting a shadow over my initial excitement. Everything felt like an uphill battle, and despite having a circle of expat friends, a lingering sense of loneliness remained.

Eventually, this feeling of unease gave way to acceptance. I reminded myself that this move was temporary, and I could choose to leave after a year or two. Living abroad is not like being on a never-ending holiday. No matter how much I tried to explain this to my friends back home, they seemed to misunderstand this concept. "You're in ASIA. That's so exciting. You can sunbathe and go to the beach every day," they would exclaim. Even if you move to a country or continent that may be seen as a holiday destination, you still must work, go food shopping, pay the bills and clean the toilet. You'll also probably be doing it in a completely different language and surrounded by those with a completely different cultural reference point.

Chapter 28. A City Under Siege

Sunday 14th February 2021

Dozens of neighbourhood watch groups have emerged across the country, formed to safeguard anti-coup activists from arrests by the security forces. Defying the overnight curfew, crowds are taking to the streets, emboldened by the knowledge that they are being protected and watched over. Yesterday marked the seventh consecutive day of magnificent rallies. The Association for Political Prisoners (APP) group has documented an alarming rise in arrests, with the number nearing four hundred. Despite the growing crackdown, the people of Burma are standing firm, declaring they are "not afraid."

In a blatant display of power, the military junta has suspended laws that previously restricted the security forces, now granting them sweeping authority to detain suspects and search private property without court approval. Additionally, three sections of the laws "protecting the privacy and security of the citizens" have also been temporarily suspended. The military seeks to identify and apprehend critical figures supporting the mass protests against the coup. The hunt for the sources of dissent has become its primary objective: to sever the roots of resistance.

Among the vibrant sea of protestors, Myanmar's youth stand at the forefront. Many of them speak of the dilemma faced by their parents, torn between their fears of speaking out and refusing to accept life under military rule. They carry the weight of their hopes and aspirations for a better future, demonstrating for themselves and their parents.

Living under military rule for the second weekend since its beginning, the days off have brought both exhaustion and introspection. The absence of teaching allows ample "thinking time," which I do not like.

This morning, Nilar and Kyi confirmed that the once-dismissed rumours circulated among Yangon's streets were horrifyingly true. More than 23,000 prisoners, ranging from petty criminals to hardened convicts, have been set free by the military, shattering any illusion of order. It's chillingly clear that this calculated manoeuvre serves a sinister purpose: to create space within the overcrowded prisons, enabling the military to incarcerate a growing number of defiant protesters.

Fear and uncertainty now envelop Yangon like a dark cloud, intensified by the military's alleged agenda and their reported encouragement of released prisoners to engage in destructive acts. Fires rage, and whispers of poisoned water bottles circulate, fuelling a volatile mix of desperation and lawlessness. The military aims to undermine the legitimacy of the protests and justify their violent crackdown, portraying the demonstrators as the ones who are being destructive.

The nightly internet blockages, enforced until later and later in the morning, allow the military to operate with impunity. Atrocities are committed under the cover of darkness, evading the scrutiny of the world. Yesterday witnessed a horrifying act of violence as soldiers mercilessly opened fire on protestors outside a power plant in Kachin, who were desperately trying to safeguard their lifeline to the outside world.

Today, alongside law suspensions, new laws are in place, requiring people to report overnight visitors to their homes. This scares me. Adding to the unease are reports of China's backing of the military junta, accompanied by the appearance of new soldiers in bluer uniforms, reminiscent of Chinese attire.

On February 2nd, the UN Security Council (UNSC) convened to propose a joint statement condemning the military's actions in Myanmar. However, the efforts were thwarted as China and Russia exercised their veto power to block the decision. Then, on the 10th, leaked photos and flight records emerged, revealing a Chinese plane landing in Myanmar allegedly transporting "Chinese technical personnel" to assist with the internet blackout. China claimed the flight was for delivering "seafood," a questionable explanation given the circumstances.

China has long been Myanmar's biggest ally, repeatedly defending the country from international criticism, particularly regarding the military's crackdown on the Rohingya. The historical ties between the countries are deep-rooted, encompassing cultural, economic, and political interactions. The extensive border they share and Myanmar's abundant natural resources, including oil, gas, minerals, and hydropower potential, make it of great interest to China. China's ambitious Belt and Road Initiative (BRI) further solidifies its role as a financial supporter of Myanmar, with secretive contracts for projects under the Economic Corridor holding strategic importance.

In the aftermath of the coup, China significantly escalated its support for Myanmar, taking advantage of the country's growing isolation. This move serves China's economic interests by enabling greater exploitation of Myanmar's resources. Additionally, China remains Myanmar's largest arms supplier, perpetuating this cycle of support.

Speculations and conjectures abound. One protester, Su San, a twenty-four-year-old medical student, captures the prevailing sentiment: "*The junta wouldn't have dared act without China's blessing. As long as Myanmar moved toward democracy, Beijing would try to forestall it.*"[4]

Amid the deepening crisis and rumours, foreign embassies, including those of the United States, Australia, and Cambodia, have taken action to ensure the safety of their citizens. They have advised them to take shelter and remain vigilant, with talks of evacuation flights.

The Philippine Embassy in Myanmar was among the first to express concern, urging all "Filipinos in the country to remain

---

[4] McLaughlin, T. (2021). *China Is the Myanmar Coup's 'Biggest Loser'*, [online] The Atlantic.

calm and to stay at home." However, the British Embassy has remained relatively silent, offering no concrete plans to assist their citizens. We have been left feeling vulnerable and anxious as we witness other embassies taking proactive measures. I don't like the contrast in responses. We feel like sitting ducks.

"It's outrageous," my mother lamented over the phone earlier. "Why aren't they doing anything to help you come back home? Haven't you heard anything else from the school?"

Taking a deep breath, I tried to steady my trembling voice. I was supposed to be wishing her a happy birthday. "It's… it's fine," I managed to utter, but while talking with her, I was also watching a video that India had sent. As its content sank in, I exclaimed, "Oh shit!"

"What. What happened?"

"A friend sent a video. She's experienced an arson attack."

My mother's voice grew more anxious. "Is it bad?"

"The video is loading."

India also shared the video in the charity group chat. She lived in Golden Valley, a luxurious condominium compound in Bahan township. This highly sought-after neighbourhood serves as a mini sanctuary for the affluent residents of Yangon, including many international schoolteachers and their students. It's very worrying that such violence has breached this seemingly secure haven.

The footage started with a shaky frame, capturing the dimly lit streets outside India's apartment. The usually serene atmosphere had been shattered, replaced by chaos and danger. Flames danced with ferocity, devouring the facade of a nearby building. Thick plumes of smoke filled the air, obscuring the surroundings in a menacing haze.

My heart sank as I watched the scene unfold. The intense orange glow of the fire illuminated the terrified faces of onlookers gathered nearby. Shouts and cries echoed through the night, mingling with the crackling of the blazes, and sirens wailed in the distance.

In the left-hand corner of the screen, armed soldiers moved with purpose. Their uniforms bore the unmistakable insignia of the military junta, leaving no doubts about the perpetrators behind the violent act. Their cold and indifferent demeanour sent shivers down my spine.

As the video continued, I saw brave individuals attempting to extinguish the flames with feeble hoses and buckets of water, their efforts futile against the raging inferno. Some wore masks to shield themselves from the acrid smoke, while others stood unprotected, facing the danger head-on.

As the video ended, I sat in stunned silence, tears streaming down my cheeks. My mother's voice snapped me back to reality. "Liddi," she said. "You need to come home."

I'm torn. This is possibly the most challenging decision I've ever had to make. It's only been fourteen days. Fourteen days is nothing in the grand scheme of things.

Chapter 29. The Great Traffic Jam Protest

Monday 15th February 2021

Dear Diary,

Today unfolded like a rollercoaster—a whirlwind of emotions, each twist and turn leaving my heart racing. The day started off fine. Ivy and Matt's rearranged flight—scheduled for the morning of February 18th—is just three days away. They have a lot to do in a short time. Their departure is not an ordinary journey; obstacles lurk around every corner.

Their first hurdle was finding an airline that offered relief flights to Kuala Lumpur. The options were limited, and the tickets can only be purchased in person. Adding to this challenge, payments for these special flights can only be made in cash, a daunting feat in a city grappling with a shortage of accessible funds due to the ongoing unrest.

The journey to the ticket office, usually a thirty-minute drive, turned into a nerve-wracking ordeal as protestors manned roadblocks, bringing traffic to a standstill. The demonstrators' ingenious tactics impressed and frustrated Ivy and Matt, who found themselves stuck in a taxi for nearly an hour, just a stone's throw from home.

[Ivy] Protestors and cars that have 'broken down' have blocked all Sanchaung roads around City Mart.

This latest form of peaceful protesting has captured attention. Cars have intentionally 'broken down' precisely at 11 a.m., causing a complete standstill in the city. This clever strategy effectively disrupts daily life and immobilises the city's movements.

[Ivy] I have no idea how we will reach the ticket office.

[Amie] Oh dear, I do not envy you in a hot and stuffy car. Did you manage to get cash?

[Ivy] Yes, Min from school lent us some of my wages. We will also close Matt's bank account so we will have that cash.

As Ivy shared updates with us, I decided I wanted to see the spectacle myself. Quickly changing into more appropriate attire—long, baggy trousers and a light pullover—I ventured out, securely locking my apartment door behind me. The building's balconies were filled with curious onlookers, and the air buzzed with animated conversations in Burmese as I made my way downstairs.

Passing by the cleaning ladies, who had momentarily paused their work, I exchanged greetings with them. "Mingalabar," I said softly. They cooed the same in return and laughed. Were they laughing at me? My energy was draining, and I found myself becoming more self-conscious, spiralling into a cycle of self-doubt and negativity.

Pushing aside those thoughts, I continued my journey,

opting for the stairs over the elevator. As I passed the condo shop with its half-empty shelves, a testament to the resident's efforts to stock up on essentials, I noticed all the benches near the entrance were occupied. The security guards remained vigilant, their watchful eyes scanning the surroundings. I waved at the regular guard on duty, and he smiled, offering words of caution, "Be careful, Miss."

Stepping outside, I surveyed the street, my gaze darting left and right. Life seemed relatively normal on the left side of the street, with small shops lining the passage, offering an array of knickknacks. Older men pushed carts heavily laden with delicious Burmese street food. On the jagged pavement, children and women savoured bowls of mohinga—noodles in a fish sauce—for a late breakfast. It was a peaceful scene.

To the right, a row of bubble tea shops and small supermarkets bustled with motion, leading towards the large City Mart supermarket and the cash exchange at the end. This side was louder and busier, filled with crowds of locals and foreigners alike, all chanting and chatting—perhaps trying to make sense of the situation.

I settled on turning right and made my way to the end of the road, where makeshift barricades had materialised. Constructed from sturdy wooden slats, plastic tarpaulins, bricks, and metal, they formed imposing barriers strategically designed to keep the police at bay while allowing passersby to squeeze through. As I edged through them, the noise grew louder, signalling the proximity of the protest.

As I approached, cars that had filled the adjacent highway had been transformed into impromptu platforms for protestors. They raised their voices in unison, shouting slogans and chanting while police attempted to restore order. Despite their efforts, the sheer number of protestors overwhelmed the authorities, and cheers erupted each time the police failed in their attempts to make an arrest.

Mesmerised by the spectacle yet feeling slightly out of place, I didn't linger long. Instead, I decided to pick up a watermelon from City Mart, now craving fresh fruit. Although the shelves were even more barren than usual, observing the generosity of others lifted my spirits. Food and water were being distributed to protestors free of charge. A well-organised system ensured that each protestor, even the children, received a T-shirt, meal, and water.

The entire experience was overwhelming. This was a situation I never anticipated witnessing, one that dismantled any preconceived notions and laid bare the fragility of life. The protestors—men, women, and children alike—have had their lives upended by uncertainty. Yet their unwavering resilience shines through. Instead of buying a watermelon, I bought some sweets instead. I handed them out to the young children beside their protesting parents, their innocent eyes reflecting the hope and determination surrounding them.

Remembering it was a weekday and mindful of my upcoming phonics lessons in just twenty minutes, I quickened my pace back home. The images of the protest lingered in my thoughts, making it challenging to concentrate during the class. I tried to engage my students in games and light-hearted discussions about the upcoming half-term holidays. Still, my mind kept wandering, especially when I noticed an email notification from the headteacher. The final five minutes of the class felt like an eternity. The children bombarded me with countless questions, each one adding to the weight of my own uncertainties.

"Miss," Mya piped up. "Why are people jumping on cars?"

"Well, Mya," I began, choosing my words carefully. "Have you heard of a protest before? Sometimes, when people feel strongly about something, they gather together to show their feelings in different ways."

Another student, Kyaw, raised his hand, his expression serious. "Miss Goldman, my daddy said everything is fine. Is it?"

His question caught me off guard. How do I respond in a way that's both honest and reassuring? My teaching handbook didn't address these kinds of questions. "Kyaw," I said gently, meeting his gaze. "Things are happening outside that are causing people to be worried. But please remember that your parents are working hard to keep you safe. And we're all here together, caring for each other."

The class fell silent momentarily until Win's voice cut through the quiet.

"Miss, it's so loud. I don't like it."

I wished I could offer her a comforting hug—I wanted to hug all of them. Instead, I said, "I understand, Win. It can feel overwhelming when there's a lot of noise around us. Remember, we're here for each other."

Though I couldn't fully address all their questions, I hoped my words had offered some reassurance. Waving goodbye to each student, I wished them a safe afternoon. Their innocent smiles provided a brief respite from the concerns weighing on my mind. As the last child exited the virtual classroom, I took a moment to collect myself before opening the email that awaited me, bracing for whatever information or instructions it contained.

> Dear teachers in Yangon,
> We have come to the decision that you may leave the country if you feel unsafe and continue to work from your home countries. This comes after the British Embassy has updated its guidance stating, "If you have concerns for your welfare, you should consider leaving."
> You must return to Myanmar once the school reopens, and it is safe to do so. As the situation is stable, with no violence, the costs for outbound, return flights, and quarantine will be at your own expense. The school will only pay if there is a threat to life and you have to be evacuated.

We discussed this on the chat, of course.

[Me] Well, that is the decision made for me. Do they really think we can afford to leave?

[Ella] What would it cost? What, two to three months' wages?

[Me] COVID-19 tests are two hundred pounds alone.

Yesterday, following the guidance of my parents, I forwarded concerning messages from the Hope Haven chat to the school's leadership team, "The military is trying to cause a divide. I have just been sent footage. Several civilians were killed in the night (yesterday), and women have been kidnapped. The Tatmadaw is using the blackout to kidnap young girls to give them to visiting parties (mainly Shan and Karen girls)." Perhaps this helped sway the school's decision. It will look poorly on them if they ignore the threats. And besides, people are being murdered; they just don't seem to believe it.

While I still grappled with the nuances of Meg's message, the words "killed" and "kidnapped" were as clear as day. We were all angry. While technically we could hold onto our jobs, the imposed conditions felt like a financial straitjacket. We had been coerced into agreeing to wait until there was a "threat to life" before we could leave. As a teaching assistant, the exorbitant cost of the three-flight journey home and mandatory COVID-19 tests in Myanmar and London seemed insurmountable. It was infuriating to be thrust into such an impossible predicament.

"It might be best if you come home, Liddi," my mother suggested persistently.

"I'll miss it here," I replied during our phone call. "Besides, it's too expensive."

"I can help you," she offered.

"It's okay," I smiled, already aware that my parents would support me if necessary. "There's no immediate threat to our lives, as the school claims."

"Hmm."

I rolled my eyes, "But if anything changes, I'll let you know. At least we have the internet during the day now. Small victories."

The news, at least, was a relief for Ivy. As soon as she read the message, fresh from her four-hour journey to the relief flight office, she declared her intention to reclaim her position. Ivy was an outstanding teaching assistant, and the leadership team must have appreciated the importance of maintaining consistency for the children—I hoped. She'd already informed her class about her departure, and I couldn't help but picture their joy when they saw

Ivy's familiar face on their next Zoom call. Unlike the younger children in my class, Ivy's eleven-year-olds were much more acutely aware of the situation. I hoped, for their sake, that she could keep her job.

Chapter 30. Voices of the Rohingya

Tuesday 16th February 2021

The coup has further exposed the deep-rooted inequalities and ethnic divisions within Myanmar, with the Rohingya people facing increasing hardship as time goes on. The pervasive militarisation in minority areas like Rakhine highlights ongoing tensions and the emergence of new ethnic armies.

In August 2018, a series of coordinated attacks by the Arakan Rohingya Salvation Army (ARSA) on security forces in Rakhine State prompted brutal retaliation from the Tatmadaw. This resulted in a large-scale campaign marked by indiscriminate killings, mass rape, torture, and deliberate destruction of Rohingya villages. While the Tatmadaw justified their actions as a response to ARSA's attacks, it was the Rohingya population that bore the brunt of the violence, actions that many have characterised as genocide. Although the Myanmar government initially denied these allegations, substantial evidence has since emerged corroborating accounts of widespread violence against the Rohingya.

The same generals responsible for the 2018 crackdown now hold positions of power in the country. Once again, the Rohingya are at risk, and the fate of the 600,000 Rohingya remaining in Myanmar hangs in the balance, subject to the whims of the military.

"The Rohingya had hope when the National League of Democracy first won in 2015," someone told me. "But Aung San Suu Kyi did little to stop the Tatmadaw and protect the Rohingya."

"She even won the Nobel Peace Prize," someone else added, "and defended the military against accusations of genocide in 2019 at the International Court of Justice."

During the coup, fear among ethnic minorities is particularly intense. The international community and the NLD's previous inaction in 2018 had raised concerns about their ability to address the ongoing challenges faced by these communities. With over one hundred and thirty-five tribes and ethnic groups, Myanmar is a melting pot of cultures and traditions. And it was not only the Rohingya that had been subjected to systematic and brutal violence by the Military.

Among these ethnic groups, the Kayan tribe, often referred to as the "long-neck tribe," stands out for their distinctive practice of adorning women with multiple brass coils around their necks. These coils, weighing up to twenty kilograms, gave the appearance of elongated necks. The origins of this tradition are shrouded in mystery, with various stories suggesting they descended from a man who fell in love with a female dragon or that they were formed by planting a banana tree in a gold mine. Another tale recounts a tribe leader breaking his daughter's neck to prevent a prophesied tiger attack.

Despite the discomfort, the tradition serves as protection against kidnapping, as the elongated necks make these women less appealing to potential captors. Girls as young as five begin wearing a few rings, gradually adding more as they grow older. However, the cost of these rings—sometimes as much as two hundred pounds each—poses a challenge for many families. Conflict in the 1990s forced Kayan tribe members to flee, leading some to mistakenly associate the long neck tradition with Thailand due to refugee camps along the Myanmar-Thailand border.

Now, the Kayan tribe's unique cultural practice has become a tourist attraction, drawing visitors eager to witness the "spectacular neck-ringed women." Fewer women within the tribe continue to wear the rings and those who do live in more isolated and remote communities. Modern development and gender discrimination within the tribe threaten their cultural heritage and limit their decision-making opportunities. They are often seen as objects of entertainment, existing to support and receive appreciation rather than being allowed to lead or express their opinions.

Similarly, the Chin tribe faces extinction due to the ban on their distinctive full-facial tattoos, known as *Apuyea*, which means "beautiful" in the Chin language. For many women, these tattoos symbolise beauty and cultural identity. However, as each generation passes, the artistry and knowledge of facial tattooing fades away.

Finally, the Moken people, living along Myanmar's southern coast and neighbouring countries like Thailand and Indonesia, lead a sea-roaming lifestyle reminiscent of sea nomads. Their children grow up surrounded by the ocean, honing remarkable underwater skills through activities like swimming, canoeing and free diving. Their unique lifestyle is anchored by their wooden boats, called 'kabangs,' which serve as both homes and transportation, connecting them intimately with the marine environment. The Moken's livelihood depends on the sea, making their way of life a true Moana experience.

However, the Moken have faced significant hardships. In the 1970s, the Tatmadaw fabricated a story of lost pearls as a pretext to enter Moken villages. This tragic plot allowed the military to carry out an "area clearing" operation, resulting in the murder of several villagers. In 1988, the military forcibly evicted the Moken people from multiple coastal areas, driven by economic development interests. During this period, the military even resorted to using pirates to murder Moken individuals, then justifying their aggression as a response to the pirates.

Despite these adversities, the Moken maintain their deep connection with the marine environment. However, their numbers have dwindled over the years, with the latest population census in Myanmar revealing only 1,727 individuals remaining.[5] Efforts have been made to raise awareness of the Moken people's struggles and protect their rights. NGOs and advocates have worked alongside the community to preserve their cultural heritage, safeguard their ancestral lands, and support their pursuit of a sustainable way of life.

On the ground, there is little to report today. I am counting down to the half-term holidays—not because I'm excited, but

---

[5] *The Coming Extinction: The Moken People of Burma's Mergui Archipelago A Research Report.* (2020).

because I dread them. I have three more days of teaching left. Hopefully, I will be able to get through the lessons for my class's sake.

Chapter 31. Don't Be Long

Wednesday 17th February 2021

Dear Diary,

Ivy and Matt's departure is imminent; they are leaving tomorrow. Tonight, I attended a small farewell gathering in their apartment. It was bittersweet; while I'm thrilled for Ivy, knowing how eager she's been to leave, it feels as if a part of us will be missing. We assembled on their eighth-floor balcony, glasses of wine in hand, soaking in the breathtaking hues of the sunset. Inside, the living room was chaotic—clothing, toiletries, and various bits and bobs scattered everywhere. Maeve, Ella, Amie, and I were privileged to select what we wanted. The coveted British toiletries were the initial point of contention, with Soltan sunscreen, hairspray, and Simple moisturiser emerging as the prized spoils. Ivy also gifted us some beautiful garments that couldn't find space in her suitcase and wouldn't suit the chilly English weather. The rest I took to donate to Hope Haven or the school administration.

"What's the temperature right now in England?" Amie asked,

Ivy chuckled, before saying, "Bloody cold, around ten degrees?"

"Twenty-five degrees colder. Good luck!"

"My dad has already bought me a hat and scarf," Ivy said with a laugh. "All I care about is trying the new Greggs vegan sausage roll."

The conversation seamlessly transitioned to our longing for British food. We felt a tinge of envy as Ivy tantalised us with vivid descriptions of the delicious treats and chocolates she couldn't wait to devour upon setting foot on English soil. As the sun dipped below the horizon, we gathered on the balcony one final time, capturing our laughter and bittersweet expressions in snapshots taken by Matt.

"I will miss you all so much," Ivy said with a smile. "But I won't miss being here. Come home soon, okay?"

That night, like countless nights before, I attempted to quell my restless mind through meditation. I had always been intrigued by crystals, spirits, and even witch doctors.

I first visited a witch doctor in 2015 when living in Jakarta. My body had been ravaged by relentless sickness, symptoms plaguing me for months with no relief in sight. Headaches, unexplained weight loss, and a bone-deep ache left doctors perplexed, unable to offer a definitive diagnosis within the confines of modern medicine.

Jasmine, the mother of an affluent friend, urged us to seek the aid of a renowned witch doctor in outer Jakarta. Despite my scepticism, the allure of a potential remedy drew me in. So, the following day, my mother travelled to the small village with Jasmine and the President's wife, Sweta, to view her 'treatment' and receive my diagnosis.

The Dukin, as he was known, commanded reverence among his villagers, and his reputation preceded him. The drive took three hours, and we set off early. We travelled through picturesque hamlets, where children played in the mud and women stooped by the riverside, laboriously washing clothes in water tainted by its own murkiness. Our friend told us incredible stories of the Dukin and his wonders.

"Sweta had seen countless doctors at the hospital," Jasmine proclaimed. "They told her that her cancer was incurable and were now in awe at the shrinking of her tumour."

Our arrival was met with a throng of eager hopefuls waiting for their chance to seek his healing touch. The mustard-coloured building where 'patients' were admitted welcomed us, offering respite from the scorching sun.

We sat in the tranquil confines of the building, feeling privileged to have been seen immediately because we had travelled with the President's wife. Conversations ebbed into hushed tones, heads bowed, and eyes averted.

Then, a figure emerged from the shadows, a small and fragile form enveloped in a flowing blue robe. His bare feet glided gracefully across the floor, belying the weight of his age. With short, white hair and a face etched with wrinkles, the Dukin's gaze held a captivating blend of intensity and kindness. Jasmine acted as our translator, relaying his words of reassurance. "Do not be afraid," she said. "He knows you are feeling scared."

Sweta was first, and we quickly followed her as she was led into the treatment room. She reclined on a taut rug and sipped from a seemingly ordinary glass of water. Almost immediately, her eyes grew heavy, and her body surrendered to the hard, earthy floor. The Dukin wasted no time, swiftly gathering a needle, scissors, and cotton wool. My heart raced with concern for the sterile conditions—or lack thereof—surrounding the impending procedure. Yet, a gentle smile from the Dukin seemed to assuage my fears as he embarked on what I would later come to understand as 'psychic surgery.' It was a surreal spectacle—a surgical incision performed without physical instruments. His fingers disappeared into the folds of Sweta's abdomen; her eyes closed in silent repose. The air was filled with the melodic hum of the Dukin, resonating with otherworldly power as he mimicked the motions of tumour removal, deftly stitching her up without leaving a trace. The healing process was quick, and Sweta was soon stretchered to the adjacent room for recovery.

Now, it was my turn to occupy the spot where Sweta had just lain. My muscles tensed, my eyes darting nervously toward my mother. The Dukin's penetrating gaze fell upon me as he examined my abdomen. His touch seemed to penetrate my flesh without causing any pain, though I could definitely feel his presence.

Jasmine translated his observations. "You have a lot of pain all over," she relayed. "You are tired a lot, and your kidneys hurt. You are so sad. Why are you so sad?"

But what he said next left me dumbfounded. "He says you have lupus, and your next blood test will show the anti-nuclear antibodies for this," Jasmine continued. With a deft motion, the

Dukin extracted a tiny droplet of blood from my ear, sharing the exact count my hospital blood test would reveal. "You don't need to go to the hospital," I was told. "Three operations here, and I will make you all better."

As I slowly rose to trembling feet, I joined Sweta in the adjoining room. Together, we sipped from the holy water blessed by the Dukin, feeling an unfamiliar sense of lightness wash over us.

In the days following the profound encounter, I delved deep into research on spiritual healing. The term 'fraud' repeatedly leapt out, painting these age-old traditions as nothing more than pseudoscientific deception. It was undeniable that some individuals exploited the vulnerable, resorting to deceptive tactics like fake blood and mystical illusions to prey on the desperate, often charging exorbitant fees for their services. Yet, the Dukin sought no monetary gain, offering his healing abilities freely and only accepting donations of food and water.

When I returned to Western medicine, subsequent tests conducted at a reputable hospital in Singapore confirmed the elevated levels of antibodies he had discerned.

When I first moved to Myanmar, I hoped to relive the healing experience. That dream remains elusive and my chance at finding a healer has dwindled. Still, Myanmar's medical system continues to captivate me. While traditional Western medicine remains scarce in rural regions, herbal remedies are an accessible and affordable alternative. Despite Western scepticism, these remedies carry cultural significance, with roots tracing back centuries. Alternative healing has even found its place within Myanmar's hospitals.

My personal experiences with Western medicine have left me disillusioned, with its reliance on symptom suppression and the prevalence of sometimes debilitating side effects. The medication prescribed for my chronic pain offered only fleeting relief, exacerbating my condition once discontinued. But I know the lack of stringent regulations and limited drug trials makes people apprehensive about being unwitting guinea pigs to more herbal and lesser-known approaches.

Three-quarters of Myanmar's population still turn to herbal treatments. Institutions like Mandalay's University of Traditional Medicine boasts extensive herbal gardens, nurturing ancient wisdom alongside modern knowledge. Among this, some practices appear nonsensical to me—like the Astrological or *Nekhatta* system, which claims to cure illness based on the patient's astrological chart and planetary positions, prescribing specific diets accordingly. Dubiousness aside, I remain receptive to any avenue that offers a glimmer of hope.

Following a severe bout of Typhoid in November, accompanied by numerous hospital stays, my pain has only intensified, both physically and mentally. Each passing day seems to add another layer of fog over my mind while my weary body bears the weight of an unforgiving agony.

Chronic pain has been an invisible foe, its grasp unyielding, sapping my strength and, sometimes, will to live. It's a burden that defies easy explanation. On days when I may appear relatively healthy, well-intended individuals often remark, "You seem better," or "You can't feel too unwell." Their words, though intended to comfort, highlight the isolation of enduring pain without a visible cause. I realise their lack of understanding isn't malicious; they simply can't grasp the complexities of an unseen torment.

Chapter 32. Electric Days, Sleepless Nights

Thursday 18th February 2021

Sleep was elusive yet again. Ivy's departure that day was sad and strange, keeping me awake through the night. Also knowing that we had eight long days ahead, devoid of our usual work routine to keep us occupied, only added to my racing thoughts. That day's email from the school informed us that an additional day might be tagged onto the end of the half-term holidays for "wellbeing." The last thing we wanted was an extra day of solitude. This holiday didn't quite feel like a respite, and I anticipated most of our time would be spent indoors, playing *The Sims* or attempting to stay active on the gym's treadmill. Any instances of violence had remained relatively contained, and perhaps my anxiety had gotten the better of me, causing me to label myself as irrational.

The shops were closing earlier and earlier—between four and five in the afternoon—and I found myself going shopping every day; a daily ritual disguised as a front to witness the protests up-close. During the daytime, supermarket workers continued their acts of kindness, distributing hot noodles and water to the protesters. First aiders stood ready to respond to any inadvertent trampling or violence that might arise.

The energy in the air was always electric, and I had to remind myself not to linger too long. Entrenched by the sights and sounds, I enjoyed searching for new protest signs—that day, my favourite was one that read, 'It's too BAD!! Even introverts are here!' I yearned to be a part of it all, to protest alongside Nilar and Kyi. However, as a foreigner, engaging in protests was strictly prohibited by law, with severe repercussions.

The law banned foreigners from even expressing political views. The military had banned several friends from social media for expressing their views and had visited the homes of those who had commented or "raised fear" around the ongoing issues, both foreigners and natives. Nonetheless, I was clinging to the hope of finding another way to contribute. I needed to do something. And when Meg announced the food donation event for Hope Haven on the 20th of February, I instantly knew that would be the way I could help.

During my visit to the supermarket earlier, I saw an elderly man along the way, begging a shopkeeper in a 7/11 for a bottle of whiskey. He was already drunk, his body swaying softly as his eyes pleaded for more alcohol.

People were on high alert, unsure of who was good or bad in the situation at the time. Undercover military personnel could have been present, watching our every move.

Chapter 33. Blood-Stained Pavements

Friday 19th February 2021

Dear Diary,

Mya Thwe Thwe Khaing died today. Her death came ten days after a brutal round of live ammunition had been fired on the ninth day of the coup. Mya was only nineteen years old when she was brutally shot—murdered. She was more than just a name among the sea of protestors; she was a daughter, a sister, and a valiant warrior standing up against the dark forces of oppression. She was full of dreams for the future, all mercilessly shattered by the piercing bullet that tore through her tender flesh.

Days before her twentieth birthday, a phone call between Mya and her brother resonated with an air of apprehension. Growing increasingly anxious as he tried to find a stable enough internet connection to hear his sister's voice clearly, he pleaded with her to stay away from the frontlines. The police were not to be trusted. Their last conversation ended with Mya insisting that the police would not shoot anyone. The police would never resort to violence against their own people.

At 1:30 in the afternoon, Mya stood among a row of protesters, their voices rising synchronously, echoing through the streets of Yangon. Chanting slogans of defiance, "Let's together oppose the dictator who kills the people," the rhythm of the cacophony of voices pulsed through the veins of those around her. Mya stood tall, adorned in bright red, her eyes filled with determination and hope as she gazed upon the crowd.

The atmosphere crackled with anticipation. The crowd was flourishing, and banners and placards bearing bold slogans were held high.

Suddenly, chaos erupted as water cannons were fired through the crowd. Mya, undeterred, tried to get up. A woman beside her gripped her hand, yet the brunt force of the water cannon kept her down. Panic gripped the crowd, and losing control, the military fired.

Mya celebrated her twentieth birthday, unconscious and on life support. The vibrant spirit that once filled her eyes now lay dormant. After ten days of life support, Mya succumbed to her injuries. Thousands of mourners gathered for her funeral. Vigils are being held in her honour all over the country. Protestors describe her as a "martyr," holding aloft photos of Mya following the war crime.

At age twenty, I was in my second year of university. My worries would have been trivial: the grade of a module paper, deciding whether to work a six—or ten-hour shift. I had my whole life ahead of me, and the thought of being caught in a round of ammunition never crossed my mind.

Tomorrow is the food donation day, and I am nervous. It feels like ages since I last saw my fellow volunteers. It has also been a considerable amount of time since I stepped outside the boundaries of Sanchaung Street. Weighing up the circumstances and deeming it 'safe enough,' I have decided to join the group and keep my intentions hidden from my mother, who has explicitly instructed me to remain within the confines of my apartment. I know it's a risk, but I also know that by the time she sips her first cup of morning tea, the day of volunteering will already be a thing of the past. I will be back home, nestled safely, far removed from harm's reach. I can't just sit here and do nothing.

I messaged Meg earlier.

[Me] Do you think it's safe?

[Meg] Yes, don't worry. We are only going to safe areas. Stay with the native volunteers, and you'll be fine.

Kyi has told me that our meeting point will be at Manny's house. Manny is the kind-hearted owner and driver of the bus responsible for ferrying volunteers and donations, with a wonderful wife and two lovely children who occasionally join us on donations. Earlier, I quickly visited the supermarket, carefully selecting fresh fruit, vegetables, sweets for the children, and sanitary towels. Due to our restricted access to cash, my purchase was limited, but I made sure to buy whatever I could manage.

The United States government is organising the departure of non-emergency American government employees and their families due to the heightened risk of violence, communication restrictions, and limited flight options. The government is arranging these flights at their cost, not financially burdening those stuck in

Myanmar.

Japan has also taken decisive action, arranging the first flight to evacuate Japanese nationals from Yangon today.

Chapter 34. A Risky Mission

Saturday 20th February 2021

The day of volunteering has drained me completely. I'm utterly exhausted and feeling constantly on edge. The journey home felt like an eternity, with passionate protestors again flooding the city. Army tanks lined the streets, blocking our way and allowing only a trickle of cars to pass at a time. The ever-increasing presence of the massive, armoured vehicles sends a clear message, and my heart leaps every time I see one.

This morning, I had to rely on Kyi to communicate with the taxi driver waiting outside my complex. I had no clue where we were headed, utterly oblivious as to whether I was being taken to the correct location or falling into the clutches of potential abductors. In hindsight, I was stupid to have even left my apartment in the first place. However, trying to summon the mantra of 'trust the process,' as my younger brother often advises, I finally eased myself into the back seat after a lengthy exchange between Kyi and the driver.

I was instantly relieved when I noticed a small child, presumably the taxi driver's son, in the front passenger seat. The boy looked exhausted, his restless legs betraying the weariness that gripped him. Catching a glimpse of the driver through the rear-view mirror, I saw the heaviness in his eyes, reflecting the immense burden that he, like countless other mothers and fathers across the nation, is carrying on his shoulders. For many, the coup has meant an abrupt loss of livelihood, whether due to participating in the civil disobedience movement or staying home to care for their children who can no longer attend school. Worries about limited access to essential resources like food, water, and medical supplies weigh heavily. The taxi driver smiled at his son, muttering something in Burmese before our journey began. They were good people.

Sitting in quiet contemplation, my eyes fixated on the window, and I watched the ceaseless stream of protestors passing by. A young woman caught my eye, and I blushed, smiling as I turned away.

After what felt like an eternity of manoeuvring through congested street traffic, I finally arrived at Manny's house. Kyi greeted me with open arms, signalling the taxi to a halt. We embraced, happy to see each other again,

"Yay, you made it!" she exclaimed.

"I was so nervous," I admitted. "Thanks for helping me. Where's Nilar?"

"I don't know. She is not talking to me."

Nilar's temperament is always tricky to predict. Today, her anger burned with an intensity that spoke volumes about the collective trauma experienced by the volunteers. Beneath her fury lay a deep well of grief, frustration, and a desperate hope for an eventual change.

When I approached her, her tension was immediate, and her body language seemed resistant.

"Hi, Nilar," I said tentatively.

Her response was sharp, cutting. "I don't want to talk to you!"

The rejection stung. Was it because of my potential departure? My inability to truly understand their struggle? I felt not only hurt but also embarrassed; I spoke little Burmese and Nilar and Kyi were supposed to be my friends.

"Fine," I whispered, my voice barely audible.

I turned away and greeted Lenny, who had just arrived, and diverted my attention to helping load the van.

Once the van was loaded, we all piled in, ready for our volunteering expedition. I hoped my presence, as a white foreigner, wouldn't feel intrusive or overwhelming. I wanted to be a comforting presence and provide much-needed food and water.

These thoughts weren't new. They'd flitted through my mind during our first volunteering trip to an orphanage on Yangon's outskirts, back when I was still learning to navigate the intricate landscape of this unfamiliar country. The approach to the orphanage had been marked by a worn-out sign, its letters faded and illegible. From the outside, it seemed quiet, but before long, a sudden burst of energy had erupted from within.

Children of all ages and sizes had burst through tall brown doors. Boys surged forward with unbridled excitement, while others hung back, curiosity wrestling with reservation. Many appeared be in their late teens, a stark contrast to the baby-focused donations we would collect. My heart sank at the potential disappointment.

Yet, despite their circumstances, the children appeared genuinely happy and full of hope.

Before moving to Myanmar, I was naive to the negative impact of orphanage tourism. It was understandable why some tourists would want to visit one of the many orphanages in the country, believing they could bring joy and attention to vulnerable children. But many left without fully considering the long-term consequences of these children's true needs.

Data on unregistered private orphanages in Myanmar was scarce. Shockingly, many children who lived in these establishments were not even orphans; as few as a quarter genuinely had no family. Fortunately, the three I have visited thus far seemed to emanate love and warmth, and I hope what I saw wasn't a facade.

Even so, I had fallen in love on my first visit to one of the orphanages. The caretakers welcomed us warmly, guiding us through corridors alive with children's laughter. We distributed toys, books and sweets, bridging the language gap with smiles and gestures.

After some time, I quietly slipped outside. I walked across the open courtyard to a smaller building nestled in the corner. The building housed a playroom for the younger children. As I entered, a kaleidoscope of colours greeted me, emanating from the plethora of toys, books and art supplies scattered across tables and shelves. Amidst this riot of hues, my gaze was drawn to a corner where a young boy lay on the floor, his delicate features bathed in the soft glow of sunlight streaming through a nearby window.

Approaching cautiously, I noticed the attentive eye of a staff member nearby. Sensing my interest, she shared a glimpse into the boy's life. "He has a rare chromosomal disorder," she revealed softly. "He is four years old."

My heart swelled with empathy as I crouched beside him, careful not to disturb his peaceful pose. His small hand clutched a toy car, his imagination weaving intricate tales as he navigated imaginary roads in his mind.

"He likes to be tickled," she told me. "You can tickle him."

With my fingers trembling, I extended my hand, tracing delicate movements along his sides. This elicited a giggle that seemed to dance like music in the air. His laughter, pure and unrestrained, echoed through the playroom.

"He's gorgeous," Maya whispered, her voice soft with emotion as she appeared beside me, drawn in by the boy's infectious laughter.

I nodded in silent agreement, unable to tear my gaze from the boy, his face aglow with genuine delight. "He's so sweet. They seem to take such good care of him."

"I spoke to the staff earlier," Maya said. "His parents abandoned him."

The weight of those words settled. In this landscape of persistent hardship, I found myself wrestling with the unimaginable—the profound desperation that could drive parents to such a heart-wrenching decision. Poverty isn't just a statistic here; it's a relentless force that pushed countless families to the razor's edge of survival, compelling them to make choices that would shatter most hearts.

I tried to imagine the depth of their pain, the impossible calculus of survival that might lead parents to believe an orphanage would provide a better life than they could.

Today, the young boy's laughter still echoes in my memory. He was just one of the many children I've met this year, and last, each with their own story of survival.

***

This evening, I lay in my bed, gazing at the ceiling above as I struggled to put words to paper. It wasn't too long ago that our day of volunteering ended. Manny dropped me home—as near as he could before the minibus had reached its limits. Disembarking a few blocks away from my apartment building, I wove through the chanting crowd, marvelling at the ever-improving intricate structures that had sprung up like an agility course. Finally, reaching home, I kicked off my shoes. I drank the last of my large twenty-litre water bottle and slipped into bed, depleted. I need to remember to buy some more water tomorrow. If there is any to buy. It is warm; however, I am too tired to move and turn the air conditioning on.

I watch the dancing patterns on the white ceiling—the fairies dancing in the shadows formed by the half-drawn curtains. My thoughts inevitably return to the families we had encountered earlier today. Some children played with blissful ignorance while I endured their curious gazes, tiny faces filled with awe and hesitant waves revealing their fascination with a foreigner.

One housing complex in particular has stuck in my mind. When our bus pulled up, families retreated into their apartments, doors slamming shut in our faces. The other volunteers and I looked around in worry. Were we in danger? Was there a lurking presence of police or military? Confusion swirled as we surveyed our seemingly empty surroundings.

Determined to fulfil our mission, I grabbed food boxes and followed Kyi up the narrow staircase leading to individual apartments. The air was thick and suffocating, the humidity clinging to our skin as we struggled for breath. Step by step, we ascended to the highest floor, where Kyi approached Apartment 52. With trepidation, she knocked gently on the door. An elderly woman, weariness evident in her dark-circled eyes, cracked it open slightly before quickly slamming it shut upon seeing unfamiliar faces. Kyi pleaded with her in Burmese, urging her to let us help and provide them with food boxes, but her pleas fell on deaf ears. Then, a young man, likely her son or grandson, cautiously opened the door and uttered words in Burmese, later translated to English as: "Leave. Everyone is scared. You have to leave."

Back in the safety of my bed, as fatigue overcomes me and my eyelids grow heavy, I allow my mind to wander to what a typical Saturday night in London would look like. I conjure the vision of a fire crackling in the fireplace, drinking hot chocolate with marshmallows, and snuggling underneath a thick, soft blanket while arguing about which movie to watch with Zach—safety and comfort found in the predictable routine of home.

However, my reverie is fleeting, shattered by a deafening bang that dissolves my marshmallow-soft dream clouds. Panic seizes me as I hear terrified screams outside. I rush to the balcony, eyes scanning the darkness for signs of danger.

To my relief and confusion, I see only the familiar sight of people huddled behind the safety line, shouting and banging pots in protest. Perhaps the sound was of a car backfiring or a drunken brawl.

I glance at my watch: it's half past nine in the evening. I experienced my usual angst and awe at those who were brave or stupid enough to cross the safety line after curfew. Then, sighing heavily, I turned away from the balcony and securely locked the door behind me. Another restless night awaited, filled with fitful sleep and uneasy dreams.

Chapter 35. Murder in the Night

Sunday 21st February 2021

This morning brought the grim realisation that the loud bang and piercing screams I heard last night were not mere disturbances but the sounds of another murder, this time alarmingly close to home. The violence was not a random act, but a deliberate assault orchestrated by unseen hands. The military, with their heinous tactics, had struck again. The streets of Sanchaung were stained with blood.

When the internet connection flickered back to life, group chats overflowed with messages, each one recounting the horrifying crime. I learned that a man on night watch had been ruthlessly shot and killed by a sniper—a man who had taken it upon himself to protect this community, Sanchaung. He likely left behind loved ones who depended on him. Perhaps he had a wife waiting at home, children who would never see their father again, or an elderly mother whose trembling hands would now fend for themselves. His selfless heroism had cost him everything.

The news had spread like wildfire. Neighbours whispered in hushed tones, their anger simmering beneath the surface. Democracy, already battered and bruised, had been violated once more. Rights trampled; voices silenced.

"Tomorrow is the revolution day," Nilar's voice crackled through a voice note.

When I called her for more details, she emphasised the significance of the upcoming protests. "It will be big," she asserted, citing the increasing number of casualties in Mandalay as another driving force for the growing anger.

"More deaths?" I asked, my voice trembling.

"Dozens injured and a few killed," she replied, her voice filled with deep-seated anger. I learned that a violent crackdown occurred in the Maha Aung Myay Township, where protesters and innocent people guarding a shipyard had been subjected to rounds of live ammunition, water cannons, and horrific beatings. Even nurses and doctors who had rushed to help the injured were targeted and shot.

"If they want to play dirty," Nilar declared, her voice seething with anger. "Then they will get dirty."

Nilar warned me that small and large shops would remain closed, and if all went according to plan, the "revolution" would extend beyond a single day. She advised me to stock up on necessities. Knowing I couldn't directly participate in the protests, she suggested I buy snacks and drinks to distribute to the demonstrators tomorrow. I was desperate to help however I could, so I was grateful for the suggestion.

The military has made explicit threats of violence against the protestors. Friends whispered comparisons to the past—the fateful year of 1988. The "888 Uprising," etched in blood and memory.

Back then, Myanmar seethed with anger. General Ne Win's coup in 1962 had birthed rapid economic growth. However, this progress was marred by inefficiencies and mismanagement. Corruption seeped through the cracks, and the currency reissuance in 1985 left people's savings worthless—a cruel twist of fate.

So, students, monks, everyday people flooded the streets. Their grievances, like stones in a slingshot, propelled the movement. Hope surged, crashing against the walls of oppression. But mid-September brought tragedy—three thousand lives lost; dreams shattered.

Nilar's voice cut through. "The revolution will be known as the five-twos revolution," she declared. "To mark the date 22nd February 2021 (22.02.2021)."

The Sanchaung girls have dismissed my fears, not wanting to propagate the anxiety themselves. Their perspective holds some truth—the circumstances were distinct from those in 1988, and we now have open borders and advanced technologies. Undoubtedly, the world will be watching.

[Maeve] Not like 88 at all; the contexts aren't comparable, and we're not looking at the slaughter of hundreds of people. There's no reason to be scared just yet, my love...

[Ella] Jax's parents lived through the bloodshed. There are open borders and technologies. They can't get away with it now. The whole country and foreigners can share what's happening here in Myanmar.

[Me] I didn't mean it like that—sorry. Just in the way they are

protesting tomorrow.

Ella's new boyfriend, Jax, a popular Burmese TikTok star, has quickly become a close friend to all of us. He will know what is happening. But the nightly internet shutdowns serve a purpose beyond giving us a temporary respite from social media. The deliberate disruption has a deeper reason, which extends far beyond our immediate understanding.

The news of the death in the street over from ours has also not sparked any change in opinion from the school's leadership team. Their silence speaks louder than any protest.

"It's revolution day tomorrow!" I exclaimed to my mother during our daily call.

"What does that mean?"

"I am not actually sure," I faltered. "Somebody was killed last night. Everybody is angry, and tomorrow is the day that the Burmese take back control…I guess."

"Do not step foot outside of your apartment tomorrow," my mother warned. "Promise me, Liddi."

"I promise," I sighed. I'd finally caved and told her about my day of volunteering. I couldn't keep anything from her, secrets spilling from my lips the moment I promised myself to keep them.

"I know I went out yesterday," I said. "But I promise I won't tomorrow."

Taiwan has evacuated its citizens today. We have yet to hear anything from the British embassy and I don't suppose that will change anytime soon.

Chapter 36. The Revolution Has Begun

Monday 22nd February 2021

Good morning,

That day was as monumental as anticipated. The city, awakening early and defying the imposed curfew, pulsed with an undeniable energy. Dragging myself out of bed, I was drawn to my familiar perch by the window in my spare room. I sat there, a silent observer of the unfolding drama on the streets below.

Before me lay a tableau of change. Generation Z—fearless, unyielding—led the charge. College students and children, their faces etched with determination, stood shoulder to shoulder. Proudly, they brandished signs and wore whimsical T-shirts adorned with the symbols of the Milk Tea Alliance.

The Milk Tea Alliance—a digital phoenix from clashes between Chinese nationalists and democracy advocates in Thailand and Hong Kong. A potent emblem of unity. Across social media, users embraced milk tea as a metaphor for diverse cultures and political ideologies.

Yet, beneath the veneer of rebellion, I detected an undercurrent of desperation in their eyes. It was a desperation born of years of oppression and injustice, a collective yearning for a better tomorrow.

As I tore my gaze away, a pang of hunger hit me. I needed to find some food. Cupboards bare, I had ventured to the shopkeepers the day before. "New stock?" I asked. Their answer: a shrug, an "I don't know." I would try again that day.

And so, I filmed. Documenting the pulse of rebellion, the heartbeat of defiance. Though I might soon find myself forced to leave this place behind, I would carry the stories with me, sharing them with the world as a reminder of the realities faced by those caught in the throes of unrest.

***

16:00

Hours have passed, and having missed my morning coffee, I am hungrier than usual. My head is pounding. Earlier, I feebly attempted to find sustenance. My water tank was empty, and my cupboards held only meagre supplies. With little hope of finding provisions, I knew I still had to force myself into making the two-minute journey downstairs to the small shop. It should have been an effortless task, yet the mere thought of it made me queasy. The preceding days have drained me both physically and mentally. My hair unkempt, I hastily threw on a jumper to conceal my bare arms and midriff. I double-locked my front door as I left my apartment.

The corridor outside was loud, and the small outside viewing gaps between apartments were again lined with watchers. I shielded my eyes behind sunglasses in an attempt to become invisible. My pace quickened as I walked along to the lift, with the two-hundred-metre distance feeling more difficult than it should have. I wanted to complete the task as quickly as possible so I could return to the safety of my flat.

My lack of choice to restrict food is what scares me most when I see the bare shelves of the downstairs shop. My earlier inquiry about new deliveries had been answered; the absence of restocked goods a haunting confirmation. Empty cardboard boxes and discarded packaging littered the floor. The aisles that once held rows of canned goods, cereals, and rice were now barren, with only a handful of stray items scattered here and there. Fortunately, I managed to secure the last tank of water, which would last me at least a week.

Every few hours, I descended the four flights of stairs in a futile quest for hope, only to be met with the same desolate scene. The streets outside remained barricaded, barring the passage of both delivery trucks and people. No Grab or Food Panda deliveries were possible. In my kitchen, the lone tin of baked beans in sugary sauce remained from my welcome pack in August as a testament to my declining options.

Our daily gatherings in Sanchaung had evolved into a food-swap huddle.

"Does anybody have any tuna?" asked Maeve when we last regrouped.

"Does anybody have any baked beans?" Ella asked.

"I am saving the tuna, and you can have my baked beans," I told Ella.

Some days, I succumb to eating raw oats out of a bowl. Though a scant amount of milk remains, I hoard it jealously, reserving it for the small comforts of tea and coffee.

In the past, restricting my intake would have been a source of perverse satisfaction, a means of exerting control in a world gone awry. But now, as hunger gnaws relentlessly at my insides, I find myself longing for sustenance. I am hungry—ravenous even.

With each passing day, as my hunger grows more insistent, so too does the relentless assault on my body image. I'm spiralling—spiralling back to some of the darkest days of my life. Five years ago, I found myself ensnared in the merciless grip of anxiety and depression, my struggles manifesting in a harrowing battle against my eating disorder. The mirror became a twisted reflection of my inner torment, distorting my perception until I saw myself as a monstrous creature despite the evident sharpness of my protruding collarbones and ribcage. Though logic attempted to offer reassurance, the demons of self-doubt and loathing waged their own vicious campaign, their barbed words shredding the fabric of my fragile confidence.

My battle with eating only intensified, reaching a crescendo one Christmas when my family and I returned to the UK from Indonesia to visit my dying nana. My faltering attempt to confront the disorder was met with a crushing blow as my mother's accusatory voice echoed through the bathroom door, "I know what you're doing in there."

"I'm just brushing my teeth," I croaked, flushing down my dinner and splashing my face with water. Another meal flushed away in a desperate bid to reclaim control. This time, it was Christmas dinner. The meagre portion of a single roast potato, carrots and turkey had been too much for me. It had to go.

Dignity became a distant memory as my disorder morphed into a twisted coping mechanism, a way to navigate the overwhelming challenges life had hurled my way. Though I had hoped to leave behind my struggles when I began university, the relentless foe refused to be vanquished. A huge decline in my mental health marked the bleak conclusion of my first year at university in Bristol, as did my dwindling weight.

Seeking help, I found myself met with the reality that my BMI was not yet low enough to warrant immediate referral for treatment, despite losing twenty kilograms. The message I internalised was that I was not "sick enough" and didn't deserve the help I desperately needed.

Finally, after a referral, I was admitted to the day patient service at the Maudsley Eating Disorder unit. My twenty-first birthday party, days before my admission, consisted of me explaining why I wouldn't be returning to university for the next term.

Days at the unit blurred into a monotonous routine of structured meals and therapeutic sessions designed to equip us for "normal" life beyond the unit's walls. Anorexia had taken over my life, stripping away not only my friendships but also my ability to function as a normal human being—so much so that I had to be monitored for half an hour after meals, with no bathroom breaks. Weigh-in Mondays became a dreaded ordeal. Gaining weight would inevitably lead to a meltdown, while losing weight increased the risk of being expelled from the unit. It was a lose-lose situation.

On my first day, a whirlwind of health checks awaited me in the nurse's room—weight, blood pressure, heart rate, breathing and blood tests. Without pause, I was whisked into the kitchen for snack time. I was met with the anxious faces of fellow patients pouring their milk and painstakingly selecting their biscuits in silence. "How did I end up here?"

The therapist at the dining table attempted to coax small talk from our muted group, urging us to finish our snack within the allotted time. Lunchtime brought a trolley laden with the week's menu choice; my first meal was an oversized portion of the infamous rice 'salad,' a running joke among patients. My stomach, accustomed to meagre portions, protested in agony by the end of the meal. There was still a pudding of two yoghurts and granola to be consumed, and the thirty-minute eating period was almost up. Finishing even a minute too late meant being sent home. It seemed harsh, but the strategy worked. The embarrassment and guilt of being sent home motivated us to finish our meals. Most patients had to put their studies or work on hold, so wasting the opportunity to recover was not an option, however painful.

While in the unit, I encountered eight new faces—eight individuals who left an indelible mark. Olivia joined us in my second week, and Grace followed in the third. Together, we navigated the labyrinth of crumbling cornflake cake and the solemnity of psychotherapy sessions where silence reigned until someone dared to break it—a silence that could stretch on for forty minutes. Community group sessions were another peculiar experience, resembling an episode of Jeremy Kyle, with patients storming out and doors slamming shut.

My time in treatment was a mosaic of contrasting memories—moments of camaraderie juxtaposed with the harsh realities of battling an eating disorder within a strained NHS. The nurses, burdened by administrative demands and dwindling resources, struggled to provide the level of support we desperately needed, their efforts often overshadowed by the weight of bureaucracy. The decline in the quality of NHS food mirrored my own internal struggle; the irony of being encouraged to enjoy food again while being fed unpalatable meals was not lost on us.

Treatment felt like a return to the regimented confines of school, where our table manners were scrutinised and packed lunches inspected. Moments of rebellion brought a fleeting sense of liberation—whether sneaking Weight Watchers bread or conspiring with friends about cafeteria choices. As treatment progressed, I learned that my habits of speed walking around the field during lunchtime, slipping biscuit crumbs into my pockets, or loading up on water on weigh-days only affected me and my recovery. However, it still makes me smile when I recall how the girls and I were reprimanded for learning TikTok dances or being too energetic.

Therapy itself was a challenging process.

"It's a grieving process," my therapist would say. "You are losing a part of yourself and are having to build yourself back up again."

Recovery was far from a linear path. Each step forward brought me closer to healing, yet recovery remained a winding road fraught with setbacks and tears. The day of my discharge was marked by hugs and laughter, a joyous celebration of progress made, and challenges overcome. As kind words of encouragement filled the room, I struggled to accept the praise, my mind still wrestling with years of self-doubt and insecurity.

Now, back in my apartment in Yangon, I cling to the memories of my time at the Maudsley, determined to stay on course and resist the pull of my disordered past.

***

22:00

It's dark now, and the evening has descended upon us. My day has been a grim cycle of watching the protests outside my window to distract myself from hunger.

At several points throughout the day, screams punctuated the air, each one a shard of fear, followed by hurried footsteps racing into the distance. News filters through—a relentless tide of arrests, an act to dispel further protests.

The military responded violently, unleashing live ammunition, rubber bullets, and tear gas upon the courageous protesters. I strain to gauge the proximity of gunfire—is it just beyond my window or miles away? I haven't been able to tear my eyes away. I don't want to watch, but I feel like I must.

The Hope Haven group chat, which had remained relatively subdued over the past few days, now buzzes with activity. A stream of messages flood in, sharing vital advice on how to protect oneself in the face of potential attacks:

[Meg]

1. If attackers have sticks and bats, keep your distance. Use personal protection items to strike back in vulnerable spots.

2. If you are being detained, do not fight the police. Shout out your name and try to make sure someone sees your face. Help will come.

3. If they have rocks, they are dangerous but hard to aim with. Keep moving and try to cover your head. Stay low and zigzag.

4. Try to get children out of the danger zone. Run and try to hide them.

5. If they have a slingshot, stay low to the ground and keep moving.

6. Gas—Tear gas. Avoid contact with the cloud of tear gas as much as possible. Close your mouth and (if possible) your eyes while seeking high ground away from the chemical powder. Tear gas will settle to the ground, so moving uphill and picking small children up helps. Wash your eyes out with water, wash your clothes, and remove traces of the gas.

I find it devastating that Meg had to write that message.

As I delve deeper into the sea of videos capturing the unfolding protests, an overwhelming surge of footage inundates my screen. I am endlessly scrolling, fixated on the array of perspectives. Many of the videos and images still show protestors carrying pictures of Mya Khaing, the 19-year-old who had tragically been shot in the head on the 9th of February. Today, thousands of people march the streets of Mandalay, Naypyidaw, Chin State, and other cities and towns across the country. In a show of heightened security, embassies in Yangon have taken precautionary measures by fortifying their premises with barbed wire, recognising that they've become focal points and potential targets of government backlash.

But one video seized my undivided attention. It depicted what seemed to be a peaceful march, with teachers and students standing united in their call for change. Suddenly, the tranquillity shattered as a swarm of police and military forces descended upon the scene.

Chaos erupted instantly. Panic rippled through the crowd as protestors scrambled for safety, ducking into nearby buildings. The air transformed into a toxic cloud of tear gas, its acrid fumes stinging their eyes and searing lungs. The sound of brutal beatings reverberated through the tumultuous scene.

The forces surrounding the protestors showed no mercy. They ruthlessly apprehended and detained anyone within their grasp, indiscriminately targeting individuals who, moments before, had been peacefully expressing their desire for change. This was not an isolated incident—the videos I received rapidly transformed scenes of peaceful protests to landscapes of violence and terror.

Kyi informed me about a chilling military announcement broadcast on state television the previous evening:

"It is found that the protesters have raised their incitement towards riot and anarchy mobs on 22 February. Protesters are now inciting the people, especially emotional teenagers and youths, to a confrontation path where they will suffer the loss of life," the Tatmadaw declared.

The stakes had been raised, and the warning of more loss of life was scary. The entire country seemed to be engulfed in flames of dissent.

Maeve, who had eagerly awaited her half-term trip to Mandalay, shared that she would cancel her plans. Given the escalating situation in Myanmar, this was a wise choice—one I deeply appreciated. Whispers were circulating about arrests targeting those attempting to travel within the country, accompanied by stricter security measures and mandatory COVID-19 testing.

A Western teacher from another school tested positive for the virus before a trip to Bago. Swiftly, the authorities had descended upon the teacher's apartment after being alerted by the testing centre, whisking him away to a government healthcare facility, leaving him with nothing but the clothes on his back. The grim reality of potential confinement in such a facility loomed heavily, overshadowed any boredom from the lack of travel during the holiday.

Meanwhile Ivy, now recovered from her jet lag, had been tantalising us with photos of Robinson's squash and delicious food we all missed.

[Ivy] I saw on Facebook that many restaurants are opening up. Is it not dangerous?

[Maeve] Despite all the tests, COVID doesn't exist in Myanmar now. haven't you heard? It is ridiculous; I am so glad I spent all those months inside.

[Me] That's what my dad thought when he saw the protests. COVID?

[Maeve] I know, haha, and they are not reporting any new cases because the test centres are closed.

Chapter 37. His Sealed Fate

Tuesday 23rd February 2021

Dear Diary,

I re-watched an Anne Frank documentary today—don't ask me why. Our surname, Goldman, is a telltale sign of our Jewish identity. Thoughts of Anne Frank's hidden annexe in Amsterdam have consumed my mind. I've visited her home twice, once as a ten-year-old on a school trip from The Hague and more recently during a holiday with friends. Over the years, I've observed a subtle change in the atmosphere of the house—less personal, more commercialised.

As I write this, a familiar question resurfaces. Nearly everyone knows the story of the Frank family and the brave friends who aided in concealing their refuge. Those who sheltered Jews risked severe punishment if caught. Yet, Miep Gies and other helpers did not hesitate to protect their friends, offering not only lodging and sustenance but also risking their lives for even the most minor acts of assistance—whether transportation or trading in

Jewish possessions.

I've playfully asked friends if they would have hidden me in the 1940s. Without hesitation, they replied with a resounding yes. But now, faced with the reality unfolding around me, would I say yes now if someone banged on my apartment door in Sanchaung during a raid? I say this after a scene from yesterday.

I ventured down to the shop in our building, hoping to find any remaining supplies. However, as I navigated the dimly lit corridors, food scarcity mattered little compared to the startling eruption of gunshots that shattered the air. The sharp cracks echoed like thunderclaps, reverberating through concrete walls.

Chaos descended instantly. There was panic, followed by people running and screaming. Desperate for safety, I pressed myself against a cold, stone pillar, my breaths shallow and rapid. My eyes locked onto the complex gates where a surge of protestors was flooding in like a breaking dam.

Inside the building, everything fell silent. The guards stationed at the entrance stood paralysed, horror etched on their pale faces. They exchanged futile glances; fully aware they held the power to grant entry to the terrified demonstrators or condemn them to the brutality waiting outside.

Some protestors had already managed to enter, taking shelter in the shop, which dimmed its lights as people ducked behind counters. Others dashed for the stairwells, their footsteps a fanatic staccato against the polished floors.

I stood rooted to the spot; every muscle tensed until, unable to bear witness any longer, I turned and raced to my apartment. Once inside, I locked the door behind me. I moved cautiously toward the window, careful to stay hidden behind the curtain's edge. From my position, I could see the entrance to our building clearly.

I knew all too well that the armed military forces would be conducting spot searches, barging into flats in search of protestors, reminiscent of the dark days of the 1940s. A lone protester, a youngish-looking man, remained nearby while I saw others in shops across the roads and beneath cars. I dreaded that if I could see them, the Tatmadaw could also. As the man banged on the gate, begging to be let in, the guard shook his head, aware of the approaching military. Though I couldn't discern the guard's facial details from my distance, I imagined a torrent of worry, fear, and guilt washing over him—particularly guilt. I envisioned a trickle of sweat dripping down his forehead, mirroring the adrenaline surging through his veins. Perhaps they both had loved ones waiting at home, desperate for their return. But fate was sealed, beyond the guard's control. The military descended upon the trembling individual, restraining him while a gun was held to his head. One soldier delivered punches to the man's abdomen; his lips contorted in a burst of chilling laughter—a sound filled with pure malevolence that echoed through the now silent street. I turned away, unable to look any longer. Gunshots followed, and his lifeless body lay motionless on the cold, unforgiving pavement.

Today, a haunting stillness envelops everything around me. It feels like a heavy weight has settled over the city, dampening even the slightest sounds. Perhaps yesterday's events have left people too afraid to raise their voices and too cautious to draw attention to themselves. The echoes of those gunshots continue to reverberate within me. Now, this is war.

I find myself torn between conflicting desires. Part of me yearns to be at home, but another part of me resists, compelled to stay and offer whatever help I can, even if I am unsure of what form that assistance should or could take. My being elsewhere could serve a greater purpose: using my voice to raise awareness.

As night has fallen, large spotlight beams pierce the darkness, illuminating our building with an intensity that sends shivers down my spine. The darkness, once a friend, now holds a threatening aura, concealing the sinister acts of murder and abduction that happen under its cloak the moment one steps outside a mere minute past curfew. The sanctuary of the night has been stolen away.

Chapter 38. Terror at Twilight

Wednesday 24th February 2021

Last night, as the sun bled crimson across the horizon, chaos erupted outside. The air crackled with tension, and I found myself drawn to the balcony again. I didn't dare step outside; instead, I parted the curtains just enough to peer into the night.

The other apartments, once warm with life, plunged into darkness. Their residents were hidden, but I could almost hear the collective hold of breath.

Then, the night shattered. The distant echo of gunfire tore through the silence, interspersed with desperate screams. Each shot a jolt of terror slicing the air. And then, like a malevolent dance, flashes of light illuminated the streets below in a hellish strobe. Each illumination revealed a snapshot of terror: a figure darting for cover, a shattered window, and buildings scarred. The city, once familiar, had transformed into a battleground.

But it was the sound of a grenade being thrown that stole

the breath from my lungs. Its metallic thud reverberated through the concrete. Then came a voice—a command—sharp and unyielding, shouting something incomprehensible yet unmistakably threatening.

I pressed my forehead against the cold glass, torn between fear and curiosity. What was happening out there? The night seemed endless. I could hear the faint rustling of my neighbours, whispers barely audible through the walls. Suddenly, another loud crash echoed from the street below, followed by a series of rapid footsteps. A group of figures moved swiftly through the shadows. They were not just random looters or frightened civilians; they had a mission.

As the first light of dawn began to creep through the curtains, I breathed a sigh of relief. But it was fleeting. The sounds of conflict had not ceased; if anything, they had intensified.

Lydia

Chapter 39. The Shadows of Paranoia

Thursday 25th February 2021

I am slowly coming to terms with the need to prioritise my mental health, and that realisation is gut-wrenching. Living in the epicentre of the military coup, a constant state of panic has taken root within me, intensified by the now constant sound of gunshots and the harsh thuds of tear gas canisters hitting the pavement.

Just hours ago, a phone call from my mother shattered the fragile composure I had barely managed to hold onto. Tears streamed down my face uncontrollably for the fourth consecutive night. Fear is a reigning emotion: fear for the safety of my Burmese friends, the children I teach, and the precarious state of democracy in Myanmar. But today, the tears stemmed from a profound inner conflict, a battle between the instinct to stay and the acknowledgement that leaving is essential for my wellbeing.

I'm acutely aware of my privilege—the privilege to be able to leave when so many can't. This privilege is a sobering reminder of the disparities that exist. I know that my departure will disappoint Nilar and Kyi. "Everyone can return to their home countries and leave us alone," they would message. If only I could bring them with me, tucked safely in my suitcase.

My depression grows stronger as I grapple with the undeniable truth of the world's inherent unfairness. The pervasive belief that no goodness is left in the world burdens me. How can senseless acts of violence go unpunished? How can those in my home country turn a blind eye to the suffering of others? I find myself questioning everything I thought I knew.

The world's unfairness is not new, so I'm not sure why I'm surprised. Even during an unrelenting pandemic, a time of upheaval and trauma, racism managed to rear its ugly head in a shocking act of murder. The news of George Floyd's death in May 2020—the image of a white policeman in Minneapolis kneeling on his neck for eight long minutes as Floyd struggled for breath until his last, harrowing gasp, served as a reminder of the injustices that still plague us. I was overwhelmed with shame as I turned on the news later that day and witnessed the heart-wrenching scene of his family, including his young daughter, unable to find words as tears streamed down their faces.

In today's world, it's astonishing that someone can face violence simply because of the colour of their skin.

In the Euro 2020 final, Italy emerged victorious over England. Their win was well-deserved, with a possession rate of sixty-one per cent to England's thirty-nine per cent. While the defeat was painful, a prevailing sentiment of pride should have emerged. After a challenging year, England's performance offered a much-needed sense of hope. However, keyboard warriors unleashed racist slurs without any consideration for the consequences. Online racism is often followed by statements from government bodies, public figures, and officials. It dies down, and anger subsides until the next wave of racism hits, often even stronger than before. It begs the question: Have we not learned from the lessons of incidents like George Floyd's? Why must anything good in our country be transformed into something purely negative and avertable?

After England's loss, a video depicting hostile English fans resorting to violence emerged. The scenes showed attacks on Italians, innocent children, and anyone with differing views. Shockingly, a man intervening to protect a teenage Italian faced police trouble, not the aggressor.

Today, I saw a similar video. However, the angry English football fans were interchanged by the Myanmar military, and the victims being beaten were medics in Yangon, who were desperately trying to provide life-saving treatment to those wounded by the military's gunfire.

Racism extends beyond explicit actions or words; it lurks in subtle biases, whispered remarks, and unconscious attitudes ingrained in society. Is racism only "true" if overtly expressed? Or does it encompass all forms of discrimination, even the hidden and insidious ones?

Watching a play titled *Seven Methods of Killing Kylie Jenner* shed light on the exploitation of Black culture by white women, prompting reflections on privilege and identity. It's worth a watch. Experiencing life as part of an ethnic minority in Indonesia and Myanmar and being unable to voice opinions or participate in protests has offered a tiny insight into the discomfort and anger that can arise from the lingering stares, the curious glances, and the names sometimes directed towards outsiders. We all need to take responsibility for tackling racism. It starts with introspection.

***

Today, sounds of gunfire have again been constant. The street opposite ours is always filled with smoke now. The same pattern persists: gunfire, smoke billowing, frantic footsteps, screams, and then, an eerie silence.

I think of the children in my class hearing and witnessing the same things. Their eyes wide, their small hands trembling. How do we protect them from this reality? They're only four and five years old, for goodness' sake.

Outside, the number of protestors attempting to break into our condo is also increasing. I always make sure I double-lock my door and bolt the security gate outside of it. Every time I hear the bang of a gunshot, my body freezes up. Sometimes, the sounds are far away, and sometimes they are nearby. I can't believe how much has changed over the past few days.

Within a week, my mind has oscillated endlessly between the desire to book a flight back home and inner anger directed at myself for even contemplating it. How can I even consider leaving when others are fighting for their lives?

Chapter 40. A Decision Made

Friday 26th February 2021

Yesterday, on the third day after the 'revolution day,' I made the decision to leave. The British Embassy still hasn't announced any evacuation plans, and neither has the school. Isolation within my apartment has resurrected my eating disorder, undoing the progress I fought so hard for, and self-destructive thoughts have taken over, clouding my judgment.

As the coup rages on, time feels like it's slowing down to a painful crawl. It's been twenty-six days since its onset, and each day feels longer than the last, distorting my sense of time.

"Book the flight, Liddi," my mother urged. "I'll make your bed up all nicely. It's cold here, so you can have a double duvet."

I tried to joke, my tears held back by sheer will. "Oh, so I'm allowed to live at home then?"

"Book the flight now while I am on the phone with you," she insisted. "I need to make sure you actually do it."

I placed my phone on the floor, opened my laptop, and returned to the Qatar Airways website—a tab that had remained open for the past week. The cheapest flight available was for the fourth of March, giving me six more days to organise my life before departure. The to-do list is long, with priority actions of sorting my belongings, closing my bank account, and navigating the increasingly challenging process of obtaining a COVID-19 test. Logically, it makes sense. Emotionally, the journey ahead looms like a storm cloud.

With the Qatar Airways flight departing from Kuala Lumpur, I must first secure an emergency flight out of Yangon Airport. Memories of Matt and Ivy's hurdles in reaching the flight office worry me. I know that I'll have to manoeuvre through protesters in a taxi and traverse through a city gripped by protests, all while silently praying that the military will remain at bay. And now, there's violence to worry about, too. Plus, my cash reserve is running low. But that's a problem for tomorrow.

I was about to tell the Sanchaung girls about my decision this morning, but before I could, I received an urgent message from Nilar and Kyi. Without hesitation, I shared it with the girls.

[Me] Hello, the school has confirmed this, so it is not random news. I have spoken with the school; it will be very dangerous downtown this weekend as the military has announced they will make a stop to the Civil Disobedience Movement and have been ordered to shoot and scare everyone. The internet will likely be down for 24 hours tomorrow or Saturday. I wanted to warn you, as it is confirmed news.

[Maeve] Confirmed by the school. What do you mean?

[Me] That the news is valid. They have confirmed the

information.

[Maeve] Bloody hell, where's the info from?

[Me] I found out from the charity, and then I told Sophie. She said to inform the Senior Leadership Team, who confirmed it. Basically, don't go out this weekend and prepare for an internet shutdown.

[Maeve] Haha, same old then, bloody hell.

[Me] There's shootings going on right now *sad face*. We'll be fine; I'm just worried about everyone protesting.

[Maeve] Saffie has gone to ask the bloody owner of the shisha shop what he knows.

I briefly stepped away from my phone, but Kyi pulled me back with a video showing a shooting near her house. My heart raced as I watched the horrifying footage captured through the lens of her bedroom window. Military forces fired indiscriminately into the air while people scattered in a frenzied panic, their screams deafening. Though the details were blurred, the message was crystal clear.

The video left me unsettled, so I did not share it with the group but mentioned that I received it. Still, Ella asked for the video privately. I hesitated, mindful of its impact on her fragile emotional state.

Maeve's response, tinged with passive aggressiveness, did not go unnoticed.

[Maeve] Thanks for letting us know about the internet. The chaos we will deal with when it happens. No point bringing the anxiety forward x.

Her dismissive words, marked by the appended 'x,' hurt. Nonetheless, I replied, clarifying that I only meant to inform everyone in case they planned to venture out that weekend. I also suggested downloading the official International SOS (ISOS) app, which has provided us with continuous, updated information concerning the escalating violence.

Tonight, the alert level on the ISOS app has been updated to the highest level. I am exhausted and struggling to sleep, and gunshots and bomb-like sounds are keeping me awake.

I rang Daniel earlier. It has been a while since we have spoken. It is not that it is intentional; the time difference and volatile internet make it difficult to connect. We should make more of an effort, though.

"I'm so happy you're coming home soon," he said.

I paused for a moment. "I know; I'm not sure how I feel about it," I replied, a mixture of excitement and uncertainty lingering in my voice. "I'm very excited to be seeing you, of course."

Daniel's expression shifted slightly, sensing my hesitance. "I'll need to quarantine for a bit, though," I continued.

"I guess. Are you going to get the vaccine?"

The first COVID-19 vaccine in the UK was approved for use on December 2nd 2020, and the rollout began shortly after. I shifted my body as I lay on the hard tiled floor, with sounds of unrest in the background.

"Of course I am." I took a deep breath, fully aware of his apprehension towards the vaccine, and the virus in general.

"Look, Lydia, I know you're worried about the virus, but I've been doing my own research, and I'm not convinced," he sighed, frustrated. "Besides, the vaccine was developed too quickly for my liking. I don't think you should have it."

My heart sank, my eyes pleading for understanding. "I

respect your opinion, but people are suffering, and lives are being lost."

"Young people are fine," he said, his exasperation seeping through from my phone. "I think there are other ways to stay safe. You may not be able to have kids if you have the vaccine. I don't want you to be a guinea pig for something I'm not convinced about."

"It's my body," I retorted. "I don't want to talk about this anymore. There are other things on my mind."

The fundamental differences in our approach to the virus have planted seeds of doubt in my mind. We have agreed not to discuss the virus anymore, as every conversation recently has reverted to it.

Yesterday, supporters of the Tatmadaw launched violent attacks on those peacefully protesting. Disturbing photos and videos show pro-military individuals using slingshots, rocks, and even knives to target innocent civilians. The police have remained relatively passive, failing to intervene. Concerns mount as Aung San Suu Kyi, absent since 1st February, remains missing, prompting worried citizens to gather for prayers outside her residence in Yangon.

Also yesterday, Facebook announced that it would ban all accounts associated with the military, including advertisements linked to Tatmadaw-owned companies. Meanwhile, during this morning's UN General Assembly briefing on Myanmar, the UK strongly condemned the military coup. They demanded the release of arbitrarily detained individuals and assurances of their wellbeing. The UK also urged the military to stop using live ammunition against unarmed protesters. Of course, that won't happen.

Chapter 41. In the Eye of the Storm

Saturday 27th February 2021

Yesterday, our fears turned to reality. Against all warnings and pleas for caution, Maeve ventured out to the supermarket in the afternoon. Echoing my earlier concerns, Ella urgently reminded everyone to stay indoors as reports flooded in about police deploying tear gas in other townships and making arrests. We anxiously awaited Maeve's return, hoping she would heed Ella's words if not mine.

The group chat, usually filled with conversation, fell eerily silent throughout the day. Poor internet connectivity contributed to the silence, which also reflected our dwindling hope and despair. The usual snippets of banter were replaced by a sombre atmosphere, with everyone grappling with their emotions.

In the morning, desperate to find solace or distraction, I scoured my surroundings for any form of escape. My books have been exhausted, and streaming services have been rendered useless.

I was worried and angry and couldn't hide it, however much

I tried.

[Ella] Has anyone seen Maeve?

[Me] Is she by the pool?

[Ella] No, she went shopping an hour or so ago. She said she would text me when she was back.

[Me] Are you serious?

[Ella] Maeve is back. Please stay inside today or move only when it's safe.

The news of Maeve's whereabouts sent a ripple of concern through the group. Maeve sent a voice note to the WhatsApp chat explaining what had happened. She had visited the supermarket down the road with Saffie, supposedly to exchange currency. The supermarket had two entrances and exits; one could be accessed via the backroads, and one was the main road, where protests were commonly held. Maeve and Saffie had entered through the back entrance, completed their shopping, and then decided to catch a glimpse of the ongoing protests from the front.

She told us that the crowd at the protest was larger and more spirited than usual, filled with passionate individuals determined to make their voices heard. Maeve and Saffie lingered briefly, observing the energy and fervour. Then, they began their journey home, weaving through streams of people shouting slogans and waving signs. But in an instant, screams pierced through the air, disrupting the chants. People scattered in panic, clutching their loved ones and running in all directions.

Maeve's voice trembled in the recording as she described their frantic retreat. They hurried back into the supermarket, which was the safest option, with multiple doors and security guards. The street outside was swarmed with the military, their presence accompanied by deafening police sirens and an unsettling tension.

As the girls reached the top level of the supermarket, they cowered behind a cashier's desk, hearts pounding with fear. They noticed hundreds of protesters desperately trying to gain entry and find cover. The sound of gunshots flew through the air. In broken English, they were informed that the military was chasing an ambulance that had attempted to rescue injured protestors.

The security guards swiftly closed the shutters and turned off the lights, plunging the supermarket into darkness. The only sound was the military and police shouting. Imagining the scene, I thought of the unbearable tension that must have gripped the space. Mothers clinging tightly to their children, silently praying that the fortified doors would hold firm as the police banged and tried to force their way in.

After what would have felt like an eternity, the military presence gradually diminished, offering a small window of opportunity for Maeve and Saffie to escape. They had been trapped in the supermarket for over an hour. With trembling steps, they decided to make their way down the backstreets, silently running all the way home.

The ordeal had left us all shaken. It was eye-opening, and I have struggled to contain my anger, realising that my petty remarks and frustrations will only add to the heightened tension. I need to remember to stay calm.

Today, Myanmar's military rulers made a brazen move. They announced the dismissal of Myanmar's UN ambassador, a courageous individual who had dared to urge the international community to take decisive action.⁶

Meanwhile, the situation on the ground continues to deteriorate rapidly. This morning, authorities arrested over 470 individuals who had protested nearby. I've seen more disturbing footage, this time of medical personnel fleeing as the police officers launch stun grenades near a medical school.

As the crackdown intensifies, we increasingly rely on VPNs to access vital communication channels. Without them, WhatsApp has become inaccessible, making it even more challenging to stay connected with loved ones and gather news about ongoing events. The sounds of pots and pans being banged continue. What once was a nightly ritual at 8 p.m. has now escalated to occur sporadically throughout the day, each instance signalling another arrest or the advancement of troops.

Our lives during the half-term holidays have fallen into a disorienting routine. We stay up until one in the morning, taking advantage of the internet when it is still accessible. Then, we try to sleep, only to wake at nine, anxiously check messages, and scour the news for any developments that have transpired overnight. It has become a cycle of restless sleep and constant vigilance as we have to stay on full alert.

Knowing I am leaving soon has immersed me in a whirlwind of hectic preparations. These preparations are distracting, and that is what I need. My room is filled with items I need to sell, from paintings and art supplies to clothes and shoes. I have many clothes—too many. I have contacted HR to ask if they can collect

---

⁶ Myanmar coup: UN ambassador fired after anti-army speech. *EBC News*. [Online] 27 Feb.

the bags I've filled with clothes once it is safe to do so and donate them to charity or the school cleaners. I managed to sell my nearly new oven a few weeks ago in anticipation of the challenges of traversing our now infamous road. It was a stroke of luck, and I can use the money toward my relief flight.

This morning, a lady purchased my beautifully crafted fusion covers from the beloved Hla Day shop. She had to travel a long journey on foot to reach me. Touched by her effort, I insisted on giving them to her as a gift, refusing any payment. She initially protested but eventually accepted my offer. Another lady from America, who had only been in the country for a month, also received some of my items for free.

Meanwhile, in the UK, the most vulnerable individuals have received their first doses via the newly established COVID-19 vaccination programme. My parents, concerned for their safety, have told me that they will not hug me upon my arrival and have insisted I quarantine for two weeks in my bedroom. Exhausted and overwhelmed, I reacted irrationally, lashing out at their logic.

"Me flying home is safer than going to the supermarket," I pleaded, longing for a hug from my mother. "I will have had a COVID-19 test and quarantined before flying, as well as being on a flight with passengers who also will have been tested. It is the safest way to travel."

The media has instilled fear surrounding air travel, tarnishing its reputation. However, accounts from numerous doctors indicate that flying is safer than being in an office, classroom, or other modes of transport. Researchers from Harvard have even published a paper explaining that the highly efficient air filters, and consistent compliance with mask rules make air travel an unlikely source of infection.[7]

I am not looking forward to the flight myself. Memories of our outbound flight, sweaty and exhausted from wearing visors and masks for seventeen hours, haunt me.

***

This afternoon, I had a surprise visitor. Despite the risks, Nilar was determined to bid me farewell before I leave.

Her message came in a terse whisper. "I'm outside."

I rushed to the window, my pulse racing. The street below was a chaotic tableau, and I was momentarily angry at her for coming to visit me.

"Coming," I replied. "Is it crazy out there?"

Her response was swift and resolute: "It's fine. Come quick."

Without hesitation, I bounded down the stairs, two at a time. I brushed past the curious onlookers, their eyes wide with fear or curiosity—I couldn't tell which. The condo's shop shutter was half-closed, a silent witness to the turmoil outside.

And there she was—at the front gate—Nilar, her eyes alight with determination. "I can't believe you're here, Nilar," I whispered, my voice catching.

She laughed a musical sound that defied the chaos. "I walked one hour to get here. Buses weren't moving because of the protests. Your street is so busy."

A smile tugged at the corners of my lips. "Tell me about it."

---

[7] Marcus, L, J., (2020) Assessment of Risks of SARS-CoV-2 Transmission During Air Travel and Non-Pharmaceutical Interventions to Reduce Risk. Aviation Public Health Initiative. *Harvard T.H. Chan School of Public Health*

"Well, there were so many people—"

"Sorry, it's an English expression," I interrupted, laughing, and pulling her into a hug. But I'm very glad you made it."

The first foreigner that we know of was detained yesterday. A Japanese freelance journalist, Yuki Kitazumi, found himself at the heart of a flash protest in Yangon. Plainclothes police descended upon the rally, seizing him. Witnesses spoke of fists raining down on Kitazumi's head—a desperate attempt to silence the truth he sought to report on. Fortunately, he was wearing a helmet that absorbed the worst of the blows.

Chapter 42. The Deadliest Day

Sunday 28th February 2021

Today has etched itself as a haunting milestone in the ongoing coup, earning the grim title of the "deadliest day" since its onset. This morning, the Sanchaung group chat was noisy.

[Maeve] Is everyone okay?

[Amie] Honestly, no. How are you?

[Maeve] No, not at all. But it's okay. We're safe here.

[Maeve] What's everyone thinking?

A sudden noise broke the flow of discussion.

[Maeve] Saffie just called to say (as I freaked) and said she looked, and the noise was smoke bombs, and it didn't look as scary as it sounds, and the people aren't hurt, and the military hasn't advanced yet.

[Ivy] I hope everyone is okay. Have you all got supplies to keep you entertained indoors? Are there any updates from the school?

[Me] We just got an email.

The email stated:

Dear All,

After receiving two video clips showing events outside Sanchaung and Gems today, I contacted ISOS for the latest advice. Please stand fast until further notice. Do not leave your apartment or house for any reason.

Various reports are circulating on Facebook and Signal indicating that live rounds are being used. ISOS has not yet confirmed whether these rounds are being used as warning shots or targeting individuals. The ISOS app updates two to three times per day. Keep monitoring and await further advice.

The email likely followed a video I sent to one of the leadership team members yesterday evening. The video showed one of the numerous scenes of ongoing chaos and violence I captured. With constant gunfire and murder over the past few days, why has it taken them this long to address our concerns? The British Embassy has also finally advised its citizens to leave. If we don't make plans to leave now, they will not help us in the event of an emergency.

Also, yesterday, Maeve spoke with a different member of the leadership team, expressing her worries and frustration. She explained how she should not be forced to choose between depleting her financial resources or remaining in an unstable and potentially life-threatening environment.

Maeve recounted the exchange in a voice note shared with us. "I told them I was living on the first floor or the apartment block," she said. "Their response? They simply said, 'I hope your windows are closed.'"

The callousness and disregard exhibited by the leadership team have left us stunned and disheartened. I've made a mental note that we are in it alone.

The rest of today has passed by slowly. It is sunny, a humid and sticky type of sun, with a heavy cloud of sorrow hanging in the air. The ever-constant stream of news is damaging, yet I cannot avoid it; my brain ignites a neuron every time a ping emanates from my phone. Further news of the 'Milk Tea Alliance' has spread, even to the UK. They are holding rallies across Asia. From Taipei to Bangkok, Melbourne to Hong Kong, voices are being united against oppression. Online protests are also being held in Indonesia and Malaysia. However, amidst this display of solidarity, the violence has escalated, leaving devastation in its wake. News of increased violence and deaths has spread, reaching our social feeds and inboxes. Among those recently killed in Yangon was Nyi Nyi Aung Htet Naing, an internet network engineer who had bravely posted his concerns on Facebook. Just the day before he was shot, his poignant words echoed with a plea for action, "How many dead bodies UN need to take action."[8]

Videos have circulated, capturing the haunting moment when Nyi Nyi lay lifeless outside the gate of the Kamaryut township high school, his builder's white hard hat still on his head, his phone tightly grasped in his hand. As protestors sprinted by his motionless body, crouching low in fear, a small group mustered the courage to carry him away, their hearts heavy with the realisation that it was too late to save him.

Tragically, the loss has not ended there. Again, in Yangon,

---

[8] Reuters (2021). *'How many dead bodies?' asked Myanmar protestor killed on bloodiest day.* [online] 1 Mar.

Tin New Yee, a middle school teacher, succumbed to the violence unleashed by the authorities as they attempted to disperse a peaceful teacher's protest, resorting to the use of grenades. The echoing explosions shattered the peace, leaving only anguish in their wake. Grenades were also hurled outside a Yangon medical school. Reports begin to surface from the Whitecoat Alliance of Medics, revealing that over fifty medical staff have been unjustly arrested for their involvement in the protests.[9]

Yesterday, a brave front-liner took to Facebook, exposing the malicious intent that seemed to drive the authorities, capturing their menacing words; "We shoot because we want to. Get inside your homes if you don't want to die."

In the face of these increasingly hostile circumstances, the brave protestors seek ways to protect themselves. From my balcony, I can see them donning plastic helmets, with makeshift shields and masks to conceal their identities. Their forearms are marked with their blood group and a contact number for their next of kin, ensuring that vital information is readily available in an emergency.

The streets have fortified their safety measures, setting up additional roadblocks at strategic locations and utilising whatever resources are available. Garbage bins, lighting poles, and concrete blocks have been repurposed to impede the progress of oppressors and shield the innocent.

Hearing of Nilar's visit the previous day, Kyi decided that today, "the deadliest day," was the right time to visit me.

---

[9] Reuters (2021). At least 18 killed in Myanmar on the bloodiest day of protests against the coup. [online] 28 Feb.

"I am outside," Kyi said urgently as soon as I answered the phone.

"Coming," I yelped, pulling on a jumper and slipping into my flip-flops. "How did you get here? Is it safe?" I echoed into the phone.

"It's fine," she said. "Be quick."

I rushed down four flights of stairs, relieved to find Kyi chatting with the security guard inside the building.

"Hello, Miss," he greeted me as I approached. "I recognised her face."

"Ce-Zu tin-ba-deh (thank you)," I replied in broken Burmese, hugging Kyi.

She grinned. "I have bubble tea."

"My favourite," I smiled back. "I will miss these."

In the safety of my flat, Kyi and I catch up. We talk of past and present. We half-watch an Adam Sandler film—something light-hearted to distract ourselves.

"I can't believe you're actually leaving," she whispered. "Why do you have to go?"

"I have no choice," I reply. "If I don't leave now, the British government will not help me. I'm sorry."

"It's so quiet outside," she sighed. "Too quiet."

"Let's look," I said, stretching my cramped muscles and stepping onto the balcony.

Dusk is approaching, and the sun casts an orange glow over the city streets below. Kyi is right. It's eerily quiet—no usual clamour of pots and pans, singing or shouting.

"I should go soon—"

"Fuck," I hiss. "Get down!"

My heart races, not just from the sight of armed soldiers patrolling the streets below but from the unsettling atmosphere and the tension in the air.

"What's happening?" Kyi's voice trembles with fear as she rises to her feet.

"Oh shit," she whispered, quickly crouching back down again.

Carefully peering through the gaps in the balcony, we spotted a figure. Clad in black, the form blended with the backdrop of old buildings and faded streetlights. A rifle, an ominous extension of their lethal intent, lay casually over the person's shoulder. Daring to steal another glance, I saw fingers, calloused and disciplined, coiled around the trigger. The streets below lay subdued, the rifle representing the constant vigilance of those in power, ensuring obedience to their every command.

"Get inside," I hissed, guiding Kyi back through the balcony doors, still keeping low. Softly closing the door, I turned to Kyi. "You can't leave yet."

Seated far away from the balcony doors, I called my mother.

"Mum," I cried as soon as she answered. "There are people outside with spotlights and rifles."

"Get away from the fucking window," she shouted. "Shut the curtains."

Her sudden use of profanity shocked me into action. I closed the curtains and turned off the lights, casting the room in a dim, flickering glow from a candle. Shadows danced on the walls as my mind raced to find a solution.

The silence outside was deafening, broken only by the distant echoes of sporadic gunfire and the muffled voices of military personnel.

"I should go," Kyi whimpered.

"You can't leave here and be killed on your way home," I pleaded, desperation in my voice. The mere thought of Kyi navigating the perilous streets, each corner a potential threat, chilled me.

"If they raid the building," she replied softly, "we may both be imprisoned. I'm not supposed to be here after dark."

"I don't care."

"I do."

Kyi knew the risks all too well, as well as the harsh reality that awaited her outside my home. As the moment of parting drew near, I fought to hold back the tears that threatened to spill from my eyes. She wouldn't stay, as much as I begged.

After waving goodbye to Kyi, those tears finally came. The weight unleashed a whirlwind of gratitude, admiration, and sorrow. With no word from Kyi, uncertainty gnaws at me. The internet was cut off early tonight, leaving me in anticipation and dread as I await the morning when communication might be restored.

Chapter 43. A Dangerous Game

Monday 1st March 2021

The end of the half-term break marked the return to teaching, a comforting return to a sense of normalcy. After having endured a week filled with fear and monotonous boredom, the familiar routine offered a glimmer of hope. This morning, the students and their anxious parents seemed visibly relieved to have the structured environment of online school once more.

The day before, I found myself yearning for school to resume. But that day, I felt drained. My energy reserves had been depleted, drained by the constant vigilance and emotional labour that the current situation demanded. Kyi was home though; safe for now.

In our maths class that morning, the children voiced their worries, loudly sharing their concerns. Their eyes darted between the screen and something beyond my view, their attention fractured.

"Miss, Miss!' one child exclaimed. "I hear gunshots, Miss.

I'm scared." My heart clenched at her words.

"I know it can sound scary," Alexa replied, her own body visibly trembling as multiple gunshots were fired outside her apartment window. "But your parents will keep you safe."

As teachers, we face the daunting task of providing constant reassurance and stability in a world that feels anything but stable. We find ourselves repeating the same phrases, like broken records. "It's going to be okay," we say. "Let's focus on our lesson."

"I don't like it. It's so loud," Mya chimed in, her lower lip quivering. She clutched a stuffed animal to her chest.

"Let's take a deep breath," Alexa suggested. "In through your nose, out through your mouth." A few children followed suit, their small shoulders relaxing ever so slightly. "Remember, we are all here for each other."

Later that morning, in my phonics lesson, which I usually conduct solo, the questions persisted. I mistakenly asked about their half-term holidays, hoping for answers like "We went swimming" or "We visited the park."

Instead, their responses centred around soldiers, scary noises, and seeking refuge in safe houses. A lump formed in my throat. I glanced at the grid of faces—tiny boxes filled with innocence. What could I say?

It's been a few days since Maeve's experience at the supermarket, and the girls have unanimously decided it's time to leave Yangon. Ella, Maeve and I will fly back to London, while Amie has been offered a relief flight home to the Philippines. There are still seats available on the flight I've booked, and I secretly feel relieved that they've chosen to take the same one. While I don't mind travelling solo, the thought of having familiar faces by my side has lessened the burden of anxiety threatening to overwhelm me. We had embarked on this journey together as the Sanchaung crew, and now we'll be returning to Heathrow Airport side by side.

Another silver lining in their decision to join me is that I won't have to face navigating the coronavirus testing process alone. Despite the safety warnings issued by ISOS and the British Embassy over the past few days, urging non-Burmese citizens to evacuate, we are still bound by stringent travel requirements. To board our relief flight, we must present proof of a negative COVID-19 test taken within 48 hours of departure. The tests come at a steep price—a hefty sum of two hundred dollars. However, only cash payments are accepted for the relief flight and the testing fees. With funds not entering the country since the first of February, cash reserves are running perilously low, putting pressure on civilians and humanitarian and aid groups.

The CDM movement and low cash funds have essentially paralysed Myanmar's banking sector. Transferring money into or within the country has become a near-impossible task. I've read accounts from aid workers struggling to provide for large groups of displaced individuals, particularly in the Kachin and northern Shan states, who share their worries as they struggle to provide food for them, "Many of us cannot operate."[10]

We've scheduled our trip to the testing centre for tomorrow. In normal times, this would be a mundane errand, but now it feels

---

[10] The New Humanitarian (2021). *Post-coup cash shortages put the squeeze on Myanmar aid.* [online]

like traversing a minefield. The roads are unpredictable. We have meticulously planned our journey, endlessly discussing what to bring and attempting to ease Ella's worries.

[Maeve] What do we need?

[Me] I am bringing my grab bag, but you should also bring your bank card, passport, flight tickets and a good nostril.

[Maeve] I have plans to say goodbye to Tomas tonight, so I am ensuring we return, haha.

As I read her light-hearted remark, I missed the Maeve I once knew, who brought laughter and joy to our conversations. The weight of our circumstances has changed us all, casting a shadow over even the simplest moments of levity. Ever since her ordeal at the supermarket, tensions have lingered between us, a rift that I hate myself for.

Finally, our employers are starting to grasp the gravity of the situation. They've now provided armed security and transportation to ensure our safety wherever and whenever we travel. The school has been transformed into a safe house, with rows of mattresses, pillows, and duvets on the lower ground. Some of our Burmese colleagues, maintenance staff and cleaners already live there. Yet, despite these measures, evacuation still hasn't been deemed "necessary."

Living in our guarded building in Sanchaung offers a degree of security, shielding us from immediate danger. But for those in traditional houses or flats, the situation is fragile. Expatriate teachers who opted to live in houses have been relocated to secure compounds, and many have been repatriated or relocated to neighbouring countries like Thailand.

I reach for my journal and flip to a blank page. I let the pen flow, spilling my anxieties onto the paper. I then scribble down a list of things to remember for the next few days—a practical attempt to regain some control.

- Passport and copies
- Negative COVID-19 test results (once obtained)
- Embassy contact information
- Emergency cash (if I have any)
- Medications

I draw a line beneath the list, which seems so clinical against the backdrop of the emotional storm inside me.

It's now late in the evening, and the usual chorus of banging pots and pans didn't occur at its customary eight o'clock hour. It's strange.

Chapter 44. Safe House

Tuesday 2nd March 2021

Dear Diary,

Earlier today, we set off for the testing centre at six in the morning; forty-eight hours before our flight. Dawn had broken over the city of Yangon, signalling the end of the curfew and our time to depart. We hoped to avoid the bulk of the protests. A car was waiting for us a few streets over, as our street is entirely inaccessible at this point. Two armed security men greeted us at the entrance of our complex, where Maeve, Ella, and I were waiting. The street was beginning to wake up, meaning we had to move fast.

    The scent of tear gas lingered in the air, blending with the acrid smell of fear and defiance. Symbols of resistance adorned the walls and roads, defiant marks against oppression. Images of military general Min Aung Hlaing stared back from the pavement, each one marked with bold white crosses.

    On the streets, a group of men worked tirelessly to rebuild

the maze of crumbled barricades that had been destroyed by the military the previous day. Despite the odds, protesters persisted, strategising and planning how best to undermine the opposition with the limited resources at their disposal. Beneath our feet, shattered glass and debris littered the ground.

An elderly man hunched on the pavement; his eyes fixed on the scene unfolding before him as he took the final swigs from a whisky bottle in his hand. Nearby, children as young as four or five were graffiti-ing on the pavement. As we passed by, I kept my head down, feeling a pang of guilt, knowing that we would soon be leaving, leaving behind a community bravely fighting for their rights.

"It will be hard to get back in," one of the guards said. "They will completely block the street."

"They are very clever," Maeve replied.

Once we reached the small white van, we all felt comforted. We were surely safe with security men in the front two seats and Maeve, Ella, and me in the back. Water bottles were passed around as we braced ourselves for the long journey ahead.

Seated in the middle, I couldn't tear my eyes away from the view outside the front window. I watched as a convoy of armoured vehicles patrolled the streets. Even at this early hour, soldiers, faces hidden behind masks, stood stoically at every corner with rifles in their hands. Their gaze pierced through the darkness of the morning light, scanning the surroundings for any sign of dissent.

"I hate this," Ella said. "I can't look."

Arriving at the COVID-19 testing centre, we were greeted by a scene of bustling activity. At seven in the morning, the queue, snaking like a winding serpent, stretched around the battered pillars, likely a football pitch in length. Most of those waiting were Burmese, perhaps seeking refuge in another, quieter area of Myanmar. Restless children fidgeted; their energy was barely contained as they shifted from one foot to the other. Conversations were subdued, punctuated by anxious glances that darted around the room, wary of unseen threats.

In the queue, a familiar face brought a small sigh of relief, reassuring us that we weren't the only foreigners in the centre.

"Take a number," he shouted, sensing our unease, "and sit."

Following his instructions, we scanned the area for the number dispenser.

"Demur," a young man behind a desk called out, gesturing at the numbers.

"English?" He asked as we nodded. "Sign here. Fill in the form."

He handed us forms to fill out, and with pens that were running out of ink, we improvised, using each other's backs as makeshift tables. We grabbed a questionnaire each and filled it in as best as we could. Flight details and cold and flu symptoms were asked. We left the section "reasons for leaving" blank. Returning the forms, we exchanged them for numbers, all of which were in the high two hundreds.

"How long?" Maeve asked, pointing at her watch.

The man simply shrugged. "One, two hours."

The white van that transported us to the centre was now out of reach. We stood huddled in a corner, observing the testing procedure unfold. A father held his young son in his lap, restraining his flailing arms as a figure in a white hazmat suit approached with a swab. The boy cried as the swab was inserted into his nostril, and his mother pleaded for him to stay still. I turned to Ella and told her not to look anymore, her face worryingly pale.

"Right, let's sit over there," I suggested, attempting to shield Ella from the distressing scene. I pointed at rows of seats in a nearby building. It could be hours, and we'll hear them announce the numbers from there."

We settled into the white plastic chairs, each engrossed in our phones. Despite the weak signal, messages and emails trickled through. Witnessing the outpouring of love for the Burmese on Facebook was heartening. Campaigns were being launched, and funds poured in from around the world. Yet, the true depth of the unfolding crisis remained elusive. Outside news provided only a narrow view, downplaying the scale of the suffering—reporting tens of deaths instead of hundreds and thousands.

Moments later, my phone buzzed, signalling an unexpected email—a response from UCL. Over the past few months, I've been applying to universities for my master's degree, but previous rejections and the current situation have discouraged me. With bated breath, I opened the email. UCL has always been a dream university, especially after failing to secure a place as an undergraduate. With trembling hands, I read the contents of the email:

Dear Lydia,

This email is to inform you that there has been a change in the status of this application. Please log into UCL's portal to view your new application status.

My body trembled as I tried to hide my growing dread, crossing my legs and turning my face away from the girls. My first attempt to log into the portal failed. The internet was too weak. On my second try, I struggled with my password, growing increasingly frustrated. Just then, our colleague from the queue interrupted us, exhaustion evident in his weary expression.

"Hey guys," he sighed.

"Hi mate," Maeve greeted him. "How's it going?"

"As good as can be," he replied, a wry smile on his lips. "I just had my test—it was brutal."

"When's your flight?" I asked, my voice betraying my underlying anxiety.

"The fourth," he said. "You?"

"Same," I replied. "I think most people are aiming for that relief flight. I bet it will be crammed."

As we engaged in small talk, my mind was consumed by thoughts of my university application status. Refreshing the portal repeatedly, I hoped for a breakthrough. However, our turn for the test again interrupted my attempts.

"Ahhh," Ella screeched. "My nostrils are not ready for this."

"Think of the nice bacon and McDonald's you can get at home," we said, grabbing her hand and guiding her to the mass of people. Frustratingly, our number called for us to join a shorter queue, offering a clearer view of the procedure. Shielding Ella, I glanced down at my phone. The signal appeared stronger, prompting another attempt to access the portal. My fingers trembled as I entered my login and password. The page refreshed, and I barely had to read more than "congratulations" before bursting into tears.

"What's wrong?" Ella gasped.

"I got into UCL; I am doing a Masters!" I blurted out,

overwhelmed with joy.

The girls squealed and hugged me tightly. I felt a renewed sense of purpose in that moment, knowing I had something to return home to. I am beyond relieved.

With our tests complete and the familiar sting of discomfort lingering, we were handed slips to bring back to retrieve our certificates. Given my experience at Heathrow Airport, the promise of receiving them within 24 hours feels uncertain. Gratefully, our driver volunteered to collect them on our behalf, sparing us another venture until our departure.

"Let's head home, chicks," sighed Maeve as we climbed back into the van. With the afternoon sun casting long shadows, we prepared for a lengthier return journey now that the city had awoken.

On the way home, we made a detour to the school to use the ATM, one of the city's last sources of cash. Our March wages had been deposited, and we needed to withdraw the remaining funds. Once inside the secure, gated building, our phones buzzed incessantly with messages from Amie:

[Amie] Things are heated here in Sanchaung. I hope you're all safe where you are.

[Me] We are coming back now…or trying to.

[Amie] The gunshots are nearby, and people are running and screaming. Stay safe! I can smell the smoke from where I am on my balcony.

[Me] Oh god.

[Amie] Please stay safe.

[Amie] The shots are even closer now.

[Me] Okay, we are staying here.

[Amie] I can't see it from where I am, but it sounds like they're on the road just across from us.

"We stay," our driver declared firmly.

"It's a good job I brought my grab bag." I chuckled, trying to lighten the mood. "I wish I'd brought snacks, though."

"We may as well get comfortable," Ella added. "I hope Amie is okay."

With a silent nod, I sank into the worn-out, plush brown sofa in the staff room. Like the school itself, the space had been neglected for far too long. Once vibrant with children's laughter, it now sat empty, a mere shell of its former self. The hallways were eerily quiet, devoid of youthful energy. It had been over a year since students had filled these corridors, a reminder of the havoc wreaked upon the education system.

Hungry from skipping breakfast due to the early start, we raided the staff room cupboard for food and coffee. We found plenty of dry, tasteless crackers, which we shared as we anxiously waited for an update on the situation.

Restless and with a sense of finality, I decided to take one last walk through the halls. Tiptoeing past a barely familiar classroom, a dim light from the lower school nursery caught my eye.

Approaching cautiously, I heard the hushed sounds of a Burmese family inside. The room had been transformed into a makeshift shelter, with books pushed aside and a row of mattresses in the centre. A woman sat on the floor, cradling an infant, her gentle fingers stroking the baby's forehead in an attempt to soothe its troubled mind. Their few possessions, carried in a bag or two, lay beside them, along with a lone baby bottle.

Our eyes met unexpectedly, and I blushed. In her gaze, I saw pain and fear. I offered a feeble wave and a small smile, knowing it could do little to ease their suffering. Yet, in that vulnerable moment, I felt a fragile connection. The woman's eyes held an extraordinary determination to protect her child—a spark of hope in the face of adversity, a testament to the resilience of the human spirit.

Leaving the family to their makeshift sanctuary, I retraced my steps, contemplating the impact of the situation. They were just two among many displaced souls, forced from their homes. I thought of the children in the orphanages, their innocent faces etched in my mind, wondering how they were coping.

Eventually, we received the signal to return to Sanchaung. The journey back was unsettlingly swift, and the streets were unnaturally deserted, tainted by the bloodshed. Passing a convoy of military tanks, Ella trembled with fear, her hands visibly shaking.

"It's okay," one of the guards murmured, glancing back at us with a strained expression. "But we have to get out of the car soon. The roads are still blocked."

We nodded, exchanging a brief look of apprehension. The obstacle course of barricades ahead of us had grown more complex. Street signs leaned precariously against battered lamp posts, creating impromptu barriers. Rusted barrels, repurposed, stood as silent sentinels. Wooden chairs and tables, perhaps once part of someone's home, were piled high alongside doors torn from their hinges. Sticks and metal rods were lashed together with fraying ropes and strips of cloth.

As we weaved through this labyrinth, chanting filled the air, growing louder with each step. The crowd had swelled; it was larger than ever. Brave individuals, their faces concealed behind masks, stood guard at each barricade. With gleaming eyes, they wielded whatever weapons they could find—sticks, metal rods, slabs of wood...

As we passed through, a young man stepped forward, his eyes locking onto mine. Dirt smeared his cheek, and a cut above his brow oozed a thin line of blood.

Reaching Sanchaung Residence felt like emerging from a fever dream. Curious eyes tracked our arrival, watching from the viewing spots. The hum of generators filled the air, a low drone that barely masked the tension thrumming just beneath the surface.

"You made it," the guard said, smiling. "Good job, it's going to be crazy tonight."

I documented every detail for Ivy, sending her hourly updates.

"That's wild," she had just replied.

***

23:45

I couldn't sleep again. My mind was racing as I recounted the events of that day. Earlier, as I stepped onto my balcony for the nightly ritual, a shroud of eerie silence enveloped the street. The absence of sound was deafening, swallowing the usual clatter of pots and pans, the hum of the streetlights, and the whispers of passing convoys.

Every apartment around me was cloaked in darkness; even the streetlights were switched off. My own breath sounded unnaturally loud in my ears. Then, a sudden explosion shattered the stillness—a sound grenade fired into the dark sky. Instinctively, I recoiled back into my home, locking the balcony door behind me.

I crouched low, inching toward the spare bedroom window. Peering through a sliver where the curtain didn't quite meet the wall, I waited for my eyes to adjust. The soldiers were here. Even in the darkness, their presence was undeniable. They fanned out across the street, methodically approaching the adjacent buildings.

I watched in silent horror as they breached a neighbour's home. Doors splintered under the brute force of authority, rifles gleaming in the scant light. A spotlight swept across our apartment complex, illuminating the building.

Then came the gunfire—a staccato burst that echoed off walls, each crack like lightning. I pressed my back against the wall, knees drawn to my chest, fighting the urge to scream.

I tore myself away from the window, seeking consolation in the mechanical whirr of the air conditioning, a feeble attempt to drown out the outside noise. I tried to listen to music, hoping it would help me fall asleep, but I couldn't. Beside my pillow lay my grab bag. It had everything I needed in case we needed to stay in the safe house.

Chapter 45. The Final Day

Wednesday 3rd March 2021

I woke to the soft light of dawn filtering through the curtains, casting shadows across the room. I lay there for a moment, cocooned in the transient peace that comes just before the world stirs. A pang of bittersweet nostalgia washed over me, reminding me of all the moments that led to this day.

I rose slowly and made my way to the balcony, where I watched the warm, yellow sun rise majestically over the horizon. The first rays of sunlight glinted off the Shwedagon Pagoda, casting a radiant glow.

From this vantage point, I could see the familiar sights and sounds of the city. In a previous life, children would have been laughing on their way to school, vendors haggling with early customers and monks collecting alms with bowed heads and serene expressions.

The news this morning that our COVID-19 tests have

come back negative and the impending departure from Myanmar in twenty-four hours has brought a mix of emotions. It dawned on me that today would officially be our last day here, not by choice but by circumstance.

Leaving behind Amie is worrying. She will remain for a few more days, awaiting her relief flight organised by the Filipino government, having turned down the first one out of fear of losing her job. We don't know when she will be leaving Myanmar, and it's tough to say goodbye to a friend without knowing when she will be safe. But then again, I'm leaving my Burmese friends.

The timing of our departure feels significant, given recent events. Reports emerged overnight—disturbing whispers that the military and police have been given authorisation to use excessive force, including lethal projectiles, against those in opposition to them.

Today also brought news of a brutal crackdown in Mandalay, claiming the lives of at least thirty-eight innocent people. Among the fallen was nineteen-year-old Ma Kyal Sin, affectionately known as Angel[11]. Angel had become a beacon of hope and resilience, a fearless activist who stood at the forefront of the struggle, shielding others from the onslaught of police advances and tear gas. I saw photos of her this morning, her dark hair pulled back and a pair of goggles around her neck. She stood as the sole girl in a group dominated by men, yet her courage knew no bounds. In the haunting video that captured the moment of her death, Angel's voice

---

[11] Centre for Information Resilience (2025). Myanmar Witness – Centre for Information Resilience [Online].

rang out, "People at the front, please sit down. You cannot be allowed to die." Her words were a rallying cry, a selfless plea for the safety of others.

As she turned her head towards the line of advancing security forces—faceless men clad in riot gear—a single, sharp crack split the air. In an instant, she crumpled to the ground, the life slipping from her body before she even hit the pavement. A bullet had pierced her skull, a merciless ending to a young life dedicated to justice. She had been wearing a t-shirt she had made with the slogan "Everything will be OK."

Fellow protestors rallied around, racing against time to whisk her away on a motorcycle to a makeshift clinic. She was pronounced dead at the scene.

The tragic death sent shockwaves across the globe, resonating beyond the borders of Myanmar. Today has now been declared as the new "bloodiest day" since the coup began.

Today, I have seen countless images captured by bystanders, portraying heart-wrenching scenes of lifeless bodies strewn across the streets, surrounded by pools of blood. The chaos of protestors desperately fleeing for their lives as the police unleash a torrent of violence is a nightmare brought to life in disturbing videos.

The toll of innocent lives lost is staggering, particularly today. The brutality is escalating, with police openly firing at demonstrators mere streets away from where I stand. Even more horrifying are the accounts of young women being dragged away to prisons, where they face sexual assault. The very thought makes my blood run cold. In response, protesters have been blocking off more and more roads to try and prevent the women from being taken.

The reported casualties represent only a fraction of the actual number. Among the victims are at least five children mercilessly murdered, with four others left severely injured. Shockingly, over five hundred children have been detained. I can't bear to look at the images and videos anymore, yet turning away won't erase the horrors unfolding. The world needs to know the truth, and I am committed to sharing their story, no matter how difficult it may be.

As the afternoon waned, a new wave of terror gripped Mandalay. The low, ominous roar of fighter jets shattered the relative quiet, their sleek forms slicing through the sky at intimidatingly low altitudes. Videos circulating on TikTok reveal soldiers threatening protesters; "I will shoot whoever I see."

Another video is even more direct, showing a man in army uniform aiming a rifle at a camera as he tells protesters: "I will shoot you in your fucking faces…I am using real bullets." He continued, a sinister edge to his tone. "I am going to patrol the whole city tonight, and I will shoot whoever I see…If you want to become a martyr, I will fulfil your wish."

With Facebook blocked by the military, TikTok has rapidly become a favoured social media platform in the country. It is a battleground for both truth and propaganda, with courageous individuals using it to expose the atrocities while others exploit its reach to spread fear and incite further violence.

At midday, yet another video emerged—a civilian mercilessly gunned down in the street. The footage was gut-wrenching in its rawness. The man was unarmed, his hands raised in a gesture of surrender as he was led away from a protest. Without warning, a gunshot rang out, and he fell, his body lifeless on the pavement. The camera shook as the person filming gasped, the harrowing reality too much to bear.

Equally disturbing was a video depicting a medical crew being savagely beaten by soldiers. The assailants laughed as they struck them with batons and rifle butts, the cruel mockery in their eyes a stark contrast to the cries and pain of their victims. The sanctity of humanitarian aid was disregarded entirely; a line crossed that underscored the depths of the regime's brutality.

Against the backdrop of this appalling and heart-breaking series of events, the response from our leadership team is shocking. Despite the overwhelming evidence and mounting atrocities, some schools have chosen to downplay the severity of the situation, asserting that there is no "threat to life." I want to know which news outlets they're reading.

Chapter 46. "Please, tell our story."

Thursday 4th of March 2021

Dear Diary,

I am writing this as we wait to board our plane to Kuala Lumpur. The plastic chairs in the terminal are cold and unwelcoming, and the fluorescent lights cast a harsh glare over the nearly empty space. The usual hustle and bustle of travellers, the murmur of conversations, and the rolling of suitcases are conspicuously absent. Instead, an eerie silence hangs in the air, broken only by the occasional crackle of the intercom and the distant hum of machinery.

Yesterday evening, at nightfall, Myanmar's security forces invaded the cemetery where Angel had been buried. They ruthlessly discarded the carefully arranged flowers and wreaths, desecrating her final resting place. With shovels in hand, they dug up her grave, leaving behind a scene of macabre destruction. Razor blades were strewn around haphazardly, glinting menacingly under the pale moonlight. Bloodied plastic gloves littered the ground, grotesque reminders of the callousness with which they handled her remains. And then, in a final act of desecration, they filled her grave with unyielding cement—a thick, grey slab sealing away not just her body but the very essence of her memory beneath a cold, unforgiving barrier.

It was disgusting.

We weren't sure if we'd be able to make it to the airport that day. We had left early, as soon as the morning curfew had lifted, driving past the familiar streets lined with tanks and soldiers. Even now, as we waited in the terminal after passing through security, it seemed abandoned. Our plane was the only one departing today. The departure board flickered overhead, a stark reminder of the halted movement and the isolation gripping the country. Boarding was imminent; however, we were anxious about taking off. Rumours swirled of fighter jets and drones prowling the skies above. I couldn't shake the gnawing anxiety until we were safely airborne, bound for Malaysia.

The world's gaze was now fixed on Myanmar as the harrowing videos had *finally* begun to circulate across the globe, exposing the atrocities unfolding within its borders. Images of peaceful protestors facing off against armed soldiers, of smoke rising from makeshift barricades, of blood staining the streets. These were not mere clips; they were cries for help, pleas for recognition and intervention.

Tom Andrews, the UN's special rapporteur on human rights, had urged members of the UN Security Council to watch the videos before their meeting the next day. He called on them to bear witness to the atrocities, see beyond political rhetoric, and grasp the cost of idleness. Yet hope waned with each passing day of inaction, leaving many here disillusioned with the prospect of international intervention. After all, it had been over thirty days.

When we arrived at the airport that morning, the driver stopped the car, and for a moment, none of us moved. Finally, he turned to face us, his eyes glistening with unshed tears that traced silent paths down his weathered cheeks.

"Please," he said. "Tell the world what is happening here. Do not forget us." His shoulders sagged slightly, a man carrying the weight of uncertainty and fear for what the future holds.

I will never forget.

Chapter 47. Thirty-Three Hours

Friday 5th of March 2021

As the wheels of the plane began to turn, and I felt the familiar feeling of the aircraft taking off from the hot tarmac, the tears fell involuntarily from my eyes. Seated by the window, I turned my head to witness the sprawling city of Yangon coming into view, concealing my tears and quivering hands. Each tear carried a multitude of emotions: regret, relief, sadness, and guilt. Especially guilt, knowing that I was fortunate enough to return to a country where such acts of brutality would never be tolerated. But above all, they symbolised helplessness, a feeling of abandoning my friends in their time of need.

The journey to Kuala Lumpur airport was brief—a mere hour and a half. Most seats were occupied by expats and their families, creating an atmosphere of shared experiences. I closed my eyes, seeking solace in the temporary respite of darkness and attempting to gather my thoughts.

The airport in Malaysia was a ghost town, and few were travelling, except for the passengers on relief flights. I'd almost forgotten that COVID-19 is still a prevalent concern. Since the beginning of the coup in Myanmar, social distancing had become a relic of the past, disregarded in the face of more immediate threats.

We gathered in the quiet solitude of a nearly empty cafe. With hours to spare before our next flight, Ella, Maeve, and I huddled together alongside a handful of colleagues. While our trio was bound for London, others had final destinations ranging from Australia, Germany, and America. We sipped our beers and coffees and shared stories of the past seven months. Gradually, country by country, we were called for our ongoing flights until, finally, it was our turn to make our way to the Qatar Airways boarding gate.

The plane was sparsely populated, operating at only twenty-five per cent capacity. With an entire row of seats to myself and the gentle hum of the engines, I was lulled into a drowsy state of relaxation.

A short stopover in Qatar provided a fleeting moment of respite, a chance to stretch our legs and recharge before the final leg of our journey. The anticipation of reaching our final destination grew, as did our weariness. As we prepared to board for the final time, exhaustion weighed heavy in Maeve's voice. "Almost there. See you on the flip side."

The second leg of our journey from Malaysia was slightly more crowded than the first, but to my relief, I had an empty seat between myself and my neighbour. As we took off, the excitement of finally heading home kept me awake. I found it impossible to shake the restless energy that pulsed through my veins. As the plane ascended towards the clouds, the aroma of the plane food wafted through the cabin, sparking a hunger that had lain dormant for weeks. With each bite, I savoured the taste of normalcy. It felt like a small victory, a sign that I was moving towards a place of stability and comfort.

But as we began our descent into London, the thunderous hum of the wheels being released from the aircraft triggered an intense pounding in my chest. My feet tingled, and my fingertips grew numb. My vision was distorted, and beads of sweat began to form on my forehead. I started to panic and instinctively gripped the armrests of my seat, digging my nails into the fabric. The mask covering my mouth had become suffocating. Breathing became difficult, and despite long deep breaths, oxygen felt like it was being sucked from my body, my throat constricting. My mouth felt like sandpaper, and I desperately wanted to scream, yet no sound escaped my lips. I tried to calm myself, repeating, "I am not dying" in my mind. I found it odd that a panic attack had hit me once I had reached safety and not before. I knew the symptoms, living with anxiety, my rational brain reminding me that I could breathe. Time seemed to stretch out, each minute passing by slowly, gradually easing the grip of panic. Then, with a sudden jolt, the wheels of the airplane landed on the runway, shaking me back to reality. I wiped the tears that stained my cheeks and quickly gathered my belongings.

The off-boarding process was long and drawn out, reminding us that we were back in the land of coronavirus rules and regulations. Fortunately, we narrowly avoided the need to quarantine in a hotel. Still, some of my colleagues opted for self-quarantine in an Airbnb or other accommodations to keep their elderly relatives safe. I couldn't help but feel for them, as all I yearned for at that moment was to hug my mum as tightly as possible.

As I passed through passport control and baggage collection, I kept glancing at Maeve and Ella, knowing they felt the same way I did. Each step closer to the arrival hall felt like an eternity.

As I passed beneath the 'nothing to declare' sign and stepped through the revolving doors of the arrival hall, I immediately spotted my mother's short brown hair and my father standing beside her with his hand resting in the bow of her back. With tears welling in my eyes, I hurried towards them, my feet barely touching the ground. In an instant, I jumped into my mother's waiting arms, releasing all my pent-up emotions and momentarily forgetting about the hardships of the journey home. My parents didn't seem to care about their 'no hugging' rule now. In that embrace, I found solace and comfort, melting into my mum's warm familiarity. I realised that she will always be by my side no matter where life takes me.

My father took charge of my heavy suitcase and retrieved my coat that had been carelessly discarded on the floor. Finally, I was home.

Chapter 48. Home

I landed in London a different version of myself.

I found myself spiralling into a pit of red, hot anger. I was argumentative, defensive, and guilt-ridden. It was a seemingly innocuous moment in the car with my parents that ignited a fire within me. My father's complaint about a slow drive at a crossing was the spark that set off an explosion of pent-up emotions. In a fit of rage, I lashed out, questioning why trivial inconveniences matter when so many people are being murdered and facing violence in the world.

The car fell silent, my words hanging heavy in the air. My mother murmured her agreement, offering little comfort in the wake of my outburst. In the weeks that followed, my anger became a constant companion, erupting whenever my family dared to express their grievances, be it my mother moaning at the bin men, mocking how somebody spoke, or my brother complaining about work. I berated them for their perceived privilege, urging them to see beyond their petty concerns.

But as the dust settled, I began to realise that my anger was not entirely justified or fair. It was born out of the deep wounds and traumas I had witnessed. My perspective had been irrevocably altered, making it difficult to reconcile the trivialities of everyday life with the profound suffering I had seen.

Even though I had returned to the comforts of my home in London, I remained tethered to the turmoil in Myanmar, unable to fully disconnect from the atrocities unfolding there. And I didn't want to disconnect. Each day brought a barrage of news updates and messages from the charity group chat. I desperately searched for new information. Nilar and Kyi's messages swung between missing me and hating me, reflecting the emotional turmoil they were going through.

Then came a video, a horrifying testament to the violence and brutality that continued to engulf Myanmar. A lone motorbike carried two unsuspecting souls—a man and his partner. Suddenly, the tranquillity of the quiet backstreet shattered as gunfire erupted. Bullets tore through the air, ripping into flesh and shattering bones, as the innocent couple's world shattered in an instant. The screech of metal against pavement echoed like a haunting lament, and as quickly as the violence erupted, the military vanished into darkness. I have no idea who captured the footage, but they captured murder. I still think about that video regularly.

In England, news of murder and war was nothing new, often overshadowed by images of conflict in Iraq or Afghanistan dominating the headlines. While I had occasionally felt a fleeting sense of sadness and devastation for the affected communities, the distance and inability to fully grasp the reality of these situations had allowed those feelings to dissipate quickly.

However, now, whenever I encountered images or sounds of violence, whether in Myanmar or elsewhere, I was instantly transported back to the raw emotions I had experienced. It was as if I could smell the fear and taste the anguish that permeated the air, igniting a sense of guilt for not reacting with the same intensity to previous conflicts.

The relief I felt upon returning home was short-lived. Just days after my return, I received distressing news about Nilar. She had gone temporarily missing, last seen in Sanchaung, where she had assisted a friend past curfew. The silence surrounding her whereabouts sent my heart racing with worry. I prayed for her safety and breathed a sigh of relief when I learned she had found a hiding place.

But Nilar's disappearance was just the beginning. Another friend, Myo, had been arrested for participating in the protests. Uncontactable, the jail was overflowing with 23,000 protestors, none of whom were officially registered.

Then came the devastating news shared by Ivy. The military had brutally murdered a former colleague of Matt's. They raided his home, beat him mercilessly, dragged him to a cold, unforgiving prison cell, and killed him.

Messages from Saffie flooded Maeve's inbox, revealing even more horrors. The military had destroyed all security cameras in front of Sanchaung Residence and boarded up the viewing platforms on each floor to hide their atrocities. Caught in this chaos, Amie had been relocated to a hotel on the city's outskirts. The urgency of the situation prompted the Filipino embassy to raise the alert level, urging its citizens to evacuate immediately. The Swedish embassy followed suit, issuing a similar advisory to its citizens.

As anger simmered within us, the school directors, who had all remained outside of Myanmar throughout these tumultuous times, finally offered to cover the cost of emergency flights and COVID-19 tests for those still trapped in the country. Their delayed action felt like a cruel twist of fate, exacerbating our frustration and resentment. They had forced us to choose between physical and mental safety and financial stability, and their belated offer only amplified those feelings.

Amie's flight wasn't until the 16th of March, and she shared her daily experiences with us.

[Amie] Today has been an absolute roller coaster. I fly on Wednesday, but the embassy will have to evacuate those stuck in this township and move them to a hotel near the airport tomorrow. The school driver tried to pick me up, but he was stopped, and all the roads were blocked.

[Amie] I don't know how the embassy plans to get through the heavily barricaded roads.

With each passing moment, our fear and uncertainty grew heavier. And, of course, we were still teaching virtually. Granted a day off for travelling home, we were quickly thrust back into the routine of online lessons the day after we landed. Amidst it all, our only source of comfort was the fervent hope that safety and freedom would soon prevail and that our friends and students would find their way out of this harrowing ordeal.

When I returned home, the process of re-adjustment began. I was constantly alert, unable to fully relax. Even though Bromley was familiar, it initially felt foreign. For the past eight months, I'd lived alone, and despite my aversion to solitude, I'd grown accustomed to the independence it offered me.

The sense of social disconnection was palpable. With three months left of the school term, finding a moment to disconnect and breathe was difficult. The children noticed the background change, asking, "Where are you, Miss? Are you in England?" Their innocent inquiries only amplified the ache of realising that I would never get to meet the children I was teaching in person.

Chapter 49. Healing and Hope

Months after I arrived home in March, I finally had the chance to reunite with some of the girls from Sanchaung. On Monday, May 31st, 2021, Matt orchestrated an extraordinary charity cycling event called "Bike for Burma." The event consisted of three races: a three-hundred-kilometre race, a thirty-kilometre race, and a three-kilometre race.

The event embodied the three-finger salute, symbolising the fight for freedom. After being home for a while, guilt gnawed at me for what I perceived as my lack of involvement. The ride had been planned months in advance, with Matt pouring immense effort into ensuring its success. The three-hundred-kilometre ride was set to kick off on the Saturday of the bank holiday weekend, with the thirty-kilometre ride concluding around the same time on Monday. While Matt took on the longer journey, Ivy, Maeve, Daniel, and I opted for the shorter distance.

On Sunday, the four of us gathered in Bournemouth for a

day of relaxation, wading in the sea, sunbathing, and catching up on the past few months. It was a scorchingly hot day, and the beach was alive with families and friends, making the pandemic seem like a distant memory. It was freeing to be with friends and enjoy normal activities again. That night, we stayed at a hostel. I slept fitfully as I had done most nights since our repatriation, and rising at four o'clock on the Monday proved to be a struggle. While it was a bank holiday in the UK, it was not in Myanmar. The leadership team had denied us a day off to partake in Matt's charity cycle, so I continued working in the car until we set off. Alexa then kindly held the fort.

The event's hub was a spacious car park in the New Forest. I was amazed by the enthusiastic participants congregated around a large tent emblazoned with the words "BIKE FOR BURMA." Roughly a third of the participants were Burmese, eager to hear our experiences. Many had been living in England for some time, while others were foreigners who had lived in Myanmar prior to 2020 or had connections to it.

During the event, I had the privilege of hearing about an inspiring woman named Tint Tint Wai. She was a Burmese woman employed at a UK hospital who had never ridden a bike. Two months before the event, she had signed up for the gruelling three-hundred-kilometre cycling challenge and trained four times a week with the support of her doctor friends, who volunteered to help her prepare.

"How are you feeling about everything?" Ivy asked during the bike ride.

"I don't know," I replied.

"Same," Ivy said. "But we have to make the most of our

fortunate situation. Live life for those who can't."

I didn't know how to feel. Since we left Myanmar, over fifty-eight defence forces have emerged, each representing different ethnic groups and regions. In the week leading up to the Bike for Burma ride, conflict had escalated dangerously, primarily between the Tatmadaw and the newly formed Karenni People's Defence Force (PDF) and the Karenni Army. Alarming statistics from the Armed Conflict Location and Event Data Project (ACLED) painted a grim picture. In May alone, there had been a staggering 154% increase in explosions, while fatalities rose by 164%.

Ethnic armies and the People's Defence Force had begun to retaliate as reports emerged of security forces and military personnel being targeted. In Yangon, a wedding party was attacked. A bomb, disguised as a gift, had claimed the lives of four people, including the bride. The groom was suspected to be a military informant.

The education system, too, became a target for those seeking to reinforce the shutdown by the CDM. Schools across the nation were subjected to bombings, an attempt to cripple the education system and undermine the resolve of striking teachers. Despite the Junta's order for parents to register their children to return to school, half the teachers remained steadfast in their commitment to the CDM, leading to approximately 125,000 of them being suspended. Nearly 20,000 university staff members also faced punitive measures for their support of the pro-democracy movement. In solidarity, students prepared to boycott classes as a protest, witnessing the loss and sacrifice their classmates endured.

China and Russia continued to supply the Myanmar Military with resources and support. The influx of external support to the military regime compounded the already dire situation, bolstering their capabilities and highlighting the complex geopolitical dynamics.

The international community, particularly EU countries, responded to the crisis by imposing sanctions on the military leadership. However, the scope of these sanctions left much to be desired. They primarily targeted a select group of individuals and companies linked to the Military. An arms embargo was also imposed to restrict the flow of weapons and military equipment into the country.

Ivy's words hung in the air, again reminding us of our privilege and the responsibility that came with it. As we pedalled through the serene countryside, the contrast between our peaceful surroundings and the chaos we had left behind was jarring.

"Ivy, do you think we'll ever go back?" I asked, my voice barely above a whisper.

She glanced at me. "I don't know," she admitted. "We can help from here, though, in any way we can."

The images of the conflict, the gunfire, the bombings, and the suffering were etched into my mind, but so was the resilience of the people we'd left behind.

Later, as the sun set, I felt a renewed sense of purpose. We might be home now, but our hearts were still with Myanmar.

Chapter 50. Trauma

Letting go of trauma had been a demanding journey, one filled with relentless effort and countless setbacks. Motivational books often tout the mantra of "let it go" and "focus on the positives," but if only it was that simple. Whenever my mother offered her well-meaning advice of "it could be worse," I cringed. The lightness in her voice and the pinched smile on her face suffocated me, leaving me feeling unseen and unheard.

"If only it were that easy, Mum," I sighed, my frustration evident.

"But it is," she insisted. "We've all had difficult experiences, but it's up to the individual whether they allow them to affect them."

"If only I could just 'get over it' as effortlessly as you suggest," I'd replied wearily, feeling the chasm between us widen with each conversation.

Months after my return from Myanmar, conversations with family had become fraught with tension. Despite my attempts to explain anxiety, depression, and trauma, they struggled to fully comprehend how I am feeling.

I began to question why some people could quickly 'let it go' while I found it insurmountable. Doubts crept in, whispering that perhaps I was responsible for constructing my own nightmare. I wondered if the flashbacks and chronic pain were my fault for failing to release the grip of the past. But all of that changed when I underwent an assessment for PTSD therapy.

With kindness in her eyes, the therapist explained the physiological effects of the autonomic nervous system. As a science graduate, I already understood the basics. Still, I smiled and nodded as she delved into the intricacies of the back brain and automatic survival-based reactions. She emphasised that the decision-making part of our brain couldn't solve these deep-rooted responses. It rationalised the panic attacks, stomach aches, muscle pains and quickened heart rate I had been experiencing.

During that same session, she introduced me to the concept of dissociation. As we discussed Myanmar, my brain began to shut down, enveloped in a thick fog that clouded my thoughts and blurred my vision.

"Sorry, my brain feels all foggy," I apologised to the therapist. "And my vision gets blurry, too. It happens a lot."

"Do you experience dissociation frequently?"

"Dissociation?" I questioned, unfamiliar with the term.

This phenomenon of dissociation became more apparent during the darkest days of my depression. When confronted with situations reminiscent of past traumas, a wave of peculiar sensations washed over me, leaving me feeling detached and unsteady, as if I were floating away from myself.

"It's an evolutionary response," the therapist explained. "A 'flight' state in the fight-or-flight response that allows you to play dead. You find it difficult to move or speak, experiencing numbness as your body conserves resources in preparation for the inevitable shock."

"Your body can actually release its own opioids, meaning it reduces perceptions of pain, physical and emotional, producing a sense of detachment."

I learned that my brain and body were constantly hypervigilant. I couldn't simply "switch it off" and relax and just knowing that was empowering.

I began to observe patterns in my dissociation episodes, identifying triggers and implementing grounding techniques to manage them. From focusing on my breath to listing sensory experiences, I found ways to anchor myself in the present moment and alleviate the grip of dissociation. I was also told that exercise would be an excellent outlet for my restless energy. However, too much exercise was to be avoided.

During my next visit to the gym, I decided to try something different and joined a spinning class called Rhythm. I made a conscious effort to embrace my emotions and feel the energy of the room. As the instructor introduced the "Mood Track," she encouraged us to "close our eyes and open our minds," allowing us to release whatever emotions we needed. In previous exercise classes, my focus had been solely on burning calories, but on that day, I was ready to delve deeper.

I closed my eyes, tightened my grip on the handlebars, and

immersed myself in the sound of pedals churning and heavy breathing. The soundtrack was emotional, and images quickly flooded my mind.

"Cycle up the mountain," Sarah, the instructor, urged. "Don't stop until you reach the top!"

My mountain loomed steep and daunting before me. Under the bright sun and clear sky, birds chirped cheerfully overhead. But as the weather darkened and the birds' songs turned to squarks, unwelcome figures emerged. The head of the Myanmar Military charged towards me, and with a determined push, I sent him tumbling off the mountain, a symbolic act for the lives he had disrupted and the hope he had extinguished.

Next came the figures of my past, my abusive ex-boyfriend and others who had caused pain. With each one, I pushed them away, reclaiming my power. I did it for the women who live in fear every day. I did it for those too afraid to walk alone at night. Then came the objects: an emblematic dagger for infidelity, a knife for those who had betrayed me, and a heavy box representing the weight of inequalities, racism, and terror in the world.

As I cast aside these burdens, the sky brightened once more, and a weight lifted from my shoulders. The faces of loved ones appeared, and I saw my grandma, her smile radiant as she baked her signature Victoria sponge cake, and a bright glow around her. Energised by their presence, I cycled faster, fuelled by determination.

I saw my best and closest friends cheering me on, my parents, and, as I neared the top of the mountain, my late dog Tilly began to run beside me. Together, we raced to the summit, and as I dismounted my bike, I was overcome with emotion. Tears streamed down my face as I took in the breathtaking view, surrounded by the faces who had supported me through it all.

At that moment, there was less trauma and only hope. Tears ran down my face as I felt a lightness I hadn't felt in years.

Epilogue. Myanmar Present Day

On 1st February 2025, Myanmar's post-coup conflict stretched into its fourth year, and the situation remains critical. Millions of people remain displaced, and many continue to suffer under the military repression and economic collapse. The country now ranks second in the latest ACLED Conflict Index, making it the second most dangerous and violent place in the world, behind Palestine.[12]

In 2024, resistance groups made substantial territorial gains, posing a threat to the regime. In response, the military activated its conscription law, calling males over 18 into service. Many civilians have been pushed onto the front lines, "being used as human shields in combat." Rohingya civilians remain the most persecuted people in the country.[13]

The military expects to hold elections in 2025, although this

---

[12] ACLED (2024). *Conflict Watchlist 2025: Myanmar – ACLED* [Online].
[13] The Irrawaddy (2024). *Myanmar Junta Steps Up Conscription With Forced Abductions After Thingyan* [Online].

remains unlikely.

After returning to England, the girls and I continued our work at the school in Myanmar for a few more months until the summer holidays. We adjusted our schedules to align with the time difference, starting our days in the early hours, around three or four in the morning, and wrapping up by one in the afternoon. Like many colleagues, I took on a second job as a nanny for a nearby family to supplement my income. The reality was that the salary of a teaching assistant in Myanmar, amounting to roughly eight hundred pounds per month, was insufficient, especially in London.

Despite the physical separation, we made every effort to stay connected with the children we had grown to care for deeply, offering them a friendly and comforting face. Many children and their families sought refuge in neighbouring countries, their lives upended by the turmoil—their homes changed, school became unfamiliar, and friendships severed.

As the summer holidays approached, we received news that the school would resume its academic year in Thailand, ensuring continuity for the displaced children. Unfortunately, Amie lost her job despite hoping to retain her position as a teaching assistant or begin a teaching degree while working at the school.

Maeve began a teaching degree in the UK and has since become a qualified teacher. The children under her care now are truly fortunate. Ella took a well-deserved break, returning home to her loving mother, who undoubtedly will never let her move abroad again.

I began my Master's in Global Health and Development at UCL, specialising in conflict and health modules. My dissertation centred on the coup and International Humanitarian Law. Now, I work in healthcare communications. Life took its course, and Daniel and I parted ways. Meanwhile, Nilar and Kyi both managed to leave Myanmar. Kyi relocated to Qatar to work in a hotel, and Nilar went to Russia to continue her studies.

Personal Stories

Nilar

Hi, Nilar, how are you doing today? (Monday 1st of November 2021)
Mingalabar. I don't know what to say, but I don't feel fine today. It is as usual. People are dying here every day. There have been fires in Chin State over the last two days. Myanmar Junta set fire to a house in Htan Ta Lyan, which led to the loss of 40% of the town in Chin. It is not okay to say that I am fine. I am not okay.

Tell me about yourself; where are you from?
I am from Pyay (Prome), which is located by the river Ayeyarwady. I came to Yangon to finish my studies and am currently living there.

Did you know/feel a military coup would happen in February 2021?
I did not know what would happen in February. It was very

unexpected. We did not know or have any feeling that a military coup would happen. I was on a trip and just returned home on the 30th of January 2021. Then, we suddenly lost the cell phone signal early the following day. I could not call my family and friends. They cut off the signal and internet. Then we heard that our Mother Suu was detained at 3 am on the 1st of February. She was the only hope we had left, but the military junta detained her, and our president and most of the NLD representatives were detained as well.

What was your initial feeling when you heard of the coup?
At first, when I heard that the Military detained and ruled our country, I felt as if I had lost my mind. Everything vanished—I could not feel anything at all. I don't know how to explain it, but it didn't feel like anything I had experienced before. I had no idea what would happen next. People said we would have to wait 72 hours, and everything would be okay again. We stayed for those three days, and it wasn't okay. People became fed up and started taking action. We began protecting ourselves and protesting against the military Junta. We started demonstrations to free our leaders and restore democracy. After a few weeks of waiting for the Junta to give democracy back, we started the Spring Revolution, which became the 2222 Revolution. People were being killed during these demonstrations. We were protesting peacefully, but they began using guns and beating innocent civilians.

What were your main fears during the coup? Did you fear for your family, the country, or your life?

The Military is supposed to protect people and the country. But it is heading to destroy everything. What I fear the most is for the next generation. We don't want them to face and feel what we face now. There has already been a military coup which our parents faced, and students were killed. We want to end this and restore democracy, which is why we are trying our best even though most of us are detained or killed or have lost everything we have. This isn't just a small family. This is our one big family; we all are equal, and we are all trying to build the best of the best big family. Lives were taken and ruled. Freedom should be the only one above our heads, not fears and not the Junta. They ruined everything. Not only our future but also the country's.

How did you feel when foreigners, including your friends, were being told to leave the country and eventually left?

Many foreign companies and investments are in the country, but most left after the Military seized the government by force. Embassies announced for their civilians to leave the country as soon as possible. Most of my friends left the country. They were also afraid as there were always shootings, and the Military detained some foreigners.

The military coup is getting worse and worse. The Military Junta is burning down villages. Bomb blasts are going off everywhere—shootings even in big cities. The Military Junta has seized houses since the coup, and they also took all the donation money from the pagodas. It has been an unfinished revolution since 1988. First, having military power in one's country is meant to protect the civilians and the country. But now we think it is better without it. It doesn't need to be here when the Junta is killing people.

How has the coup affected you today?
We are robbed of joy and freedom as we don't know what will happen next. Lives here are not certain anymore, not safe anymore, trapped and lost in this place of nowhere. The Military Junta is not going to give us democracy back. The United Nations is turning its back on us. No one cares about us. We are being tortured. The Military Junta thinks of us like toys and puppets. We hate military Junta. We hate China. China is a big enemy for us. It supports the military through money or weapons. It is ruling us from behind. China is evil to us for so many reasons.

We won't give up till we get democracy back. Even though most of us were killed, even though we were scared, and we didn't have any support from any other countries, we will keep moving on and finish this unfinished revolution.

Kyi

Hey Kyi, congratulations on ending your quarantine in Qatar! How are you feeling today?
Hello, thank you! I have a job in Qatar (DOHA), Middle East.
I really miss Myanmar and my friends and family, first of all, as well as the Hope Haven Team the most. The weather is very hot here. It's not like in Myanmar—there is a lot less rain. I didn't get my COVID-19 vaccination in Myanmar, so I am hotel-quarantined for

seven nights in Qatar. The company arranged that, and it is very cosy.

Can you tell me about yourself and how you came to live in Yangon?
I was born in Sittwe (the Capital of Rakhine State, Myanmar), known as Western Myanmar (Burma). I have lived in Yangon with my whole family since I was eight.

Did you know/feel a military coup would happen in February 2021?
No way. Who would have known that this messy and crazy situation would happen again, like ages ago?

What was your initial feeling when you heard of the coup?
The coup happened on 1st February 2021. I had been sleeping that morning, but suddenly, I was awakened by my aunt, and she told me the Myanmar military had seized control over the country. They detained Daw Aung San Suu Kyi, U Win Myint (President) and other officials.

What were your main fears during the coup? Did you fear for your family, the country, or your life?
Now, it has been months since Myanmar has been under military control again. Many people are homeless, there are no schools for students, thousands of people are jobless, and factories are shut since there's no point in running businesses in Myanmar. There is no guaranteed health insurance for pregnant women, children, and elders, as well as other issues like detaining students and killing

innocent people—children, women, students, and elders. These are the scariest days we have had since the start of the coup.

How did you feel when foreigners, including your friends, were being told to leave the country and eventually left?
Since the start of the coup, most of my foreign friends and colleagues have been very scared, so they have had to return to their country as early as possible. I feel bad for them, some of whom I met from Hope Haven. Happy days have ended since 1 February 2021.

What were your days like during the coup? What did you do/how did you feel when there was no internet?
The students/children/pregnant/women, all people came out, even medical staff and monks. They protested all along the roads and streets daily to get Democracy back. Soldiers and police took people by force and hit them to death. The Civil Disobedience Movement against the coup began.

The detained protesters couldn't see lawyers or families in Insein Prison get their rights. Coup Leader Min Aung Hlaing cut the internet to the whole country to stop the global news flow. Soldiers still take away innocent citizens at night, killing them and asking the family members to get the dead body the following day.

How has the coup affected you today?
I wouldn't say I am lucky that I moved to another country with a job. In this very critical situation, everybody is having a tough time,

physically and mentally. However, the good point is that I can still support my country financially from abroad.

You recently left Yangon. Was it difficult to leave the country, and how did you manage to get out?

I must thank my friend, Meg (Charity Leader). Without her, I couldn't get out of there with a job visa and a visitor passport. Min Aung Hlaing (Coup Leader) doesn't let citizens get out of the country for work with a job VISA/PV Passport, but if we want to, we must have an Overseas Worker Identification Card (OWIC) known as a Smart Card here and Job passport (PJ) and work visa. Only visitors can leave with a visit visa and a visit passport. I held a PV passport and Job visa, so it was not eligible for them to let me leave Myanmar, but luckily, I got tremendous help from my friend; she helped me a lot till I got out of Myanmar. I was very worried during those days until I passed to Immigration.

Are you relieved to have left Yangon? Or how are you feeling?

Finally, I feel so relieved that I could manage to leave with so many difficulties, but I'll support my home country, Myanmar, as much as possible to restore Democracy.

List of Abbreviations

ACLED	Armed Conflict Location and Event Data Project
APP	Association for Political Prisoners
ARSA	Arakan Rohingya Salvation Army
BRI	Belt and Road Initiative
CDM	Civil Disobedience Movement
FCDO	Foreign, Commonwealth & Development Office
ISOS	International SOS
MUP	Mon Unity Party
NGO	Non-Governmental Organisation
NHS	National Health Service (UK)
NLD	National League for Democracy
NRPC	National Reconciliation and Peace Centre
PDF	People's Defence Force
SAC	State Administration Council
UN	United Nations
UNSC	United Nations Security Council

© Maxim Vinciguerra, 2024

Lydia Goldman is a London-based author, dedicated philanthropist and avid reader. Her journey from a delightfully nomadic childhood to her passion for writing and exploration has inspired her debut memoir, Red Moons and Silent Truths.

Growing up as a third-culture kid, Lydia attended eleven schools across the Netherlands, Indonesia, and the UK. She embraced the ever-changing landscape, which shaped her identity and inspired her to work abroad in Myanmar.

Red Moons and Silent Truths is Lydia's first book, and her story has already garnered attention from the Evening Standard and several podcasts committed to raising awareness for those in Myanmar who no longer have a voice.

If you are interested in publishing, writing and you love to read, then head over to
www.sleepylionpublishing.com

Otherwise, all questions can be sent to
enquiries@sleepylionpublishing.com

If you would like to submit any work, whether a manuscript, short story, article, blog post or even artwork, then send us an email at
submissions@sleepylionpublishing.com

We are always looking for inspiring work, whether it is fiction, poetry, literary, or non-fiction. We are looking for works that show great storytelling, that evoke awareness, positivity, and creativity. Don't hesitate in finding out more on our website and socials.
https://www.facebook.com/sleepylionpublishing/

On our website you will find:

-Our personal editing, illustrating and publishing services and traditional royalty contracts
- Blog posts
-Articles on writing and reading
-Essays
-Short Stories
-Poetry
-And much, much more...

www.ingramcontent.com/pod-product-compliance
Lightning Source LLC
Chambersburg PA
CBHW072045110526
44590CB00018B/3041